Distant Revolutions

JEFFERSONIAN AMERICA

Jan Ellen Lewis, Peter S. Onuf, and Andrew O'Shaughnessy, Editors

DISTANT REVOLUTIONS

1848 and the Challenge
to American Exceptionalism

Timothy Mason Roberts

UNIVERSITY OF VIRGINIA PRESS

Charlottesville and London

University of Virginia Press
© 2009 by the Rector and Visitors of the University of Virginia
All rights reserved
Printed in the United States of America on acid-free paper

First published 2009

9 8 7 6 5 4 3 2 1

Library of Congress Cataloging-in-Publication Data

Roberts, Timothy Mason, 1964–
  Distant revolutions : 1848 and the challenge to American
exceptionalism / Timothy Mason Roberts.
    p.   cm. — (Jeffersonian America)
  Includes bibliographical references and index.
  ISBN 978-0-8139-2799-2 (cloth : alk. paper) — ISBN 978-0-8139-2818-0
(e-book)
    1. United States—Intellectual life—1783–1865. 2. Europe—History—
1848–1849. 3. Revolutions—Europe—History—19th century. 4. National
characteristics, American. I. Title.
  E166.R63 2009
  973.6—dc22
                          2008046795

For Emily

Nations, as individuals, who are completely innocent in their own esteem, are insufferable in their human contacts.

—Reinhold Niebuhr, *The Irony of American History*

CONTENTS

Acknowledgments

I have accrued many debts in writing this book. Most recently I am obligated to Richard Holway at the University of Virginia Press, who accepted the manuscript but who challenged me to rethink and to clarify what the work says about antebellum America. Also to Dick's credit, readers whom he contacted provided timely and useful critiques of the work. I am indebted to Andre Fleche and, in particular, to Carl Guarneri, whose thoughtful critique of the book's organization and argument improved it dramatically.

Other individuals read earlier versions or parts of the work and shared their suggestions and wisdom with me. I am grateful in this regard to Charles Capper, Neil Jumonville, Edward Kohn, Cadoc Leighton, Larry Reynolds, Andrew Robertson, Frank Towers, Major Wilson, and the late Duncan MacLeod. I also especially thank Daniel Walker Howe, who supervised my work as a graduate student and who has continued to offer critique, advice, and encouragement. Dan's scholarship and mentoring are both exemplary.

Several institutions provided financial support for this project. I wish to thank the Virginia Historical Society, the University of Oxford Modern History Faculty, the London Historical Society, and Bilkent University for providing research fellowships. I also thank various libraries and archives for allowing me materials to study and space to work. These include the Divinity School Library of Duke University; the Houghton Library at Harvard University; the Kansas State Historical Society; the Library Company of Philadelphia; the Library of Congress; the Library of Manchester College, Oxford; the Massachusetts Historical Society; the New York Public Library; the Strozier Library at Florida State University; the Tennessee State Library and Archives; the South Carolina Historical Society; the Southern Historical Collection at the University of North Carolina–

Chapel Hill; the Virginia Historical Society; and the University of Georgia Hargrett Rare Book and Manuscript Library.

Earlier versions of the arguments made here appeared in "The United States and the Revolutions of 1848" (co-authored by Daniel W. Howe), in *The Revolutions in Europe 1848–1849*, edited by R. J. W. Evans and Hartmut Pogge von Strandmann (2002), reprinted by permission of Oxford University Press; "The United States and the Revolutions of 1848," in *The European Revolutions of 1848 and the Americas*, edited by Guy Thomson (2002), reprinted with permission of the Institute of Latin American Studies (now the Institute for the Study of the Americas); "Now the Enemy Is Within Our Borders: The Impact of European Revolutions in American Perceptions of Violence before the Civil War," originally published in *ATQ*, volume 17, no. 3 (September 2003), reprinted by permission of the University of Rhode Island; and "The European Revolutions of 1848 and Antebellum Violence in Kansas," *Journal of the West*, volume 44, no. 1 (Winter 2005), copyright ©2005 by ABC-CLIO, Inc., and reprinted with permission of ABC-CLIO. An earlier version of chapter 2 appeared as "Diplomatische Reaktionen der Vereinigten Staaten waehrend der Revolutionsjahre 1848/49," in *Achtundvierziger Forty-Eighters: Die deutsche Revolution von 1848/49, die Vereinigten Staaten und der amerikanische*, edited by Wolfgang Hochbruck, Ulrich Bachteler, and Henning Zimmermann (2000), and is republished by permission of Verlag Westfälisches Dampfboot. Parts of chapters 3 and 7 originally appeared in "'Revolutions Have Become the Bloody Toy of the Multitude': European Revolutions, the South, and the Crisis of 1850," *Journal of the Early Republic*, volume 25, no. 2 (Summer 2005), and are reprinted by permission of the University of Pennsylvania Press. A portion of chapter 5 originally appeared in "Margaret Fuller's Rome and the Problem of Provincial American Democracy," *Patterns of Prejudice*, volume 40, no. 1 (February 2006), which is available at http://www.informaworld.com.

My family and several friends inspired and assisted me in this project. My parents, Millard and Anita Roberts, and my siblings, Anne and David, and their families provided much prayer and encouragement to persist in this project, despite their bafflement at the byzantine process of bringing it to completion. Kurt and Anita Berends served up many warm meals and laughter at Oxford. Rigg and Denise Mohler offered their home and a vehicle, despite their growing family, during my many trips to Washington, D.C. The Mohlers, along with Steve Howell, Mike Poerksen, and their families, have remained friends and advocates over the years despite the long distance between us, as well as our different preferences in college football.

I finally wish to thank my wife, Emily, and my children, Sumner and Zoe, whose entrances into my life inspired me to finish this but made doing so more complicated. Thankfully, I no longer have to answer their question, "Is the book finished?" with the words of Elihu in the Book of Job: "Bear with me a little longer." The three of them are a gift to me.

DISTANT REVOLUTIONS

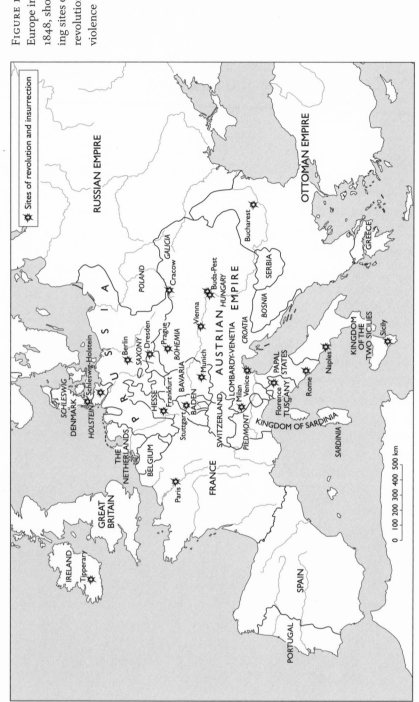

FIGURE 1. Europe in 1848, showing sites of revolutionary violence

INTRODUCTION

In 1990 the U.S. Congress paid tribute to the recent fall of communism in eastern Europe by dedicating the bronze bust of a man who died some ninety years before the Berlin Wall was knocked down—indeed, decades before the wall was built. Elected officials, foreign dignitaries, and even church ministers gathered to witness the unveiling of the bust of a Hungarian lawyer and troublemaker named Louis Kossuth—about whom we know hardly anything today, in spite of the fact that his likeness now stands in the U.S. Capitol rotunda.[1]

Who was Kossuth, and why does he deserve a permanent presence in the U.S. Capitol? Kossuth was a Hungarian freedom fighter during the 1848 revolutions in Europe, which produced a vibrant ferment in America, with elaborations in politics, popular culture, commerce, education, and religion. The 1848 revolutions brought this Hungarian rebel, as well as other European celebrities, ideas, and institutions, to the attention of Americans in a dramatic fashion. Consequently, from an American perspective the story of the United States and Europe in 1848 is fascinating because it exposes currents in nineteenth-century American society that are still with us today. These currents include how we Americans think about revolution, foreign policy, relations of race and gender, and the belief that the United States is not like any other nation, its history somehow outside the cycle of events that affects other places, rendering it superior to them. While this idea of American "exceptionalism" lately has been questioned, its influence continues in academic, policy-making, and popular circles.[2]

The Kossuth dedication ceremony had several striking aspects, only one of them the placement of a Hungarian revolutionary's bust in the Capitol. U.S. Senator Bob Dole said, "Kossuth would have been very much at home in Philadelphia of the late eighteenth century, or in Warsaw of the late 1980s." Congressman William Broomfield alluded to Kossuth's appeal for American aid in his revolution, noting, "For 200 years, Congress has struggled over . . . how much our [foreign] policy should protect America's interests, and how much it should project America's ideals." James Billington, the Librarian of Congress, used the ceremony to open a "Kossuth Commemorative Exhibition" in the Russell Senate Office Building. The exhibition showed a variety of Kossuth memorabilia, from contemporaneous portraits and sheet music written to honor his American visit in 1852, to Kossuth commemorative stamps issued by the U.S. Post Office in 1958.[3]

While Louis Kossuth had a remarkable impact on American society in the mid-nineteenth century, he was, of course, only one of many individuals who helped foster something of a shared Western politics, culture, and religion between the United States and Europe over the last five centuries. The commonality became most noticeable perhaps in the twentieth century. Richard Pells has shown how American influence in the wake of the two world wars exposed Europeans to the "full force of America's economic, political, and cultural power," following European immigrants whose learning and customs have established or enhanced American science, literature, music, and cuisine.[4]

Recently, however, transatlantic unity has weakened over questions of American unilateralism and European unification, especially in the context of the threat of international terrorism to liberal democracies on both sides of the Atlantic. While some scholars continue to find evidence of residual ties with which to maintain post–World War II affinities, others have argued that profound differences between the United States and Europe should be openly acknowledged.[5]

Amid questions of whether the United States and Europe should pursue alliance or autonomy, it is worthwhile to ask what the historical differences between the United States and Europe have been and how they originated. This book answers those questions in recounting an early episode of the impact of European events on American society and politics: the story of the European revolutions of 1848 and, especially, Americans' perceptions of them. This is a work—to use an awkward word coined by Thomas Jefferson—of "cis-Atlantic" history, defined as "the history of [a] particular place . . . in relation to the wider Atlantic world," and reflects recent scholarship that interprets American history within a transnational context, rather than treating it as separated from the rest of the world.[6]

The Kossuth dedication ceremony in 1990 suggests something about

Americans' paradoxical responses to foreign revolutions, a fundamental element of Americans' global experience since 1776. On the one hand, we are proud of our revolutionary heritage. We annually celebrate our independence, gained by violent revolution, as a civic religious experience. We have professional sports teams with names like the "76ers", the "Patriots," and the "Revolution." The title of a popular Broadway musical was simply the date our revolution officially commenced. The license plates of vehicles registered in the District of Columbia bear the revolutionary motto, "No taxation without representation." In circumstances of celebrating a national holiday, supporting a sports franchise or the fine arts, or registering our cars with the government, we Americans comfortably invoke the rhetoric of revolution.[7]

But on the other hand, we suspect foreign revolutions, especially if aspects of these revolutions seem to make them different from our own revolutionary origins. As Bradford Perkins has put it, "the reaction of Americans to revolutions abroad was essentially a projection of their vision of their own." Such a paradox—Americans' judgment of foreign revolutions based upon explicit or implicit comparison to what they believe about the means and ends of the American Revolution—unfolded in the mid-nineteenth century, when Continental Europe erupted in revolution, from France to the western boundaries of Russia.[8]

The background to the 1848 revolutions lay in the defeat of Napoleon Bonaparte in 1815. The Treaty of Vienna, the settlement of the Napoleonic Wars, arranged for four families—Hanover, Bourbon, Habsburg, and Romanoff—to restore monarchical rule over almost all of Europe. Just four families! The Austrian prince Klemens Metternich, foreign minister for the Habsburg Empire, orchestrated the treaty, by which the German peoples were spread among thirty-nine states, Italian peoples among seven. In the 1820s and 1830s a few independence movements occurred in Europe. Belgium broke away from the Netherlands, and Greece won its independence from the Ottoman Empire. A rebellion flared in Spain, leading to its invasion by France to prop up the Bourbon monarchy again, but the loss of its Latin American colonies.[9]

In America the Greek and Latin American independence movements both provoked popular sympathy and calls for U.S. intervention, and American filibusters began various ventures to invade and bring Latin American countries into U.S. possession. Events prompted President James Monroe to issue the Monroe Doctrine, asserting the right of the United States to protect Latin American independence from European recolonization, but also, contrary to some Americans' desire that the United States actively support Greek self-determination, pledging the United States not to disturb European affairs. Popular interventionism and Monroe's resistance to it reflected a division in Americans' attitudes about foreign relations that originated during the French Revolution, when Republicans and Federalists divided for a time over whether America should actively support the making of the French republic. H. W. Brands has expressed this clash in U.S. foreign relations as between "vindicationism," in which some Americans urge that the United States has an obligation and an interest to actively promote freedom abroad, and "exemplarism," in which others argue "that the United States owes the world merely the example of a humane, democratic, and prosperous society."[10]

Monroe's pledge that the United States would not directly intervene in European affairs accorded with European conservatives' interests to discourage the liberal ideas spread in Napoleon's day. But Metternich, seventy-five years old in 1848, could not stifle the "tremendous outbreak of the revolutionary volcano," as Karl Marx, exiled in Belgium at the time, later described events of the year. Following a decade of crop failures, mass unemployment, and unregulated financial crises, Europe erupted. In Paris middle-class republicans joined socialists in a short-lived coalition to topple King Louis Philippe, the last French king, in February 1848, and establish the Second Republic. The new French government, led by Alphonse de Lamartine, a moderate, and Louis Blanc, a socialist, undertook several reforms that had a mixed reception in America. The Second Republic's declaration of universal male suffrage excited most Americans, but its establishment of public works for the thousands of unemployed artisans and industrial workers around Paris, and its abolishment of slavery in the French West Indies, were highly controversial. In April 1848 France had national elections, and the Second Republic was formally established with 84 percent of the new electorate voting. Moderate republicans trumped both legitimists and socialists—Lamartine insisted that the traditional blue, white, and red *tricolor,* not the red flag preferred by socialists, would be the new regime's symbol, earning Americans' praise.[11]

The revolution in France precipitated uprisings throughout Europe. Major revolutions occurred in the German states, Hungary, and the Italian states. Britain largely was spared, perhaps on account of its liberal reforms over the previous two decades, the "safety valve" of its expanding empire in Asia, and Britons' sense of their own differences from Continental Europeans. Similar to Americans' eventual attitudes about the 1848 revolutions, the *Times* of London commented in March 1848, "We possess those things which other nations are everywhere demanding at the gates of the Palace or the door of the Legislature!" In Russia a lack of communication channels, the presence of a strong army, and political apathy combined to insulate the czar's lands from upheaval.[12]

In the German states there were two revolutionary hotbeds, one Frankfurt, the other Berlin. In southwestern Germany liberal reformers organized the Frankfurt Assembly, which sought ambitiously to unite all of the German states. Some delegates to the assembly were republicans, others constitutional monarchists. This division and the difficulty of writing a German constitution would impede the convention's work. In Berlin, the industrializing capital of Prussia, three quarters of whose residents lived in poverty, clashes between residents and royal troops killed hundreds, and King Frederick William IV was forced to salute the dead. He also granted freedom of the press, assembly, and association, leading to an explosion of newspapers, caricature journals, political clubs, and petitions. These temporary concessions preserved his monarchy.[13]

As news of the fall of the monarchy in France traveled east, it unhinged affairs of the Habsburg monarchy in Central and Eastern Europe. The Habsburgs, under Emperor Ferdinand I, ruled a crazy-quilt empire of Austrians, Germans, Czechs, Poles, Romanians, Hungarians, Serbs, Croatians, and Italians, stretching from southwestern Germany and northern Italy to eastern Russia and the Balkans, held together by the Austrian chancellor and architect of post-Napoleonic Europe, Prince Klemens Metternich. But when students and workmen clashed with soldiers outside the royal palace in Vienna, Metternich fled, joining Louis Philippe in London. His exit had a stunning effect among opponents of Habsburg rule in Prague, Milan, and Budapest, something like local celebrations over the flight of modern-day dictators from Iran, Yugoslavia, or Liberia. In Milan insurrectionists first organized boycotts of Austrian tobacco (taking as their model the Boston Tea Party) and then attacked Austrian troops in a five-day house-to-house guerrilla war. Reflecting the suddenness of the new urban growth in Europe, the cumbersome Austrian artillery proved ineffective under such conditions, and the Austrians withdrew from the city, giving way to the triumphal entry of the Italian nationalist Giuseppe Mazzini, returned from exile in London, who sought to establish a unified Italian republic. The Milan uprising also reinforced other uprisings already in motion, in Sicily, Naples, Venice, and Piedmont-Sardinia, where King Charles Albert of Piedmont declared war on Austria. For a moment it appeared all Italy might become republican or at least a constitutional monarchy. This prospect puzzled Americans, however, who tended to assume no Catholic people was capable of self-government.[14]

It was in Hungary, however, that perhaps the most significant repercussion of Metternich's fall emerged for American observers. There, on 3 March, Lajos ("Louis") Kossuth, an eloquent attorney and member of the Hungarian Diet, had called for parliamentary rule for all of the Habsburg peoples and special sovereignty for the Hungarians. Metternich's news triggered a Hungarian declaration of a bill of rights, ratified by the legislative Diet, and commencement as a de facto independent country. Americans would quickly see many elements of the Hungarian independence movement as the 1848 analogue of the American eighteenth-century rebellion against Great Britain.[15]

These stirring episodes marked the first phase of the European revolutions and became known as "the springtime of the peoples," a contemporary German phrase. But by the summer of 1848, the revolutionary tide was beginning to turn, as revolutionary groups fragmented between moderates and radicals, and imperial soldiers, who didn't like their prospects in liberal, more urban-oriented revolutionary regimes. In May 1848 a socialist-inspired mob overran and briefly occupied the French National Assembly, proclaiming a socialist provisional government in France. Republican military units, the National Guard, dispersed the socialists, but the event determined the government to terminate the plan of national workshops around Paris, offering unemployed workers either military service or work elsewhere in France. This was a match to gunpowder, because on 23 June some fifty thousand angry insurgents barricaded the city and lay siege to the government. Again government troops rallied, this time retaliating with ferocity, blowing up barricades and chasing the insurgents from house to house. Close to five thousand people were killed, either in the fighting itself or in the executions of insurgents that followed. News of these "June Days," which the liberal aristocrat Alexis de Tocqueville would call a "rising of one part of the population against the other . . . a kind of slave-war," horrified and puzzled many Americans, its specter similar to that cast by the Haitian revolution against France a half century earlier.[16] The June Days confirmed suspicions of the dangers of revolutionary socialism, raised questions as to why achievement of the franchise hadn't brought peace, and entrenched fears that France and Europe as a whole were predisposed to both socialism and especially violence. The Lincoln administration's decision not to impose martial law in New York City after the draft riots there in July 1863, or to round up rioters for summary justice, owed mainly to brittle politics between Washington and New York. As Iver Bernstein has written, however, moderation perhaps also stemmed from the memory of events during the Paris summer of 1848.[17]

Further signs of reaction occurred elsewhere across Europe by late 1848, leaving most Americans, perplexed by rapidly developing courses of events and unfamiliar issues of political and ethnic division, grasping for analogies in American history to help them understand overseas events. In Germany delegates to the Frankfurt Assembly were elected by universal male suffrage, either directly or by nomination of electors, but its composition was weighted toward the learned classes, with one quarter of its membership professors or teachers and nearly half lawyers and judges. The assembly claimed to legislate for the whole German people, labored to create a list of fundamental rights of citizenship, and invited delegates from the eastern kingdom of Bohemia to participate. But time was of the essence, and the body became "too much of a university and not enough of a political stock exchange," in the opinion of Veit Valentin. Denmark invaded two German duchies in the north, while the Bohemians refused to come to Frankfurt, on grounds that they were not German, but Slavic, and convened a Slavic congress in Prague, with students and workers prominent, precipitously declaring independence from the German states and articulating a reformed Austrian empire dominated by Slavs. The Frankfurt Assembly, which has become known as the "professors' parliament," did eventually produce an all-German constitution, but it appeared helpless as King Frederick William IV used the conflict with Denmark as an opportunity to reassert military control of Berlin, and an Austrian army bombarded Prague into submission.[18]

When the Austrians tried to deal with the Hungarians, the situation was more complicated. Habsburg authority completely broke down in

Hungary. Radicals in the Hungarian capital chased out the moderates and lynched a mediator sent by the Habsburg emperor. A Hungarian army led by Kossuth repelled an invading Austrian army, which for the moment also lost control of its Serb, Croatian, Rumanian, and Slovak regiments. News of the Hungarian resistance sparked anarchy back in Vienna, including the lynching of the Habsburg minister of war. Hungarian troops massed on the Austrian border, poised for a march to join up with Viennese insurrectionists. But at this moment dissension struck the Hungarian force, as ethnic minorities, who had been causing trouble for the Austrians, decided the Hungarian drive for national assimilation posed the greater threat. The new Austrian emperor, eighteen-year-old Franz Joseph, provided firm guidance from his temporary headquarters in Innsbruck, directing one Austrian army to march on Budapest and another to lay waste to Vienna itself. By early 1849 Kossuth's legend had swelled within Europe and across the Atlantic, but he would soon be a refugee, not a general.[19]

Meanwhile, the revolutions in Italy had begun to splinter as rival leaders emerged and Italians questioned those leaders' motivations. King Charles Albert in the north had little interest in sharing authority and even less in establishing Italian republicanism. He thus refused to ask France for assistance against Austria and alienated both King Ferdinand of Naples, who possessed the largest army and navy in the Italian peninsula, and the transatlantic revolutionary Giuseppe Garibaldi, who returned from South America to offer his services, only to find Albert jealous of his popularity. A regrouped Austrian army handily defeated the northern Italians in July 1848 at the battle of Custoza, and the Austrians occupied Milan. Italians themselves circulated reports attributing the failed independence campaign not to political division, but to incompetence and cowardice. Such stereotypes became legendary, circulating for years in Europe as well as America.[20]

With fires in northern Italy fairly extinguished, revolutionary agitation shifted to the Papal States, where the rule of Pope Pius IX stretched from the Adriatic to the Mediterranean. Beginning in 1846 Pius evinced surprising sensitivity to popular wishes—relaxing official censorship; consulting laypersons for his secular authority; and, despite the Habsburgs' Catholicism, condemning an Austrian military crackdown on a popular uprising within the papal territory. But he refused to lead or endorse any Italian independence movement against Austria. For this, in November 1848 his chief minister was assassinated, and he himself was chased from the Vatican. By January 1849 Romans had declared a republic, replacing the yellow and white flag of the papacy with the green, white, and red banner of Italy. Giuseppe Mazzini was elected Rome's first triumvir, and he governed the city with a moderate hand, ensuring protection of private property, except for the estates of the Church, which he leased to peasants at nominal rents. British prime minister Lord Palmerston observed, "Mazzini's government of Rome was far better than any the Romans had had for centuries." But the Roman republic, like its French counterpart, became portrayed as a den of violent "red republicanism." The city's secularization was probably the most astonishing of any European upheaval for those American observers who associated capacity for revolutionary success with the Protestant faith.[21]

The strength of the European reaction against the revolutions beyond Italy by 1849 also fed American pessimism about the Roman republic. The tumult of the June Days in France prepared the way for Louis Napoleon Bonaparte, the nephew of the emperor Napoleon. Because of his link to the dynasty, he had been banished from France. In 1836 and again in 1840, he made abortive attempts to claim the French government for himself, but he was in England during the June Days and so could not be held culpable for that horror. He returned to France for good in September 1848. Making subtle and effective appeals to la grandeur of his uncle's legend, Louis Napoleon was elected to the National Assembly. He soon presented himself as a presidential candidate and was elected in December 1848 by a four-to-one margin over General Eugéne Cavaignac, a devout republican who had led the suppression of the workers in June. Under the new constitution Napoleon, popular among the peasantry, was elected by direct popular suffrage, not by the assembly—ironic, since Lamartine, whom Napoleon would soon expel from authority, had largely written the constitution and guided its ratification.[22]

The tentative situation in Rome provided Napoleon a second opportunity to extend his authority. The College of Cardinals, like the pope displaced by the republic, issued calls for rescue to Spain, Austria, Naples, and France. France heeded the call, dispatching an army to restore Pius to power from exile in Naples. Rome was defended by Garibaldi's legions, but French artillery compelled the Romans to surrender in July 1849, although Garibaldi escaped dramatically with a few thousand legionnaires, whose red attire some Americans adopted as a show of sympathy; in the 1860s

Oregonians would establish the community of Garibaldi. Hounded by four armies, Garibaldi took refuge briefly in New York City but returned to Europe in 1854 and joined Mazzini and Count Camillo Cavour, a Piedmontese nobleman, to lead the Italian unification movement, not, to Mazzini's disappointment, toward a republic, but to the independent Kingdom of Italy in 1861.[23]

The French conquest of Rome provoked street demonstrations in Paris, which Napoleon used as a pretext to ban political associations, disenfranchise workingmen, and gather power to himself. Skillfully cultivating the overwhelming affection of the peasants for the name of Napoleon, he sought and achieved unlimited power. In December 1851 he executed a coup d'état, wiping out the National Assembly and declaring himself emperor. He would reign as such for twenty years.[24]

Louis Napoleon's consolidation of conservative power was a great setback to the socialist cause in Europe. Michel Proudhon, who had called for the end of government as the arch-protector of private property and had earlier sensed a socialist triumph, lamented that "the fate of European democracy has slipped from our hands—from the hands of the people—into those of the Praetorian Guard." And Napoleon's ascendance had its effects in the United States. It confounded socialist advocates such as Horace Greeley, editor of the *New York Tribune,* who, despite the June Days, had hailed the new French republic as a vindication of the rights of workers in the Atlantic world. Napoleon's triumph also discouraged proslavery radicals who were organizing "secession conventions" in the South.[25]

Back in Germany the Frankfurt Assembly had decided by now that it must hitch its unification plan to Prussia and invited Frederick William to become emperor of a newly constituted German empire. But he refused the offer because it had not come from the princes of the various German states, only the quixotic "professors' parliament." Frederick William dictated his own far less democratic constitution to the people of Prussia, and other German rulers followed his initiative. These events were fatal to the assembly. Pursued by Prussian troops, the Frankfurt Assembly desperately transferred itself to Stuttgart but, embarrassingly, found the doors of its meeting place locked by the local government. Thus, the assembly, and its effort to unify Germany by democratic persuasion rather than by "blood and iron," in the words of the eventual unifier Otto von Bismarck, was dispersed. Among those scattered were the "forty-eighters," visionaries of an all-German republic who fled to the United States, carrying their resentment of German aristocracy with them to inject into American politics.[26]

In the east the Hungarians, despite defections of the Slavic troops, continued their independence struggle against the Habsburgs, laying siege to Budapest to free the city. But in May 1849 Czar Nicholas of Russia, having no truck with secessionist movements on his borders, demolished the Hungarian cause, sending an army across the Hungarian plains to join Austrians, Serbs, and Croats. In August Kossuth, in command of the troops and also now "governor president" of the Hungarian republic, discreetly handed over authority to another general, Arthur Görgey, and escaped, first to Turkey, then to Britain, and then, in December 1851, to the United States. Görgey quickly surrendered, not to the Austrian army but to the Russian, an insult to the Austrians, who responded by cruelly executing the Hungarian officer corps, as well as a good portion of the Hungarian Diet—summary justice that would be frequently invoked in mounting American political debates over slavery. In late 1851 Emperor Franz Joseph joined Louis Napoleon Bonaparte (who now called himself Napoleon III) in officially reviving a purely absolute form of government for western and central Europe. Austria-Hungary, as the empire was increasingly termed, would divide formally in 1867. Yet the chronic intransigence of the ruling German and Magyar classes, as well as the penumbra of dissenting minority groups, mired the region in industrial backwardness and ethnic vendettas until the twentieth century.[27]

This summary of the revolutions gives a sense of the complexity and simultaneity of the European conflicts, certain ones of which Americans fixed upon to praise or criticize. Americans largely relied on their newspapers to learn about these revolutions. At the time, for the "foreign news," American newspapers normally printed stories about Europe that had been clipped from foreign, mainly British, newspapers. However, in a few cases Americans could read stories written by American journalists in Europe. The 1848 revolutions were the first overseas wars to which a few American newspapers, such as the *New York Tribune,* the *New York Herald,* and the *New Orleans Picayune,* sent their own correspondents, including Margaret Fuller, Charles Dana, Donald Mitchell, and George Kendall. Other newspapers received occasional reports from American expatriates.[28]

Americans trying to make sense of the 1848 revolutions lived in a country that in significant ways was different from Europe. The forced labor system of serfdom, extant in Eastern Europe until the 1848 revolutions (and continuing in Russia thereafter), was unknown in the United States. White laborers were free to move about the country and frequently did so. Of course, there was black slavery in the South, and slavery spread in the early American republic even as Napoleon Bonaparte was abolishing serfdom in areas of Europe he conquered. Acceptance of slavery in the United States was based on the assumption of white racial supremacy. Careers were open to talent in the United States, provided the career seeker was white and male.

The people's freedom to vote was also different on each side of the Atlantic. Before his overthrow King Louis Philippe of France, though brought to power by a liberal revolution in 1830, led a government that restricted the right to vote to the wealthiest 250,000 men out of a population of some 35 million, about twice as large as the U.S. population in 1840. In the United States, in contrast, suffrage was the most widespread in the world. The right of suffrage was determined by each state, not by the national government. But in most states native and white immigrant men alike could vote; immigrants could vote sometimes even before they became citizens, both by legal and illegal means. Enthusiasm and corruption were both widespread.[29]

The closest American counterpart to the 1848 revolutions to occur before them was the Dorr Rebellion of 1842. This rebellion erupted over the state of Rhode Island's failure to revise its colonial charter of 1663, thus denying propertyless men in the state the right to vote, a disenfranchisement increasingly conspicuous in Jacksonian America. Thomas Dorr led a popular uprising that ratified a democratic "People's Constitution" and presumed to elect him governor and to elect other suffragists to a "People's Legislature." Rhode Island authorities declared martial law to subdue the Dorrites, one person was killed, and Dorr was imprisoned. A Dorrite, Martin Luther, later brought suit against a Rhode Island law-enforcement officer for entering his home illegally, claiming that only the illegitimate charter constitution, not the "People's Constitution," provided for martial law. The case, *Luther v. Borden,* actually went to the U.S. Supreme Court in 1848. There counsel for Luther argued that should the Court reject his claim, it would "discourage the oppressed millions of the old world [to witness] a model republic [sanctioning] unchangeable despotism . . . [and be] a repudiation of the doctrines of our fathers." But Chief Justice

Roger Taney, writing for the Court, ruled that the executive and legislative branches of government were capable of determining whether the state of Rhode Island, in not broadening the state's franchise, had breached the Constitution's guarantee to every state a republican form of government, effectively denying Luther's claim. Meanwhile, moreover, Rhode Islanders enacted a much more liberal constitution, even enfranchising black men, which the "People's Constitution" had not. The Dorr Rebellion was the only episode of insurrectionary violence on the question of white men's suffrage in American history.[30]

Thus, political participation was the central action of the American ideology of republicanism. American government in the nineteenth century, especially the federal government, was hardly very powerful or active by today's standards. Still, many Americans believed voting for their leaders expressed the ideal of government by consent. Voter participation was high. In the presidential election of 1848, 73 percent of the electorate cast ballots. As the political parties weakened in the twentieth century, other aspects of American culture marginalized politics, while, paradoxically, the federal government grew larger and stronger. Voter participation declined after its nineteenth-century highs.[31]

Different from the crowded societies of Europe, the vast western spaces of North America provided an opportunity for diversity to flourish. American openness was conspicuous in religion. Although for some Europeans religious sectarianism provided the basis for their social identity, Christianity administered and funded by the state was the norm across Europe: Anglicanism in Britain and Ireland; Lutheranism in the German states; Roman Catholicism in France, Spain, and the Italian states. In the United States there were no established churches in any of the states, and churches received their financial support from lay parishioners. The last establishment of religion had been abolished in Massachusetts in 1833. Americans throughout the Union were free to have any religion or none. There were hierarchical denominations like the Anglican and Roman Catholic churches, but the country thought of itself as Protestant, and Methodists, Baptists, Presbyterians, and Congregationalists comprised the most popular Protestant sects.[32]

Partly informed by American religious beliefs, the idea of Manifest Destiny, or God's ordainment of white people's supremacy, justified westward expansion and settlement. Although much of this settlement occurred at the expense of American Indians and Mexicans, it encouraged experimentalism across American culture and geography of the mid-nineteenth century. Thus, for example, European ideas of utopian socialism, introduced from France, found fertile ground in America. Followers founded utopian communities, peopled by both immigrants and native-born Americans, largely without interference. In 1848 most American socialists did not know about or embrace the ideas of Karl Marx, who first published his *Communist Manifesto* only in February 1848.[33]

This book argues that in this dynamic age of the United States, many Americans initially responded to the European revolutions positively, on the premise that Europeans were conducting the revolutions so as to achieve results similar to those they perceived in the American Revolution. From the late eighteenth century, Americans regularly commemorated the Revolution in ritualized public ceremonies, including political elections. Within the revolutionary generation itself, these rituals at first emphasized liberty achieved through violence. But as Americans reacted to the first French Revolution, they developed a more organic image of the American Revolution. Wesley Frank Craven asserts that in the 1790s Americans portrayed the American conflict as simply a defense of "ancient ground." Sarah Purcell has argued that in the early nineteenth century commemorations of the war emphasized the patriots' unity and deemphasized the war's violence: "Public memories of violent conflict . . . were designed to downplay the bloodshed and division of war in order to bring disparate Americans together around images of shared sacrifice." And Michael Kammen has shown that "peace and prosperity" became the major theme of revolutionary festivals by the mid-nineteenth century among descendants of the revolutionary generation and immigrants.[34]

The 1848 revolutions reinforced these perceptions of the American Revolution but also clarified other aspects of how many antebellum Americans understood the war's legacy. They believed it confirmed America as a place of natural liberty, in which people embraced home rule instinctively. The Revolution established republican government largely through peaceful means, not bloodshed. It relied on Christian principles. It did not endanger private property, and it kept government interference in people's lives to a minimum. And it initiated long-term domestic serenity and prosperity. For these reasons the American Revolution, especially seen through the prism of the revolutions in Europe, was deemed a success in creating a stable republic. In 1848 the outbreak of war in Europe provoked many Americans to pat themselves on the back. The European revolutions illustrated that not only had Americans maintained the principles of the American Revolution; they had also, somehow, inspired Europeans to embrace those principles. For a moment many Americans anticipated America and Europe growing together as democratic republics.

Yet soon the European revolutions failed, at least in terms of Americans' sometimes simplistic or inaccurate interpretations of them. Europeans proved unable, or unwilling, to understand and establish stable republican governments, expand and exercise suffrage, discourage people from relying on the government for public relief, and conduct political change without resort to violence or collapse into despotism. Many Americans then responded to evidence of Europeans' failures by concluding not only that the American Revolution was exceptional, but also that, indeed, *so was* America at the mid-nineteenth century, on account of its revolutionary heritage and its apparent lack of problems in contrast to the social unrest that plagued Europe. In short, a Europe apparently unable to create peaceful republican society showed that post-revolutionary America had no problems to solve.

That the 1848 revolutions did largely end in defeat—the historian A. J. P. Taylor has quipped, "History did not turn"—bolstered the case for American exceptionalism. Many Americans consoled themselves that despite problems emerging in American politics and society over slavery, there was no chance that a violent European-style revolution against legal authority could or should occur in the United States. But over the course of the 1850s, this situation changed, driven by the question of slavery's expansion, which soon fragmented American politics and society. The problem of slavery, as well as, eventually, the Civil War itself, likely would have developed in America even without the 1848 revolutions. But the way that the American republic became unstable in the 1850s owed to antislavery Americans' perception that conditions in America had become foreign and alien—similar to conditions in Europe in 1848–52—and therefore were particularly dangerous. The growing crisis thus needed to be dealt with outside the traditional channels of nonviolent political compromise that the American Revolution allegedly had bequeathed.[35]

This book traces the path and consequences of these events in eight chapters. Chapter 1 focuses on American diplomats and civilians in Europe

in 1848, either by coincidence, as was largely the case with American diplomats, tourists, and financiers, or by intention, in the case of a few American journalists who hastened to the revolutions to tell their story, and
"filibusters," who sought to assist the uprisings, if possible. Actually, most
American eyewitnesses' inclination to sympathize with the revolutions,
much less to help them, was ephemeral, and direct exposure to revolutionary events caught these "little-r" republicans off-guard, deflecting their
reactions away from their republican professions.

The heart of the book then brings the story to American shores. Where
chapter 1 focuses on Americans close to the revolutions, chapters 2 through
7 investigate the effect of the great distance of the Atlantic between American observers and the events they observed. Unlike today, with virtually
instantaneous news coverage, transatlantic news in the mid-nineteenth
century took several weeks to arrive. It was also subject to editing by partisan American newspaper editors. Affected by distance and subject to ideological interpretation, such filtered news of the 1848 upheavals became a
theme in American popular culture and a weapon of domestic politics, as
American groups used the European news for local purposes.

Thus, these chapters interpret antebellum American society in a time of
both excitement and anxiety at the possible relationships between events
on one side of the Atlantic and events on the other. Chapter 2 focuses on
events within popular culture, including the rise of "revolutionary" clothing, theater presentations, university student debates, academic disputes,
and mass sympathy gatherings. Chapters 3 and 4 show how European
events affected the politics of 1848 and reform movements of the age. The
1848 revolutions built momentum for the international peace movement,
and American pacifists traveled to Europe to join their European counterparts to call for outlawing war. Eighteen forty-eight saw Free Soilers break
from the traditional two-party system to form their own party. They, along
with Democrats and Whigs, incorporated the rhetoric and images of the
European revolutions into the presidential campaign of that year. The year
also saw continuing challenges to the exclusion of African Americans and
women from the political realm, punctuated by the first women's rights
convention at Seneca Falls, New York. Previously, American reformers, including Free Soilers, abolitionists, advocates of women's rights, and urban
laborers, had ascribed their claims of liberty and republican citizenship to
principles of the American Revolution. Now these groups criticized the

NEW-YORK TRIBUNE.

MONDAY MORNING, APRIL 10.

City Election—Tuesday, April 11.

WHIG NOMINATIONS.

FOR MAYOR

WILLIAM V. BRADY.

ALMS-HOUSE COMMISSIONER,

JEFFERSON BERRIAN.

Whig Aldermen and Assistants.

Ward.   *For Aldermen.*   *For Assistants.*
I. THEODORE R. DeFOREST,   JOSEPH JAMISON,
II. JAMES KELLY,   SAMUEL FROST,
III. ROBERT SWARTWOUT,   JAMES E. WOOD,
V. WILLIAM ADAMS,   ALEX. H. SHULTZ,
VI. SIMON CLANNON,   MATTHEW D. GREENE,
VII. MORRIS FRANKLIN,   MORGON MORGANS, Jr
VIII. ABM. R. LAWRENCE,   JONATHAN W. ALLEN,
IX. JACOB L. DODGE,   SILAS C. HERRING,
X. ROBERT T. HAWS,   DAVID MILLER,
XII. THOMAS CARNLEY,   GEORGE F. CLARK,
XIII. WILLIAM TUCKER,   WILLIAM A. WALKER,
XIV. AARON CHICHESTER,   CHARLES E. TAYLOR,
XV. LINUS W. STEVENS,   JOSEPH BRITTON,
XVI. WASHINGTON SMITH,   WILLIAM TURNER,
XVII. CLARKSON CROLIUS,   GEORGE H. FRANKLIN
XVII. MOSES MAYNARD.   GEORGE W. ALLERTON

Whig Judicial Nominations.

Police Justice.   *Civil Justice.*
First District...(Ist, IIId and Vth Wards:)
   JEREMIAH LOTHROP. JAMES GREEN.
Second District..(IVth, VIth and XIVth Wards:)
   JOSEPH R. TAYLOR. NICHOLAS C. EVERETT.
Third District..(VIIIth and IXth Wards:)
   JAS. T. M. BLEAKLEY. WILLIAM B. MEECH.
Fourth District..(Xth, XVth and XVIIth Wards:)
   BARNA. W. OSBORNE. WILLIAM H. VAN COTT.
Fifth District..(VIIth, XIth and XIIIth Wards:)
                            DAVID RANDALL.
Sixth District..(XIIth, XVIth and XVIIIth Wards:)
   N. B. MOUNTFORT.   ANSON WILLIS.

THE TRIBUNE IN THE TENTH WARD.—An effort will be
made to have this paper delivered in the Tenth Ward at
an earlier hour.

The City Expenditures.

FELLOW CITIZENS!
   It is charged that the Whig Common Council
has wantonly and needlessly increased the expen-
ses of our City Government. We ask you to
consider the following *facts,* drawn from the Annual
Report of the Controller, (John Ewen) who is
known not to be a Whig:—
The Net Expenditure of 1846 (wholly under
   Tammany rule) was..........................$1,644,076
Do. of 1847 (partly under Whig rule)...........1,874,802
   Increase.................................$230,726
But the first four and a half months of 1847 were
   under Tammany rule, and the amount expend-
   ed therein was.............................$875,817
When the total expenditure for these months,
   in proportion with the total expense of 1846,
   would have been...........................$616,528
   Excess in the first 4½ months (Tammany)..$259,289
Exceeding the total increase of 1847 by......$28,563
   Here you see where the money has gone. The
men who were in power a year ago *squandered
your money on their own partisans,* and *now impu-
dently charge* THEIR OWN *prodigality on their Whig
successors, and thereupon ask to be reinstated in*

FOUR DAYS LATER

FROM EUROPE.

ARRIVAL OF THE HIBERNIA.

The Progress of France.

THE FINANCIAL EMBARRASSMENT.

GREAT NEWS FROM ITALY,

THE REVOLUTION IN LOMBARDY.

THE FLIGHT OF THE VICEROY.

THE CONSTITUTION OF THE ROMAN STATES.

THE CHANGES IN PRUSSIA.

BLOODSHED IN BERLIN.

The King doing honor to the Slain.

REFORM—CONCESSIONS.

A UNION OF GERMAN STATES.

The New Order of Things in Austria.

Liberal Men and Liberal Measures.

JOY OF THE PEOPLE.

DISTURBANCES IN BOHEMIA.

THE REPUBLIC PROCLAIMED AT CRACOW.

OUTBREAKS IN HANOVER.

REJOICINGS IN SWEDEN.

LOLA MONTEZ IN SWITZERLAND.

IRELAND TRANQUIL.

THE FAILURES IN EUROPE

THE MARKETS, &c. &c.

   The steamer Hibernia, Captain SHANNON, arrived at her wharf at Jersey City last evening
about eleven. She left Liverpool on the 25th ult.,
and made the passage in a few hours more than
fifteen days. We give below the leading particu-
lars of intelligence. We have, however, an ample
stock of most interesting matter relating to the
present state of Europe, which will appear as soon
as possible.

THE FRENCH REPUBLIC.

Acts of the Provisional Government.
The *Moniteur* publishes several additional official

FIGURE 2. *New-York Tribune,* 10 April 1848, reporting the first news of the 1848
revolutions, brought by transatlantic steamer. Headlines such as these facilitated
many Americans' understanding of the revolutions as a single event. (Courtesy
American Antiquarian Society)

exclusiveness of American politics and society by allying themselves with the European revolutions. Implicitly or explicitly, these groups tested belief in American exceptionalism.[36]

Chapters 5, 6, and 7 examine important aspects of American conservatism that resisted the radicalisms of 1848. Chapter 5 moves from the secular to the religious realm, indicating how radicalism in Europe provoked and, surprisingly, aligned conservative American Protestants and Catholics, who found themselves confronted not only by domestic "-isms" but also by forces from abroad. Chapter 6 examines the bitter 1850 dispute over territorial slavery—how the European revolutions influenced this critical event, called the "Crisis of 1850," and even helped defer the outbreak of civil war. Chapter 7 demonstrates how European events, especially the controversial visit of Louis Kossuth to the United States, became a point of debate in the presidential election of 1852. Exceeded perhaps only by the Marquis de Lafayette, Kossuth was the most celebrated foreigner of the nineteenth century to come to the United States. Kossuth hoped to gain substantial American military as well as financial support for the independence of Hungary. He failed to do so, and in fact, in 1852, when he left American shores, Americans seemed more certain than ever that they inhabited a unique country, based on their view that they were the inheritors and preservers of an American Revolution that was successful, yet largely peaceful, while Europeans' revolutionary tradition was one of excessive violence, culminating perennially in failure.

Finally, chapter 8 and the epilogue reveal how Americans continued to refer to the 1848 revolutions during and after the 1850s, as the country rapidly became sectionally divided. Chapter 8 concludes, however, with a new interpretation of events in the Kansas territory in the mid-1850s, whose influence by international events has been largely overlooked by existing scholarship. Kansas, on account of its reputed pristine economic opportunities, became an important symbol for how the United States was not like Europe. But when proslavery forces launched a campaign of fraud and physical intimidation to protect the territory for slavery, antislavery Northerners interpreted the conflict as signaling the outbreak of European-style violence on the American frontier. That proslavery forces seemed to have the sanction of the territorial as well as the national government made the specter of revolutionary despotism, allegedly alien to the American experience, all the more foreboding to antislavery interests.

Those interests, becoming centered in the Republican Party, were galvanized by a new revolutionary consciousness: not homage to the American Revolution for its legacy of peace and prosperity, but, instead, resistance to an alien coup d'état—by violence, if necessary. Northern antislavery commentators and partisans conflated frontier violence and recent scenes of European counterrevolution into a message that an alien form of authoritarian violence had broken out on the American plains and required a response—including defiance of standing law and order, in emulation of the European revolutionaries and contrary to answers their generation had come to understand the American Revolution could provide.

Older studies exist of the relationship between the United States and European revolutions of the nineteenth century. Several of these, however, are problematic, because they tend to view the setbacks to reform in Europe in 1848–52 as only an unfortunate delay to inevitable liberal victories of unification and national sovereignty down the road. The observation of Howard Marraro on the American response to the revolutions in Italy suggests this Whiggish determinism: "The formation of a new and complete Kingdom of Italy was watched with deepest interest in America because . . . Italy joined modern states, like America, hastening on the march of material and moral improvement." Such a rendition falsely implies that peoples on both sides of the Atlantic were not only committed to transnational solidarity, modernization, and national unification but also simply waiting for "material and moral improvement" to descend and share its blessings.[37]

More recent studies of the impact of the 1848 revolutions in America also have appeared.[38] Some of these studies focus on the experiences of Europeans who came to the United States, such as Louis Kossuth or the German "forty-eighters." Others emphasize that Americans' overall conservative attitudes toward the revolutions through the early 1850s reflected the growing tension and sectionalization of American politics; thus, Americans' reactions merely reflected preexisting, domestic interests. Meanwhile, other scholars have considered, but largely rejected, the possibility of similarities between the 1848 revolutions and the Civil War. The thrust of these latter studies is that the success of the Civil War, as the "last best hope" for the West, compensated for the defeats of the European revolutions.[39]

This book builds on these studies in an attempt to offer a broad interpretation of how the 1848 revolutions—both the news and images of those revolutions and certain significant European revolutionaries who crossed the Atlantic—affected America as a nation. It explores how Americans reacted to the European revolutions within the context of preexisting ideological and social conditions of the antebellum period. But it also seeks to show how the 1848 revolutions altered these conditions. In particular, the book interprets how the 1848 revolutions undermined faith in American "exemplarism"—the belief that America should merely preserve its status as a global model. Thus, the book explores the relationship among the 1848 revolutions, exemplarism, and the coming of the Civil War. The 1848 revolutions did not by themselves cause the Civil War, but they did contribute to its timing and its meaning for many Americans.

Finally, in contrast to the more deterministic perspective of older works on the subject, the book attempts to convey a sense of the contingent conditions of Atlantic democracy in the mid-nineteenth century. Both the United States and Europe had uncertain futures in the year 1848. Some Americans spoke about the manifest destiny of America at the time, but the success of the democratic experiment was uncertain during the mid-1800s, on both sides of the Atlantic. Many Americans, precisely because of their perception of European events in terms of their own country's revolutionary past, did not quickly acknowledge this similarity and, in fact, believed at the beginning of 1848 that the United States was an example that Europeans would follow in reforming their own governments and societies.

Yet conditions in the United States themselves were not static. Territorial acquisitions in the 1840s precipitated a sectional political alignment. Outbreaks of violence in the West, a symptom of that alignment, became significant partly because a growing number of Americans came to interpret violence—a form of revolutionary "righteous violence," in the phrase of Larry Reynolds—as signaling how America should become more like revolutionary Europe, rather than the other way around. Thus, this book shows the role of revolutionary events in Europe in directing Americans' path to the Civil War, America's ultimate response to the 1848 revolutions. The United States and Europe were drawn closer together, not in the way anticipated by Americans who in 1848 professed faith in American "exemplarism," but through shared experiences of nation-building through violence.[40]

1. THE AMBIVALENCE OF AMERICANS ABROAD

Philip Claiborne Gooch, in Paris in 1848, and Elizabeth Stiles, in Vienna that year, wrote accounts of their experiences that capture the idealism and anxiety of Americans witnessing revolution and counterrevolution firsthand. Gooch, a medical student, joined a mob that invaded the Tuileries Palace, taking a seat himself upon the throne of the deposed King Louis Philippe, and was in the streets for the "June Days" uprising, remarking at seeing Alphonse de Lamartine, attempting to mediate the conflict, wounded and having his horse shot from under him. Stiles, forced to evacuate the residence where she lived with her husband, William Henry Stiles, the U.S. chargé d'affaires in Austria, witnessed Slavic peasants mustering under Habsburg authority to put down the Hungarian liberation movement. Gooch, tending to the wounded after the June Days violence, relished the chance to witness upheavals, remarking: "Many citizens are dead. . . . Long live the republic. . . . What a good time to be here now. . . . All of Europe . . . are going to throw themselves in a great conflagration or melee." Stiles, however, had less of an appetite, confiding: "The Croats dress only in sheep skins and sleep on the floor. . . . I am not proud and will associate with anybody [but] . . . what a change from nobility when law [can] neither read nor write. . . . I am daily becoming less a republican."[1]

Like Gooch and Stiles, hundreds of American students, journalists, adventurers, financiers, artists, and diplomats—whether for vacation, vocation, or avocation—found themselves in Europe during the midcentury revolutions. For them Europe was supposed to be a static place, good for cultural enrichment or commercial enterprise, not experiments in radical politics, much less revolutionary chaos. Some Americans, like Gooch, initially embraced revolutionary action or sought to help establish, in one way or another, new republican governments, in an attempt to shape them on an American model. But many, like Stiles, recoiled from a dynamic

Europe, "in subtle flux and then sudden change, a Europe that Americans had not come to discover." These latter Americans, many but not all residing in Europe for a longer period, decided that revolutionaries seen firsthand were different from what they expected of Europeans and also different from how their American background taught them revolutionaries were supposed to act or what they were supposed to aspire to achieve.[2]

Many Americans joined the European revolutions or saluted their outbreak enthusiastically, notwithstanding threats to personal security, U.S. diplomatic policy, and even U.S. law. A first obvious sign to American travelers that revolutionary Europe would be different from both their preconceived images and the United States was the security measures to which they were subjected at international borders. "People [are] delayed [and] have much trouble with passports," wrote the poet and *New York Evening Post* editor William Cullen Bryant of his journey from the French coast to Paris. "The words Liberty, Equality, Fraternity are inscribed on the churches but soldiers with fixed bayonets are marching before them. . . . I do not see much of the change in government." The Tennessean Mary Emily Donelson, daughter of the U.S. minister to Prussia, found a search by customs officials at Naples as comical as it was bothersome. It was "amusing to see twenty men turning my shawl about [and] handing it to each other as they would carry a coffin. They kept brother's cloak for further consultation." Whereas "Americans can travel in their own country from Dan to Beersheba without being asked who they are or where they are going," the travel diarist Anne Tuttle Jones Bullard exclaimed, "the chief end of man in Italy is to attend to this most farcical of all customs, carrying a passport." William Cullen Bryant made explicit the political meaning many Americans perhaps took from the inconvenience of European authorities trying to maintain national security against dangerous outside forces: "No American can see how much force . . . has to keep up existing governments of Europe, without thanking heaven that such is not the condition of his own country . . . [and returning there] even a better patriot." The serene United States, as a result of not only its geography but its unique political sensibility—where the only persons routinely subject to search were blacks suspected as fugitive slaves—had no place for such security measures.[3]

Still, whether out of a sense of novelty or of civic duty, many Americans in Europe participated in revolutionary upheaval or expressed sympathy for its achievements. A student from New York City, George Duyckinck, joined Philip Gooch in witnessing the sacking of the Tuileries and the crowd carrying the throne through the streets "like any commonplace arm chair," Duyckinck wrote in a letter. Inspired by the chaos of 24 February, Duyckinck declared, "It is a proud thing now to be an American in Europe for our country leads the world." Likewise, 275 members of the American colony in Paris soon marched to the Hôtel de Ville to congratulate the French provisional government for overthrowing the monarchy and to present a banner of the French and American flags sewn together. The "president" of the expatriates was Samuel Goodrich, famous as the "Peter Parley" author of children's literature, who also wrote an enthusiastic report for the *Boston Courier* and the *New York Herald* of the first day of the revolution, describing "a remarkable air of fun and frolic characteriz[ing] the mob," which, Goodrich noted, cried, "*Vive la Réforme!*" François Arago, an astronomer turned French minister of war, officially accepted the American congratulations and expression of unity—although once the American press learned about Arago's intellectual background, it would excoriate his political capacities.[4]

The action of the American colony in Paris followed the initiative of the U.S. minister to France Richard Rush, who, within a week of the insurgents' sacking of the Tuileries, wound through barricaded streets to the Hôtel de Ville to publicly extend U.S. recognition to the new French government, making his country the first to do so. Rush explained himself to Secretary of State James Buchanan: "Was it for me to be backward, when France appeared to be looking to us? I was unwilling to too closely scrutinize the considerations which might war with the hope of [revolutionary] success." Buchanan told Rush that the United States normally followed a policy of "de facto" recognition, meaning recognizing governments once they had proven their capacity to exercise authority over sovereign states, in accordance with international norms. Rush's rapid recognition of the French republic hardly met such criteria, but Buchanan approved Rush's action anyway, on the basis that "[the United States] can[not] be indifferent spectators to the progress of liberty . . . especially in France. We can never forget the obligations we owe that generous nation." Like American civilians in Paris, Rush and Buchanan supported the French Revolution at its outset on the assumption that Americans and French people shared a special relationship: France had assisted the United States in its successful revolution, and now the French looked to the United States for guidance on how to return the favor. Thus, George Bancroft, the U.S. minister to Britain, joined Rush in Paris over Easter 1848, seeking to educate leaders of the Second Republic on the framework and merits of a bicameral legislature. Rush, Bancroft, and other U.S. ministers in Europe in 1848, as well as Buchanan, were Democrats, their party ideology of expanding American influence abroad reinforcing their understanding of America's responsibility to encourage foreign democratic revolutions.[5]

These premises also account for Buchanan's instructions to the U.S. minister accredited to Prussia, Andrew Jackson Donelson (the nephew of the former U.S. president), and Donelson's exuberant actions in revolutionary Germany. From Berlin, Donelson sent news in March 1848 of the Frankfurt Assembly's herculean effort to replace the thirty-nine separate German states with one unified government. Buchanan replied encouragingly, "While it is our policy to not interfere in domestic concerns of foreign nations, we cannot view with indifference the effort to unite the German States in a more intimate Federal Union." As in action toward France, Buchanan counseled Donelson to be proactive, on the prospect that the German states were seeking to erect a model of government similar to the American structure. This prospect was encouraged by such German "forty-eighters" as Friedrich Hecker, who, when he arrived in New York City, told a mass meeting that the Frankfurt Assembly was greatly interested in the American constitutional system. Buchanan even went so far as to add to Donelson's appointment as U.S. representative to Prussia the title of "Minister Plenipotentiary to the Federal Government of Germany," even though, at the time, such a regime did not actually exist. Donelson, for his part, was hardly discreet, quickly revealing his preference for the stirrings of democracy in Frankfurt. In a matter of days he abandoned the American legation in Berlin, moved southwest to Frankfurt, and offered written congratulations on behalf of the American people to the Frankfurt Assembly. President James Polk would soon add his own congratulatory message to the Germans, the only people to receive such endorsement from the U.S. president.[6]

Under the industrious Donelson the United States also embarked on providing military assistance to the Frankfurt Assembly—again the only new regime in Europe to receive such support. Donelson recommended American naval reinforcement in European waters, not only to protect

American citizens but also as part of a "clear policy to befriend measures to unite Germany by a strong Federal Government." He lobbied the State Department to help the German nationalists in Frankfurt build a navy (thus, he anticipated, to arouse German patriotism) in light of an impending war with Denmark over control of the Baltic states of Schleswig and Holstein. He arranged for Prussian and Hanoverian sailors to be trained on an American ship, the U.S.S. *St. Lawrence.* He sponsored an American military advisor's visit to Frankfurt to advise German military planners. And he negotiated the arming of an American trading ship in Brooklyn, New York, for German military use. Commodore Matthew Perry, the future American naval hero, was engaged to supervise the project. All of this happened despite the Frankfurt Assembly's lack of progress in 1848 in establishing or maintaining a new German government. It shows the extent to which U.S. diplomats, believing in a German republic established on an American model, could go to help that idea.[7]

Donelson's official initiatives to lend military assistance to the Frankfurt Assembly, probably breaking U.S. neutrality laws, were matched by other Americans' extralegal efforts to help republicanize Europe by force. Historians have provided many accounts of American "filibusters" who, despite a neutrality law of 1818 that prohibited American citizens from joining foreign independence movements and participating in foreign civil conflicts and civil rebellions, forayed against nations with which the United States was formally at peace, mainly in Central America, the Caribbean, and Canada. In 1848 several dozen young Americans, many of them immigrants, set their sights across the Atlantic. These Americans' would-be armed intervention in Europe shows us the most bellicose, if brief, element of American responses to the European upheavals.[8]

Although their views of Europeans lacked the racial justification that underlay most filibustering efforts in the western hemisphere, many Americans who sought to arm or to fight with European revolutionaries shared the filibusters' roots in the "Young America" movement.[9] George Sanders, for example, edited the *United States Democratic Review,* in which he supported his call for American intervention in Europe by arranging for the purchase, carriage on his steamship line, and distribution of forty thousand muskets from the U.S. War Department. Elsewhere, Friedrich Hecker, an ardent republican organizer from Baden, fled to the United States in October 1848. A lithograph of him costumed with plumed hat, gun, saber, and pistols became part of a transatlantic "Hecker cult" that grew to fantastic proportions. In June 1849 Hecker joined the novelist Mayne Reid, an Irish immigrant and veteran of the Mexican War, in leading an American detachment to Europe. Together they assembled five hundred German and Hungarian Americans in New York, gave each a Colt revolver, and set sail to aid the rebel cause. A handful of German Americans, led by the communist Wilhelm Weitling, left the nascent union labor movement he was helping build in New York City to return to Germany to assist in the revolution there. And George McClellan, the future Union commander, prepared to join the Hungarian army as a military observer.[10]

Irish American assistance to the Irish rebellion of 1848 was perhaps the most significant of all of these clandestine operations. Overt financial support sent to the home country of course predated 1848. Daniel O'Connell, the fiery leader of the "repeal" movement to overturn the 1800 union of Great Britain and Ireland, enjoyed Irish American backing from 1828, when he gained a seat in Parliament, the first Catholic to do so. Hibernian groups from Boston to New Orleans sent money to support the struggle for repeal. But when O'Connell died in 1847, "Young Irelanders" like William Smith O'Brien and John Mitchell, frustrated with O'Connell's ineffectual work within the legislative system, called for open rebellion amid the Continental upheavals the next year.

Hearing the call of Young Ireland, Irish Americans distributed propaganda in the United States, predicting that the Continental revolutions would spread to Ireland, and staged fund-raising rallies in the spring and summer of 1848. They formed a militant sect called the Irish Republican Union (IRU) for the purpose of "promoting revolutions for the establishment of Republican Governments throughout Europe, especially in Ireland." IRU troops left the United States for Ireland in the autumn of 1848, landing in Liverpool and making their way to Dublin. But British authorities, unlike their counterparts on the Continent, acted preemptively, effectively suppressing subversive Irish newspapers and arresting their publishers and other agitators. Police circular memoranda were distributed in Ireland, ordering that all "persons coming over from America are to be immediately arrested, and searched for treasonable papers." O'Brien and Mitchell, among other ringleaders, were sent to prison colonies in Australia.[11]

British officials complained to the U.S. minister to Britain, George Bancroft, about the meddling of the IRU—comprised as it was of American citizens—in British domestic affairs. Bancroft, who apparently did not know of the IRU's activities beforehand, officially apologized to the British government and obtained their release from prison. This was ironic. A historian by trade, Bancroft is best-known for the democratic zeal with which he wrote his ten-volume *History of the United States*. Recently returned from his political lobbying in Paris, at the time he was called upon to mediate the IRU affair, he was privately predicting that events on the Continent would trigger the downfall of the British monarchy. But apparently, if European monarchies were going to be republicanized, it would happen without direct American assistance.[12]

In general, because of the brevity of the revolutions and ideological conflicts, not much came of American filibustering in Europe. Most of the rifles that George Sanders procured were malfunctioning relics of the War of 1812 and provided little firepower in 1848. Mayne Reid, Friedrich Hecker, and their band intended to support revolutionaries in France, Bavaria, and Hungary but arrived in Europe only to witness the defeats of the revolutions at the end of 1849. Reid subsequently became a Romantic novelist in London, and Hecker returned to "the great free country," America. Wilhelm Weitling published a newspaper, took part in democratic congresses in Berlin, and distributed revolutionary pamphlets in Frankfurt. But his insistence on a communist revolution, not piecemeal reform, gained him scant support, and he returned to New York City in 1850. George McClellan, the would-be military observer, could not depart the United States before the Hungarian uprising was put down by Austrian and Russian forces. (For the first time but, as history would reveal, not the last, McClellan arrived late for battle.) Finally, many Irish Americans turned against Young Ireland. The dismal outcome of the Irish rebellion of 1848 contributed to this, as did the urging of parishioners by Catholic bishops, such as Boston's John Fitzpatrick, to avoid "secret societies," to "make ourselves American now . . . [and consider] Ireland only a recollection."[13]

The European reaction to the 1848 revolutions, in fact, not only rendered American filibusters' operations futile. The counterrevolution created a profound shift in the attitudes of other Americans in Europe at the time. Where many Americans in Europe saluted and worked for liberal reform in the spring of 1848, excited about the prospect that Europeans were embracing American ideas and institutions, by that summer American expatriates had experiences that moved them to recoil in horror, or at least skepticism, about Europeans' ability to change for the better through revolution, and then to conclude that circumstances showed the superior and unique conditions of American revolutionary republicanism.

The struggle in France between liberal and socialist forces had a profound impact on American observers, both tourists and expatriates. Thomas Gold Appleton, a Bostonian intent to improve his painting and poetry writing, had come to Paris with an attitude typical of many American cosmopolites, exclaiming, "Europe is my Boston where I am truly home." Appleton, like Philip Gooch, at first relished the chance to witness revolution: "I should not . . . miss seeing an action if one is to take place." He got his chance. In May 1848 Appleton gained a pass to the new National Assembly to witness debates on whether France should lend assistance to the popular uprisings in Italy and Poland. There workmen led by the socialists Auguste Blanqui and François Raspail, who sought to use the occasion to take control of the government and force it toward a more radical agenda, caught him in their storming of the assembly. "For more than two hours I saw France without a government and anarchy rolling over her," Appleton remarked. Leaving the assembly, he ran into a "*blouse*," a working-class insurgent, who pointed at him, shouting, "You see what work we make with aristocrats!" Appleton disabused his accuser by shouting back, "My friend, I belong to a Republic where to be well dressed is a sign of a man of the people!" Appleton scrambled up the courtyard wall, where he "enjoyed the delicious sight of a wall of bayonets . . . the respectable files of the NATIONAL GUARD wheeling in," to make arrests and restore order. Appleton's experience was a variation of the way clothing in the French Revolution of the eighteenth century manifested a person's political standing—under threat Appleton asserted that his bourgeois dress showed him to be a good democrat. More important, his narrow escape sobered his perspective: "This shocking affair has strengthened the Government . . . [although] I shall judge [its] real strength by [whether the insurgents are] immediately shot or not." Face to face with the revolutionary violence he had hoped to see, Appleton asserted his American difference and called for restoration of order.[14]

The June Days offered an even more complicated scene of revolution to Americans, significant because by the summer of 1848 several American journalists had come to Paris to cover events. Charles Dana, who earlier had resided at the utopian community Brook Farm and still sympathized with the doctrines of the French utopian socialist Charles Fourier, came to Paris as a reporter for the *New York Tribune* and four other newspapers. Dana arrived on 25 June, two days after the first barricades appeared following the French government's abolishment of the national workshops, established earlier for Paris's unemployed. Dana circulated through guarded streets and blockades, observing both worker camps and installations of soldiers being readied for the counterattack, and the fighting itself. In his reporting Dana emphasized the government's brutality against the insurrectionists, whom he did not believe were socialists or communists, although they were "no doubt operated on by the agents of various factions." He wrote, "They only cherish a conviction, which they carry to fanaticism, that justice is not and cannot be done by the existing relation of employed and employer." After witnessing the problems of European republicanism, Dana returned to the United States and embraced "the blessings" of American economic opportunity and political democracy already achieved. And he abandoned Fourierism, ironically, because he, like Karl Marx, decided its principle of cooperative work leading to social justice had done little to prevent bloodshed between the bourgeois French government and socialists and peasants. From Europe, however, Dana explained the June Days to American readers as the result of the French government's failure to help the workers establish self-run cooperatives.[15]

Other American reporters' coverage of the June Days, however, emphasized French insurrectionists' connections to both socialism and violence, linking the two concepts for American readers. The novelist Donald Mitchell was studying law when the revolutions in the spring of 1848 intrigued him with what they might suggest about the "Right to Property," different from his legal reading. He arrived in Paris shortly before the June Days as a reporter for the *New York Courier and Enquirer*, like the *Tribune* a Whig organ, but more conservative; the two newspapers sparred about Horace Greeley's support for Fourierism. George Kendall covered events in Europe for the *New Orleans Picayune*, having already made himself probably America's first war correspondent when, as an aide to General Winfield Scott in the U.S.-Mexico war, he sent reports of American advances back to the *Picayune* via an express pony service.[16]

Mitchell and Kendall represented events as macabre and sinister. Mitchell, writing about 25 June, the same day that Dana arrived in Paris, emphasized that the insurgents' "violence is equaled by their cruelty; in defiance of all civil usage, they have murdered their prisoners either behead[ing] them . . . or hanging them to their window bars. Such is the action of the advocates, of what they call a Social Republic!" Kendall, meanwhile, at first observed that Lamartine's "meet[ing the insurrection] manfully and [with] firmness has probably saved the [French] Republic." Accustomed from Mexico to bullets whistling around him, he also, unlike Mitchell, sought to get as close as possible to barricade fighting, at one point observing a charge of the National Guard while huddled in a nearby doorway. But he likewise concluded: "The most important element at work in bringing about the revolution was socialism. . . . Hardly had the smoke of the revolution of February cleared away before promises . . . were made to the working classes, assuring them . . . an abundance that maketh the heart glad . . . a perfect millennium." And both Mitchell and Kendall, probably relying on French government statements in the Paris press, spoke viscerally about rebel barbarity. They described a *cuirassier* being impaled and disemboweled and soldiers having their hands or feet cut off. Both emphasized the savagery of women: "Two fiends in female form even cut up the bodies of some of the younger lads . . . of the Guard Mobile . . . and taking the flesh to a pork butcher . . . told him to make it up into pies!" "Several women were arrested who had sold poisoned brandy to the soldiers." Kendall claimed, perhaps disingenuously, "I trust that many of these stories of atrocious cruelty may turn out untrue, but certainly they have been told," and later wrote, "The European masses lacked . . . an education which would teach them the uses of liberty." Mitchell reiterated: "Socialism . . . that shameless doctrine which instructs us that all the systems of Public Liberty now current throughout the civilized world are spurious . . . this is the doctrine which has set on the workmen of Paris to their revolt." Mitchell's and Kendall's titillating accounts, more than Dana's, registered with American readers.[17]

Satisfied that Paris was safe after his run-in with a *blouse* in May 1848, Thomas Appleton shifted his enthusiasm for revolution to struggles farther east, to the revolutions in central Europe. He used his family's name in textiles to vouch for members of the Frankfurt Assembly who wished to come to New England. Even more remote, Hungarians, and in particular Louis Kossuth, received Appleton's most romantic praise. Appleton described Kossuth as an "uncorrupted hero" and believed the Hungarian

FIGURE 3. Barricades on rue Saint-Maur, Paris, June 1848. Photograph by
Eugene Thibault. The specter of barricades and class violence chilled the atti-
tudes of Americans, abroad and at home, toward the European revolutions.
(Réunion des Musées Nationaux/Art Resource, NY)

uprising against Austria demonstrated "the gallant school-boy feeling of
fair play."[18]

Yet within Central Europe the attitudes of Americans to nearby revolutions were guided less by romantic ideals and more by reflexive self-
interest. William Henry Stiles, the U.S. chargé d'affaires in Austria, initially
expressed confidence in the potential of both Austrian and Hungarian
peoples to achieve popular government by revolution. A witness to street
fighting in Vienna, where houses were torched if they did not display window candles in sympathy for the revolution, and attacks on the Austrian
feudal assembly, Stiles, like Richard Rush in Paris and Andrew Donelson
in Frankfurt, foresaw a triumph of democracy. On 16 March, only two days
after the first major confrontation in Vienna, Stiles resolved to compile

"an entire history of that struggle by which Austria has been transformed from the most absolute to the most liberal government of Europe." He predicted that the Austrians' Teutonic character, the "remarkable patience and coolness for which the Germans are distinguished," would see them through. He conducted a correspondence with Louis Kossuth, as the Magyar led his people into battle, and offered his services to Kossuth and the Hapsburgs to negotiate a cease-fire. The Hapsburgs refused, but Secretary of State Buchanan approved of Stiles's actions.[19]

In his optimism Stiles noted only in passing a development ultimately fatal to the Hungarian cause, the arrival in Vienna of a Hungarian deputation that demanded from the provisional Austrian authority (the "Camarilla," acting as regent after the flight of Emperor Ferdinand) recognition of the Magyar language and Hungarian hegemony in Slavic Europe. This agenda quickly erupted into ethnic and class warfare among Hungarians, Croatians, Serbs, and Rumanians, undermining the Hungarians' quest to shake off Austrian authority. Stiles, a planter and lawyer of Savannah, was impressed by the severity of these ethnic and class conflicts and in fact described them for American readers in a memoir he published about his overseas experience. An example of an American using the European upheavals to emphasize the virtue of maintaining the status quo in the United States, Stiles's memoir described the struggles of embattled European serfs and the conditions that provoked them exotically, to show the superior conditions of American slaves, who had, he concluded, no such need to rise in arms.[20]

In the summer of 1848 William and Elizabeth Stiles fled Vienna when a citizens' committee seized authority from the Camarilla. At the same time they received word of the June uprising of workers in Paris and preparations by the Frankfurt Assembly for a united Germany. Now the news confirmed for them the infectious nature of malignant revolutions, not their imminent success. "The news from Paris is again very bad[:] another revolution of the workmen," Elizabeth wrote. "At Frankfort they elected the Archduke John as the Executive of all Germany when they have as yet formed no government." Earlier, William had applauded a German national trait of calmness. Now he remarked that "the Germans are a strange people both in acts and in motives by which they are impelled." Popular upheavals that did not quickly resolve themselves created uncertainties for which Americans were not prepared and could easily find fault, even to the

point, as Elizabeth Stiles admitted, of questioning the virtue of republicanism. The sordidness of European democratic upheaval revealed the advantages of popular government previously accomplished by revolution, as in
the United States, over the dangers of popular government in the process
of being enacted, as in Europe. In this context the American Revolution
was estimable because, frankly, it had already happened.[21]

American statesmen's skepticism about the various republican uprisings in Italy also reflected their formulation of U.S. policy based upon
whether Italians seemed capable of establishing regimes in an American
revolutionary tradition. In Italy the United States had established full diplomatic relations only with the Kingdom of Sardinia, its capital the industrial city of Turin. The city-states of Sicily, Venice, and even Rome hosted
only a U.S. chargé d'affaires or a commercial consulate.[22] Yet U.S. representatives, like Richard Rush on their own authority, actually tendered official
congratulations to fledgling republics established by Italians in Sicily and
Rome, the U.S. consul in Rome, Nicholas Brown, assuring the new Roman
government that officials in Washington would "take the earliest opportunity to recognize [the Roman republic]."[23]

But the response of the State Department to the actions of enthusiastic
diplomats in Italy was one of rebuke, not blessing. Despite Brown's endorsement's consistency with actions of Rush and Donelson, Secretary of
State Buchanan recalled Brown from his post in Rome on account of his
enthusiasm and issued a rebuke to John Marston, the U.S. consul in Sicily, for his precipitate action there. Buchanan wrote Marston to praise his
action and his "patriotic motives" but said that since Marston was not an
accredited U.S. minister, he had no authority to offer U.S. recognition to
the new Sicilian government. Marston was forbidden to further encourage
the Sicilians.[24]

Buchanan's posture seems inconsistent, given the lenient U.S. recognition policy exercised in France and Germany.[25] Italians' Catholicism rendered their capacity for revolution dubious in many Americans' minds. But
besides the alleged political role of Italians' religion, U.S. policies regarding
Italy also drew upon antebellum Americans' understanding of the American Revolution and its legacy. Italians in 1848 were no less likely to succeed
in an American-style revolution than French or German peoples were, in
terms of how Americans at the time conceived of such an event: establishing republican government through minimal violence; maintaining

Christian principles, property rights, and small government; and initiating long-term domestic serenity and prosperity. But eighteenth-century Italians had not helped the American patriots succeed in their own revolution, while France had; and leading Italians, such as Giuseppe Mazzini, rejected the idea of Italian federalism, unlike what Americans thought Germans might contemplate. Thus, Nathaniel Niles, the American chargé d'affaires to Sardinia, counseled that "moderation, the greatest of political virtues, is . . . a crime in the Italian mind," and John Rowan, the American chargé d'affaires in Sicily, emphasized how corrupt Sicilians were even after they declared independence from King Ferdinand II in Naples, lamenting, as "a citizen of the United States I regret that a better development of Democracy has not taken place."[26]

When the momentum of liberal revolutions did begin to flag by the summer of 1848 and into 1849, American observers in Europe in general concluded that European revolutionaries simply were not able to embrace American revolutionary principles and that reaction was what best suited Europe—rather than considering whether what they believed about the American revolutionary example was inadequate to understand European conditions at the mid-nineteenth century. Beginning in the spring of 1849, the conservative Whig administrations of Zachary Taylor and Millard Fillmore responded quickly to conditions of counterrevolution. The new Whig secretary of state, John Clayton, swiftly aborted programs toward American-German military cooperation, canceling work in progress to outfit an American ship for German naval usage and naming a replacement for Andrew Donelson, Edward Hannegan, as U.S. minister to Prussia, but not to Frankfurt. Clayton declared sternly, "We shall not renew the experiment of sending a minister to another government before it [is] organized."[27]

Whigs actually did maintain the Democrats' interest in embracing the prospects of Hungary to establish a republic independent of the Habsburg Empire. Compared to their familiarity with the history and culture of France and the German and Italian states, Americans of different political stripes were less informed about Hungary. Thus, perhaps they were even more idealistic about the Hungarian rebellion, which they greeted as a modern reprisal of the American struggle for independence against an imperial power of the previous century, an attitude that would build until shortly after the arrival of Louis Kossuth in the United States in late 1851.

Thus, President Taylor instructed A. Dudley Mann, a long-time "to-bacco agent" attached to the U.S. ministry in Prussia, to travel secretly to Hungary for a firsthand analysis of the Hungarians' prospects for establishing an independent regime. But Mann, like many of the American filibusters, did not arrive in time to be able to confirm Hungarian sovereignty. By the time he arrived in Vienna, the Hungarian struggle had collapsed under the joint repressive weight of Austrian and Russian armies, Kossuth had fled, and his successor had surrendered Hungarian forces. Secret agent Mann had written in June 1849, "I shall desire no more boundless joy than to report that 'Hungary has established her independence.'" Three months later Mann was still ebullient, but for a different reason. Now he boasted that U.S. officials were compelled "by reason, instead of passion," and toasted the secretary of state by noting that Americans never "lose sight of our true duty by becoming anarchists, monarchists, disunionists, false philanthropists, socialists, or communists." Despite his previous exposure to European political and social conditions, Mann's observations of the difficult conditions of nation-building in Central Europe induced him to embrace a typical American vocabulary about inherent or ideological differences between a flawed Europe and a superior United States.[28]

Mann's turnabout on American involvement in Hungary punctuated the rapid scale-down of American interest in Europe, once revolutionary momentum was halted by a resurgent old regime. Three years after Louis Napoleon was elected president of the French Republic in December 1848, his coup d'état gave him dictatorial authority to wipe out the foundation of civil rights the French republic had initiated. In the summer of 1849 Frederick William IV trumped the Frankfurt Assembly by offering the German people a constitution before the "Professors' Parliament" could produce its own more liberal version. In Italy Pius IX returned to the Vatican early in 1850, assisted by French military occupation of the defeated city of Rome.

American statesmen greeted these events with both regret and smugness. President Millard Fillmore (who had succeeded Taylor upon his death) ordered that the new U.S. minister to France, Richard Rives, not recognize the reorganized government of Louis Napoleon Bonaparte until a plebiscite signaled popular support for the regime. The plebiscite yielded this result, although the editor of the Albany Evening Journal, Thurlow Weed, on sabbatical in France and a firsthand observer of the voting process, described conditions that were hardly impartial or conducive to a fair representation of public opinion. Weed observed that polls were surrounded by military sentinels and that ballots for the plebiscite were printed simply: "The French people desire the maintenance of authority of Louis Napoleon Bonaparte" and "Yes."[29]

But comments of U.S. officials who witnessed the decline of apparent American-style European democracies suggest that they did not believe that Europeans deserved better. Robert Walsh, the U.S. consul in Paris, endorsed Louis Napoleon's coup, publicly quoting the *Times* of London that the French dictator's government was "the only one which offered a chance of dealing with dark doings of . . . [an] immense democratic conspiracy which threatened Europe — not France alone." Theodore Fay, the chargé d'affaires of the American ministry in Berlin, stood beside King Frederick William IV in a review of the triumphant Prussian army. Fay observed that "the strength of Prussia consists in the fear of the people of . . . the bloodshed attending the triumph of the democratic party." William Stiles in Austria concluded bluntly: "The people of Europe have been kept so long in the darkness of slavery that they are totally unfit for the light of freedom. . . . After a disastrous experience of their incapacity they [are] most ready to return to their former institutions."[30]

A final aspect of American expatriates' experience in revolutionary Europe suggests that, indeed, they prospered materially more from the revolutions' demise than from their initial successes. This indeed was contrary to the projections of American policy makers and merchants, who envisioned economic windfalls amid the onset of popular democracy in Europe. Austrian policy under Prince von Metternich taxed foreign products heavily, especially tobacco, as the German Zollverein did on goods produced outside Europe. In 1844 a U.S. representative negotiated a treaty that would have provided reductions of U.S. duties on some five hundred articles, in exchange for German duty relief on U.S. tobacco and cotton. The treaty did not entail equivalent concessions, however, and the Senate, persuaded by Whigs supporting Henry Clay's anti–free trade "American System," rejected the treaty. The 1848 revolutions raised the possibility that new European leaders might emerge, their republicanism causing them to be more sympathetic to American trade interests. Secretary of State James Buchanan emphasized to Andrew Jackson Donelson that in his approach to the Frankfurt Assembly he should prioritize achieving an adjustment of the German tariff. Freeman Hunt, the editor of the *Merchants' Magazine,* saw little difference between commercial and ideological objectives: "In western Europe the revolutions must be productive of great results in a commercial point of view. . . . The republicanizing of Europe brings its people nearer to the United States in every respect."[31]

But a break in European trade protection didn't develop, because the 1848 revolutions created financial uncertainty, not prosperity, a probability that optimistic American statesmen and commercial editors seem not to have anticipated. To the detriment of American traders, economic competition erupted in 1848 between Austria and Prussia, for example, with each side raising its tariffs to attempt to attract other German states into its orbit. And demand for American cotton dipped in the spring of 1848 when European buyers became uncertain of the availability of credit facilities. But as authoritarian governments reasserted control by 1849, cotton surpassed its former demand. In November 1849 the *New York Herald* aptly portrayed the link between political retrenchment and American economic success in Europe: "If we cannot command red revolutions, the sacking of cities . . . we can console ourselves with [a] rise in the cotton market . . . [creating] as great a sensation in Wall Street and in New Orleans as the recent revolutions did among speculators in the destiny of the human race."[32]

Recovery of European stability and the quashing of the revolutions provided the setting for an even more revealing tale of American financial, antirevolutionary success: the transatlantic venture of the Washington banker William Wilson Corcoran, of the firm Corcoran & Riggs. Following Andrew Jackson's veto of the recharter of the Bank of the United States (BUS) in 1832, Corcoran & Riggs took over many functions traditionally associated with the BUS. The firm facilitated interregional trade in financial instruments, eased foreign access to American investments, and centralized banking activity for the country—all, ironically, activities cited by Jackson in his veto message condemning the national bank.[33]

Examples of Corcoran & Riggs's activities reveal the story of American economic expansion in the first part of the 1800s. Corcoran & Riggs underwrote the investments of local and state governments and railroad and steamship enterprises across the country, including Savannah city-improvement bonds, Ohio state canal stock, and bonds of the New York and Liverpool United States Mail Steamship Company. It acted as trustee for U.S. stocks issued to indemnify the Chickasaw Indians. It was the prime bidder and underwriter for the government's sale of bonds to pay for the war with Mexico and, upon conclusion of the peace treaty, handled the transfer of indemnity funds from the U.S. treasury to Mexican buyers. Corcoran & Riggs also gave tangible support to revolutionary republics elsewhere in the western hemisphere. It acted as middleman for bonds issued by the fledgling republics of Venezuela, in 1826, and New Granada (now Colombia), in 1843. In brief, before the 1848 revolutions Corcoran & Riggs underwrote the manifestation of the American destiny, as many Americans envisioned that destiny.[34]

Despite his bank's far-flung success, however, the partner William Corcoran faced a budding crisis in the autumn of 1848. Corcoran, the main force behind Corcoran & Riggs's activities, had just acquired $14 million of a $16 million loan floated by the U.S. treasury to pay for final stages of the war effort in Mexico. This was a large sum, so large that Corcoran's partner, George Riggs, grew squeamish and quit the bank over the transaction. Compounding the problem of the large amount was the difficulty of finding buyers, at home and abroad: the national money supply in private hands, despite the wartime need for currency, was shrinking as tariff collections piled specie into the U.S. treasury. Meanwhile, a financial crisis in Britain in 1847 suppressed the British appetite for overseas securities. Corcoran faced the prospect of interest payments with little to no income to help make them.[35]

Armed with the title of "Agent of the U.S. Treasury Department" to bolster his credibility, Corcoran crossed the Atlantic in September 1848 to enlist the British investment house Baring Brothers in the loan-sale effort. Financial results of upheavals on the Continent earlier in the year had been mixed: the revolutions for a time caused European investors to seek refuge in U.S. government bonds, but that supply had been offset when revolutionary regimes, conspicuously the French Second Republic, had reneged on securities issued under old government authority, freezing European currencies. That stricture, and Corcoran's failure to charm Thomas Baring—the phlegmatic British banker called Corcoran an "overrun boaster" after meeting him—netted the American financier for his efforts a sale of only $3 million of the $14 million for which his bank had agreed to find buyers.[36]

When Corcoran returned home, he persuaded U.S. Treasury Secretary

Robert Walker, a Democrat, as well as his successor, the Whig William Meredith, to postpone collection of the 1848 loan proceeds under the guise of allowing specie to remain in the U.S. economy rather than in a federal vault. More accurately, Corcoran was trying to save his own bank. Thomas Ward, Baring Brothers' agent in Boston, wrote Corcoran: "The [European] continent politically [is] in great confusion, and no one can tell what is to come of it. . . . It affects the funds in England, and the English buy little or nothing." In the autumn of 1848 Corcoran still had most of the 1848 loan sitting in the books of Corcoran & Riggs, due to the destabilizing effect of radical democracy threatening to emerge in Europe.[37]

The swift and sometimes brutal counterrevolutions in Europe allowed Corcoran to escape. In the winter of 1848 Austrian imperial troops bombarded and retook Vienna from radical control, following Habsburg suppression of democratic-nationalistic uprisings in Prague and Milan. In December 1848 Louis Napoleon, promising order over freedom, was elected president of France overwhelmingly (receiving 5.5 million votes, compared to the American hero Lamartine's eighteen thousand). By reasserting their political and military strength, conservative regimes renewed their well-to-do constituents' confidence to invest on both sides of the Atlantic.

Accordingly, Corcoran received word from the British firm Gammon and Drinkard that "we are now anxious to 'make all the wires work' on the Continent and have the most encouraging prospects." Applications to purchase U.S. securities flowed in from leading European investment houses. Corcoran & Riggs began unloading its U.S. war bonds to Ketwick & Voomberg and Borski of Amsterdam, Hottinguer and Cie of Paris, and the Rothschilds group in England. Selling activity was so great that by the spring of 1849 Corcoran & Riggs was buying 1848 bonds to use as collateral for lower-interest borrowings to finance American railroads and state bonds. Elisha Riggs Jr., who had replaced his father in the bank in 1848, wrote Corcoran from London later in 1849 that the market for U.S. securities is "entirely supported by European demand. . . . Great excitement has prevailed regarding the French collision, which has however almost expired. . . . We are perfectly easy in money matters." Riggs concluded his message appropriately: "Everything [is] in perfect order."[38]

As the experience of an American in Europe, Corcoran's was one of the least affected by sentiments of revolutionary sympathy—or for that matter conscious sympathy for counterrevolution. Although his firm had earlier financed the growth of antimonarchical regimes in South America and the United States, this American banker now profited handsomely from the resurrection of authoritarian regimes in Europe. For many Americans such as Corcoran, when confronted with the personal or financial risks of revolution, republican sympathy was negotiable, not to say irrelevant.

Through the Monroe Doctrine the United States had pledged not to interfere in European politics, in exchange for European powers' disengagement from colonialism in Latin America. On the eve of the 1848 revolutions, however, ministers in various Old World courts, anxious over the Americans' disruptive aspirations, did not take U.S. isolationism for granted. François Guizot, the chief advisor to King Louis Philippe of France, complained about "radical democracies such as America . . . [where] public authorities are gaining ground over the rights of birth." Prince Klemens von Metternich, the prime minister of the Hapsburg Empire, felt that "the New World . . . has launched on a course such as is threatening every European government with dissolution and death. . . . [The] maintenance of peace and legitimate order in Europe is entirely foreign to the United States." Leaders of the European conservative order feared that all Americans were would-be filibusters, targeting Europe with the terror of radical democracy.[39]

Ralph Waldo Emerson, in France and England in 1848, was no political activist, much less a filibuster, but his philosophy about the European revolutions, even after witnessing socialists' meetings and violence, reflected an American attitude that European conservatives would have feared. Like other Americans, Emerson recorded in his journal that he was "heartily glad" of what he called "the Shopkeepers' victory," the defeat of socialists and workers by the French civic guard in May 1848. He acknowledged peculiarities about French revolutionaries: "The fire & fury of the people, when they are interrupted or thwarted, are inconceivable to New England." Yet he appraised events in Paris as part of a larger "Movement party," his term for the democratic idealism that, in his view, he supported. His reflections suggest what many Americans in Europe did in response to witnessing the 1848 revolutions and, conversely, what Emerson believed they should do. He wrote: "The moment revolution comes . . . the scholar recoils; — and joins the rich. That he should not do. He should accept as necessary the position of armed neutrality abhorring the crimes of the [revolutionary], yet more abhorring the oppression & hopeless selfishness of the rich, & . . . say, the time will come when these poor *enfans perdus* of revolution will have instructed their party, if only by their fate, & wiser counsels will prevail, & the music & the dance of liberty will take me in also. Then I shall not have forfeited my right to speak & act for the Movement party." Emerson was not drawn to politics and mobs, but his call for "armed neutrality" was a possible position, ideological and physical, that other Americans in Europe during the 1848 revolutions could have embraced.[40]

Emerson's attitude, however, was atypical of many American expatriates, among whom European rulers' predictions about American hostility to a Europe of inherited rights and peace through coercion were overly pessimistic. American expatriates in Europe during the mid-nineteenth century at first foresaw a new exuberant American mission in Europe, but their vision returned dramatically to a familiar, though even more isolated, American example for Europe. To be sure, Americans abroad, mostly more bourgeois than bohemian, were perhaps predisposed to the skepticism they eventually evinced about the 1848 revolutions, and the successes and then failures of the revolutions influenced their understanding of America's role in the transatlantic world. But it is worth marking the irony of Americans professing faith in republicanism and popular sovereignty as worthy outcomes of a revolution, only to backtrack from those professions when they witnessed or learned how problematic it was for others to accomplish such objectives. Such ambivalence reflected the larger tension between Americans' interest in international stability and others' emulation of an American revolutionary example. Stark or confusing differences between what American expatriates assumed a revolution should be like, and what they experienced directly, showed that for many the American revolutionary republic was unique because it protected social order and afforded economic opportunity, emphases that the direct experience of turbulent revolution did not create but did clarify. Meanwhile, Europe became less of a sentimental home for those Americans abroad like Thomas Appleton, when its peoples overreached themselves in attempting democratic revolution.

2. THE RISE AND FALL OF THE 1848 REVOLUTIONS IN AMERICAN PUBLIC CULTURE

When Philip Claiborne Gooch, the American medical student, returned to the United States from Europe in 1849, he commenced his practice in Virginia but kept up his interest in public affairs, which his experiences in revolutionary Paris had piqued. He became an organizer for a Democratic Party committed to extending American influence abroad. And to conduct his medical and political circuit-riding, he bought a horse, at fifty dollars "a very good bargain," which he named Lamartine—as a reminder of the turbulence and excitement he had experienced. Naming his horse in honor of the fallen French revolutionary allowed him to display symbolic sympathy for a radical foreign cause. But even while he displayed this revolutionary symbol, Gooch was pursuing a profitable profession and supporting one of the main political parties of the day. In his own nominal way this young Virginian reconstructed the facts of the European upheavals for his own purposes within the American domestic scene.[1]

What does it mean that Americans such as Philip Gooch "reconstructed" the European revolutions to fit the American scene? Historians tell us that with the passage of time revolutionary ideology often may be adapted to concerns different from an actual revolution, thus altering the original ideology's message of upheaval. Such a phenomenon occurred when Americans expressed their feelings about mid-nineteenth-century events in Europe. It was not the passage of time, however, that allowed Americans to adapt European revolutionary ideology, but the passage of that ideology across the Atlantic.[2]

The case of Philip Gooch and his noble horse Lamartine is only one example of the variety of ways Americans demonstrated their awareness of the 1848 revolutions. The result is a kind of panorama—a mid-nineteenth-century rolling American picture. Different from many studies that focus on a single theme in antebellum American political culture over a longer period, the picture offered here presents a wide view of American society at a particular moment, galvanized by events overseas. Many Americans participated in street demonstrations to show solidarity with the European revolutions. Others evinced sympathy in their choice of dress and popular entertainment or in renaming towns and counties in honor of European heroes. Events in Europe also became the subject of American students' assignments in secondary and higher education and provoked at least one esteemed university to punish a faculty member for his opinion of the revolutions.

These miscellaneous expressions of how Americans grasped the news of the European revolutions reflect the breadth of the evidence that many ordinary Americans appropriated some common aspects of the news from Europe. Later generations of Americans, affected by television, air conditioning, and the Internet, would more often receive and respond to news about important national or international events in physical isolation from others. But in the mid-nineteenth century Americans habitually responded to important news, gained mainly from newspapers, out-of-doors, roughly together. "By 1850," Mary Ryan has written, "newspaper offices became gathering spots for obtaining political information, and even the illiterate congregated on street corners and in grogshops for a public reading of the dailies." Thus, news of the revolutions from Europe, printed, read or listened to, and reconstructed, revealed and fostered a public revolutionary identity that united Americans, although, because they lived in a relatively open society, Americans expressed that identity in a variety of cultural forms.[3]

Michael Kammen has written about the impact of the U.S. Constitution on American culture, attempting to understand "the perceptions and misperceptions, uses and abuses, knowledge and ignorance of ordinary Americans." He utilizes a range of sources, including popular magazines, novels about the Supreme Court, holiday orations, school lessons, U.S. naturalization training textbooks and questions, cartoons, editorials, and artwork. Kammen finds that Americans' tradition of "constitutionalism, in all of its varied manifestations . . . embodies a set of values, a range of options, and a means of resolving conflicts within a framework of consensus."[4]

This chapter similarly attempts to interpret the impact and display of the 1848 revolutions on American public life, its popular path—an eclectic one, often crooked, sometimes illogical—thus tracing how a broad if somewhat misunderstood phenomenon may emerge in American cultural life. Americans' expressions of a public revolutionary identity from 1848 to 1852 shared two tendencies. First, Americans used 1848 in Europe to commemorate particular aspects of their own revolutionary past, although this meant that when revolutionary events in Europe did not conform to many Americans' commemorative preferences, the details of European events were often altered or omitted altogether. Second, individual Americans used the symbols and language of revolution to express a unity with their surrounding community, although that community changed over the course of the 1848 revolutions. Initially, the revolutionary community that Americans celebrated was a transatlantic one, promising to draw the United States and Europe closer together in republican partnership. But as the revolutions in Europe met defeat, Americans reconsidered their ideas about revolution in order to express and affirm their uniqueness: a nascent transatlantic revolutionary community thus rapidly became distinctly American. The range of ways that Americans reconstructed revolutionary events in Europe actually reveals a rough consensus of the conservative values of American society and culture at the time, rooted in an understanding of a protective American revolutionary past.

The French republic drew much American attention in the spring of 1848. The fate of the whole of Europe west of Russia, it seemed, rested in French hands. Americans like Phillip Gooch celebrated in particular the early revolutionary leadership of the French poet and national historian Alphonse de Lamartine. The American press approved of Lamartine's resistance to the adoption of the red flag of revolution over the Hôtel de Ville, the traditional center of revolutionary gathering in Paris. Soon after the French people had toppled the regime of King Louis Philippe, Lamartine issued a diplomatic circular in which he promised that France would abide by the 1815 Treaty of Vienna and not seek to reconstruct the empire of Napoleonic Europe, allowing anyone in the transatlantic world worried about French territorial expansion to breathe a little easier. The Massachusetts senator Charles Sumner wrote of Lamartine that his "position is one of incalculable influence, not only over the destinies of France, but the progress of civilization."[5]

Other Americans also paid tribute to Lamartine. Newspapers recounted Lamartine's life before the revolution, and Lamartine's romantic history of the French Revolution of 1789, *Les Girondins*, published in 1847, gained popularity. In *Les Girondins* Lamartine saluted the republicanism of the bourgeoisie and decried revolutionary violence—arguing, for instance, that Louis XVI should have been exiled, not executed. This attracted American readers to the work, one reviewer observing that it was "rendered peculiarly of interest at this time, when the experience of the past may afford instructive lessons to the present." Americans in Arkansas, Wisconsin, Pennsylvania, and, later, Colorado rewarded Lamartine's prudence by naming or renaming towns after him.[6]

But Americans hardly took notice only of events in France or limited their expressions of sympathy to municipal ceremonies. They also expressed sympathy individually, like Philip Gooch through his horse, through personal choices of consumer goods and forms of dress and entertainment. Stationed as a correspondent for the *New York Tribune* in Rome during its revolution of 1849, Margaret Fuller reported to readers: "Many handsome women wore the red liberty cap. . . . [Although] men looked too vulgar in the liberty cap . . . the noble though coarse Roman outline . . . made a fine effect." Fuller used her columns in the *Tribune* to call Americans to emulate the sacrifices of the revolutionaries in Rome and to overturn inequities in the United States. Americans by and large didn't heed Margaret Fuller the way she wanted them to, but—perhaps drawn by her description of revolutionary Romans as handsome, coarse, and noble—they did adopt clothing to simulate European radicalism.[7]

Revolutionary headgear appeared in a particularly broad spectrum of settings. The red, green, and white cockade of the Italian independence movement adorned working-class celebrants and upper-class promenaders alike in New York City, whose inhabitants tracked news accounts of republicans in Venice going to the opera dressing in red, green, and white. A journalist in Madison, Wisconsin, reported sighting the French tricolor hat, carefully specifying the order as "middle white, next blue, and outer circle red" to educate prospective wearers in their efforts at revolutionary authenticity. Americans mad in their attempts to imitate the fashion of the Hungarian revolutionary Louis Kossuth doffed the "Kossuth cap," designed by enterprising American haberdashers. Such revolutionary headgear provided a token connection with revolutionaries across the Atlantic.[8]

A more symbolic kind of headwear was the "liberty cap," whose image appeared in the recruiting literature of the American filibuster Narciso López. The liberty cap, dating back to classical Rome, was understood to have been given to slaves upon gaining their freedom. Its importance as a symbol of revolution was revived in the 1500s during the Dutch wars for independence against Spain, gaining greatest prominence during the French Revolution of the eighteenth century.[9]

In López's propaganda the liberty cap was put to new use. López was a Venezuelan who arrived in the United States in July 1848. Beginning the next year and continuing until his execution by Spanish authorities in Cuba in 1851, López mounted several "filibusters," or clandestine invasions, to liberate Cuba. López had grown up in the era of the great Simón Bolívar, the leader of the South American republics' revolt against Spanish colonialism. But López felt himself betrayed by Bolívar, whose flight from Venezuela in 1814 allowed Spanish authorities to massacre several dozen of López's townspeople, including his father. George Washington, more than Bolívar, inspired López, who, overlooking Washington's policy of neutrality during his presidency, proclaimed his cause in the 1840s a legacy of the spirit of America's founding father. López anointed his rough-and-tumble followers, typically discharged veterans of the Mexican War and numbering as many as six hundred at any one time, as "Sons of Washington . . . come to free a people [the people of Cuba]." Besides the American Revolution and the Mexican War, López also took inspiration from the European uprisings of 1848. In their audacious assaults to liberate Cuba, López's armies wore the red attire of the Italian Carbonari, the secret republican societies at the center of the Italian states' independence movements against Austria, and the attire of Giuseppe Garibaldi's famous legion. While Narciso López likely would have undertaken the liberation of Cuba even in the absence of news about the European upheavals, those events provided him a way to internationalize his cause, drawing on enthusiasm for faraway revolutions to undertake another one closer to home. López's use of liberty-cap iconography to recruit followers to invade and then free Cuba, inspired by both the American Revolution and the European revolutions of 1848, illustrates how the two episodes could work together to shape and license Americans' thought and action—whether choosing revolutionary headgear or causing trouble abroad.[10]

Americans also could connect with the European revolutions when they went to the theater—or even when they went dancing. For example, in early 1849 Mary Emily Donelson, the daughter of Andrew Jackson Donelson, the U.S. minister to Prussia and to the Frankfurt Assembly, re-

marked on the elegance she witnessed at a ball in Berlin. The event reminded her of galas in Nashville and provided a respite from the cold,
muddy streets of the German capital that she tolerated in accompanying
her father on his diplomatic mission. Mary Emily did not share her father's
interest in assisting the downfall of the Prussian monarchy. She wrote to
him that she was attracted to a striking Prussian officer at a gala that "commenced at eight and continued until four in the morning. The toilettes
were brilliant, and the whole company was gay as gay can be." Mary Emily Donelson, not unlike many American tourists, was more debutante
than democrat.[11]

In the homeland of Miss Donelson, however, dancing steps evocative of
European radicalism, not refinement, became a rage. The polka and mazurka grew popular in the late 1840s, propelled by eastern European immigrants to America, as well as movements for independence among Polish,
Hungarian, and Czech peoples, among whom the dances originated. At
first the steps were considered merely tastefully avant-garde. Benjamin
Harrison VIII, son of the late president William Henry Harrison, first en-
countered the polka when he visited Philadelphia in 1845. In response to
his sister Ann's inquiry, Harrison assured her that "there is nothing in the
polka to shock one's ideas of propriety." But soon Americans associated the
dance with the European revolutions. In his diary for April 1848, George
Templeton Strong, a New York City attorney, commented on the revolution in Prussia. A stalwart conservative, Strong disliked both rapid shifts
of power between the people and the monarch and impulsive New York
newspapers that acclaimed the triumph of popular sovereignty. "Prussia
isn't a republic after all," Strong noted dryly when King Frederick William
IV kept his authority by force. His next entry read: "[I] wish I had the man
that invented the polka. I'd scrape him to death with oyster shells." Strong
made no attempt at eloquent transitions between ideas, but the proximity
between his scoffing at the instability of Prussia and his distaste for the
polka suggests that he associated the political event in Europe with its
cultural offshoot in New York City.[12]

But besides providing such a radical cultural connection across the Atlantic, the polka and mazurka actually became activities through which
Americans could assert their cultural independence from Europe. In a
booklet on "the etiquette of dancing," a Philadelphia ballroom instructor,
Charles Durang, revealed that the charm of the mazurka for Americans

was its egalitarian appeal, noting that "the magnate and peasant" performed it in the Old World "with equal zest." Thus, American adoption of radical European dances constituted a rebellion against European high culture. "We look upon fashion centers of Paris and London with servile imitation," complained Durang. "[Americans are] the serfs of their fashionable whims." But he urged that the mazurka and the polka, "modified by . . . deviations of a *national* complexion, [to] which ardent republican sentiments . . . naturally give birth," could provide Americans a way to liberate themselves. European radical dances, with certain modifications that American republicans would incorporate instinctively, actually provided them a means to reconstruct their ancestors' achievement of political independence from the Old World.[13]

Theater performances also reflected Americans' adaptation of the overseas revolutions. Since the days of the early republic, the theater had been a repository for civic values. "It is the American people who support the theater," roared an early nineteenth-century critic. "This being the case, the people have the right to see and applaud who they please, and we trust this right will never be relinquished." A close relationship existed between the theater managers and performers and the audience. Audiences often interrupted a performance to demand a favorite song be repeated or to insist upon an entirely different song than what was scheduled. Performers typically working for a pittance had to comply and break impromptu into *Yankee Doodle,* or the French revolutionary hymn *Le Marseillaise,* depending on audiences' civic impulses.[14]

In the early days of 1848, the foreign news revealed to Americans that revolutionary passion was erupting in European theaters. In Vienna a theater critic observed, at a production of *Mary Magdalene:* "All one has to do is to know what the Burgtheater used to be like in order to appreciate such a performance. . . . The Burgtheater was . . . the private place of entertainment for a pampered aristocracy . . . [who] cast contemptuous glances through their eye-glasses at the . . . common people. . . . Now the people have in truth taken possession of the stage. . . . The performance of *Mary Magdalene* at the Burgtheater without any cuts or alterations is a political event, a manifestation of the liberated people." Elsewhere patrons evacuated a theater en masse in Milan when the famous Austrian dancer Fanny Elssler appeared on stage, and "at several [Italian] theaters . . . every Austrian officer present was tumbled headlong from the boxes into the pit." In

Europe theaters had become scenes where symbols of authority were being abandoned or literally brought level with subordinate groups. Theaters in the United States also presented dramatic scenes from the 1848 revolutions, but these latter dramas interpreted the revolutions to render them understandable, and entertaining, to American audiences.[15]

Because of its centrality to American interest in revolutionary Europe, France was the setting for many plays illustrating some aspect of the revolutions. *The Insurrection of Paris; or, The People's Triumph* opened at the Bowery Theater in New York City in March 1848, followed a month later by *The Last of the Kings*, which debuted at the Boston Museum. These productions emphasized the triumph of popular sovereignty and reflected Americans' enthusiasm. But as events in France took a more violent turn, American theater became more pessimistic. Following the June 1848 insurrection of socialists and workers against the Second Republic on account of its inadequate measures of public relief, and the brutal retaliation by General Eugéne Cavaignac and the civic guard, in September the Bowery Theater presented *The Destruction of the Bastille; or, Terror's Reign*, as well as an accompanying drama, *The Conspirators. The Destruction of the Bastille* obviously referred to the historic 1789 leveling of the great symbol of French traditional authority, but in 1848 this play alluded to the contemporaneous revolution in France. In October New York's Park Theater contributed *The Barricades*, in which the celebrated soprano Anna Bishop performed *Le Marseillaise*. Bishop was dressed, not as a street revolutionary, but in the uniform of an officer of the civic guard—a symbol of order against destruction of property and revolutionary conspiracy.[16]

After the year 1848 American plays disparaging French radicalism, especially among socialists and their American sympathizers, continued. Within the United States the most persistent advocate of French labor reform and socialism itself was Horace Greeley, the editor of the *New York Tribune*. Greeley for a time championed the ideas of Charles Fourier, the French utopian socialist who envisioned society reorganized as a system of carefully planned, self-sustaining communities, each consisting of about fifteen hundred persons. Fourierist communities and clubs, actually more prevalent in America than in Europe, dotted the Northern states at the time.

While Greeley was a widely known advocate for reform on both sides of the Atlantic, his ideas about socialism became ridiculed. The *New York*

Herald, a scandal-oriented newspaper edited by the Scottish immigrant James Gordon Bennett, caricatured socialism as promoting exotic ideas like racially mixed marriages, full enfranchisement of women and blacks, and annihilation of private property. Such a mocking attitude was also the basis for the 1849 stage production of *Socialism, A Modern Philosophy Put in Practice.* This play's setting was New York City in 1853, with "Fourier Grisley [Greeley]" as the U.S. president. "Grisley" became a socialist dictator in the course of the play, declaring work imperative for everyone; compelling the wealthy class to find work and to pay wages to the working class; and making women, children, and all real and personal property the possession of the state. The message of *Socialism, A Modern Philosophy Put in Practice* was "no one is allowed to do anything for himself; therefore, nothing is done by anybody." The inspiration Greeley took from the French socialists during the 1848 revolution provided ammunition for the American theater, inviting ridicule of revolutionary socialism as a form of popular entertainment. Associational socialism had developed something of a popular following in the years before 1848, but the revolutions that year undermined Americans' interest in such utopian experiments and distanced American reform from European upheaval.[17]

American stage representations of the 1848 revolutions reflect two ways that the revolutions entered into American society—one cultural, one political. First, Europe in 1848 became part of a broad American theatrical repertoire, within which even a single evening's offering might include demonstrations of quack science, Shakespeare, circus animals, and pseudo-historical melodrama. The Boston Museum, for example, where *The Last of the Kings* debuted, also presented "mermaids from the Fiji islands"; other "living novelties, such as Giants, Dwarfs, and Orang-Outangs, etc."; and operas—along with a panorama of George Washington crossing the Delaware River. In Philadelphia's American Theater patrons could witness in a single performance *As You Like It,* a five-member Italian gymnastics team, Spanish and French dances, and song medleys. Culturally, then, European revolutionary images could be located in antebellum American popular theater as an aspect of bald spectacle.[18]

But the European revolutions also provoked American theaters, perhaps unconsciously, to make a political expression about American society. Historians have shown that American theaters at this time were beginning to reflect class division. Certain venues like the Bowery Theater, for example, presented dramas appealing to largely middle- and working-class audiences—in Walt Whitman's words, "the best average of American born mechanics." Others, like the Park Theater, offered dramas catering to "highbrow" patrons of New York's upper crust. But depictions of revolutionary Europe went against such trends. Both the Bowery and the Park hosted plays that depicted the French upheaval of 1848 as evoking terror, not promise. Moreover, at the time both theaters even shared the same acting company, actors shuttling as necessary between the two. Portrayal of the upheavals in Europe thus cut across emerging socioeconomic lines of American theater performance.[19]

Did such "revolutionary" dramas have civic importance? William Burton, a well-known theater manager of the day, believed so. He explained his production of *Socialism, A Modern Philosophy Put in Practice* as an effort in "*American* dramatic production." The theater's interpretations of the European revolutions presented and reinforced many Americans' sense of their own peculiar revolutionary consciousness, a consciousness that, at the time, rejected the fratricide of Europe.[20]

Outside the theater Americans could witness not dramatic portrayals of the revolutions' movement but actual revolutionary battles frozen in time. Broadsides in Philadelphia in early 1850, for example, advertised a "Grand and Interesting Panorama! Of the Wars for Liberty in Hungary! Upper Italy and the City of Rome!" The broadsides showed uprisings by Hungarians and northern Italians against the Austrian Hapsburgs, and by the people of Rome against the secular authority of Pope Pius IX. In combining these three disparate events, the Philadelphia broadsides reflected at once the revolutions' broad European swath and the way in which they could be bunched together when reported by American sources. Hungarians and Italians were never allied against the Austrian empire, and the Roman overthrow of Pius had little to do with either the northern Italian or the Hungarian rebellion. But a presentation of these various struggles as one unified revolutionary story made them more interesting and coherent to ordinary Americans and also facilitated Americans' reduction of transatlantic events to familiar ideological conflicts.[21]

Panoramas such as the Philadelphia exhibit conveyed visual information on giant painted canvasses. An art form originating in eighteenth-century London, panoramas were at first stationary but were soon put on rolling cylinders to create a sense of movement for observers—a nineteenth-century newsreel. Often depicting vast scenes of the Missis-sippi River, the Western frontier, or a tour of Europe or the Middle East, panoramas displaying battle scenes also flourished in the late 1840s, show-ing, for example, the struggle at Bunker Hill or Zachary Taylor's campaigns in Mexico. Pyrotechnics or shouts of command and blares of bugles could enhance visual effects (although, because of their daring special effects, many of the most popular panoramas were eventually destroyed by fire).[22]

Such effects probably accompanied the panorama of the European revo-lutions, which contained eighty thousand figures spread over three canvas sections. Remarkable in their detail, the first two sections depicted scenes of battle between Italian insurgents and Austrian soldiers in Milan and Venice, the flight of the Pope from Roman citizens, and subsequent re-prisals against the Italian rebels by French and Austrian troops. The third section unfolded the whole drama of the Hungarian uprising, from the battle at Pakozd in September 1848 to the infamous "treason" of General Arthur Görgey—whom American newspapers labeled "a second [Bene-dict] Arnold" after Louis Kossuth published letters unfairly declaring him a traitor to the cause of Hungarian freedom—and the Hungarian surrender at Komorom to a Russian force in August 1849.[23]

Panoramas also had a strong educational function. In Philadelphia ad-vertising for the abovementioned "Grand and Interesting Panorama" in-vited teachers to arrange school visits allowing schoolchildren to attend matinees. The panorama's bird's-eye view of European struggles for liberty provided the audience with an illusory sense of being present, "chin deep in the blood of the slain," as Mark Twain would later satirically describe his sensation on hearing a rendition of Frantisek Kotzwara's sonata *The Battle of Prague*. Like Kotzwara's musical battle picture, the panorama succeeded in giving American adult and student spectators a vicarious experience of heroic revolution from a transatlantic distance.[24]

Besides visiting revolutionary panoramas, American students also stud-ied the European revolutions in other ways. By the time they were teenag-ers, most were familiar with British history and politics, having committed to memory many details about the British monarchy, especially its peace-ful restoration through the Glorious Revolution of 1688, and the British constitutional system. Normally, the history and politics of Continental Europe were less important, other than the French Revolution of 1789 and the subsequent Reign of Terror. American pedagogy also emphasized the

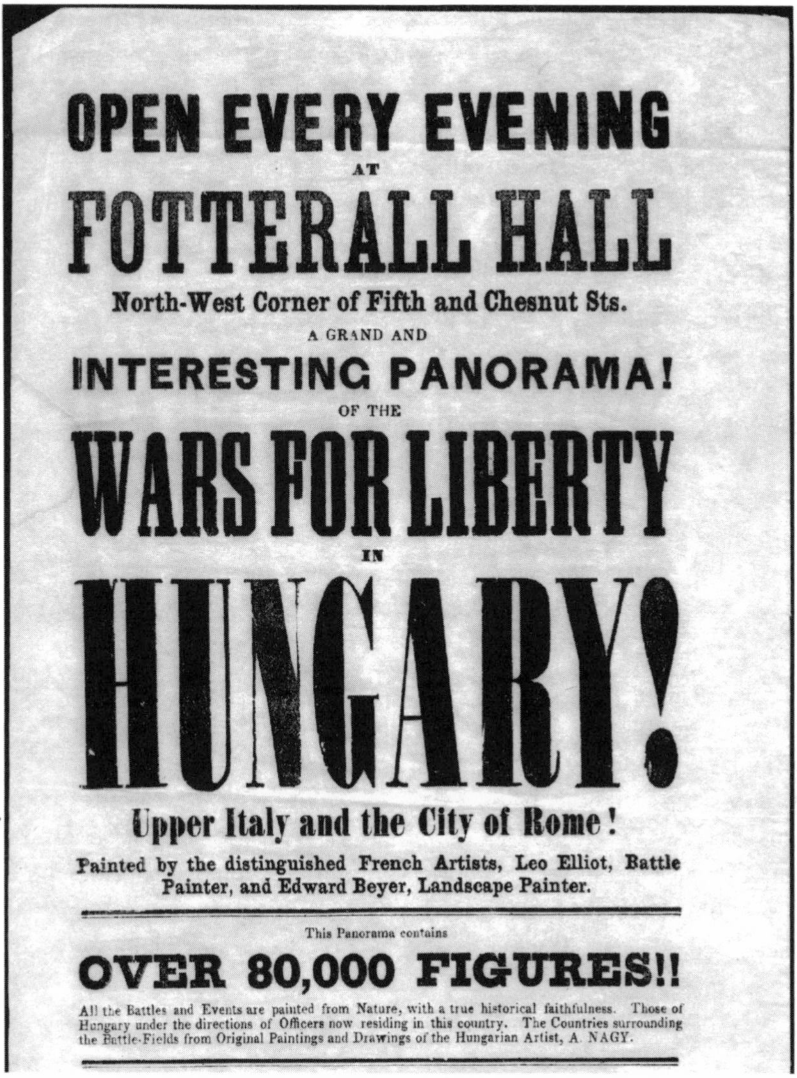

FIGURE 4. Philadelphia Broadside, 1850, showing American popular interest in distant revolutionary drama in Hungary and the Italian states. (The Library Company of Philadelphia)

history and oratory of the Roman Empire, but students, perhaps because of Protestant influence, learned about modern Italy hardly at all. Even less attention in school was given to the history of Eastern Europe, an ignorance that helps explain Americans' fascination with the Hungarian uprising against Austria. In 1848 many students, like Americans generally, were being confronted with new information about the turbulent state of affairs in continental Europe.[25]

In addition to the popularity of Alphonse de Lamartine's *History of the Girondins,* another reflection of Americans' sudden curiosity about European politics and society was Harpers' *Geography,* printed early in 1848. Upon the arrival of news of overseas turbulence, Harpers published news releases specifying that certain revisions were required by "the rapid changes in progress among the kingdoms of the Old World. . . . Under France change as follows: The government was a limited monarchy until February 1848, when a great revolution occurred, and France is now a republic. Under Germany change . . . the government was an absolute monarchy in Austria and Prussia; but in 1848 there was a revolution, and free institutions are now universally established." American geographies of the time typically provided an overview of "national categories," like type of government, dominant religious faith, and the "national character" of foreign peoples, for students to memorize; the nuances or uncertainties of a revolution lay beyond their focus. But the fact that a textbook publisher would account for European turbulence with such succinctness and finality suggests that students were trained to understand the rapid progress of revolution and, just as important, to esteem revolutions that were accomplished facts but to see revolutions with uncertain outcomes as improper.[26]

The prospect of a republican conquest of all of Europe also appeared as an academic issue on American university campuses. The Tennessean Randal William McGavock, at Harvard University's law school, was required to argue, for a debate resolution, "that the English government, in light of continental disturbances, is not likely to endure." Regarding another debate on the "all-absorbing question of the day, viz. the French Revolution," McGavock described the debate teams as follows: "The ardent and patriotic sympathized with the people, while the others contended that the people of France were too fickle for a Republic." These debates occurred in the spring of 1848, when the revolutions of Europe enjoyed their height of American enthusiasm, and Americans correlated "patriotism" with sympathy for the revolutions. But the Harvard debate on the French revolution also suggested that Americans equated republican virtue with resistance to change.[27]

The circumstances and fate of the New England scholar Francis Bowen, also in relation to Harvard, present another measure of the ambiguous way that revolutionary Europe illuminated an American public revolutionary identity. Bowen was a renowned scholar of history and philosophy, having published an important edition of Alexis de Tocqueville's *Democracy in America*. Early in 1850 he published a critique of the Hungarian independence movement in the *North American Review*, arguing that while Hungarian independence was a heroic goal, to achieve it, the Hungarians, secretly "aristocratic," were ethnically cleansing the declared Hungarian nation of Croat and Slavic minorities. Bowen's attitude was unusual among Americans, because he based his assertions on something of a detailed analysis of events in Eastern Europe and because he was able to countenance the thought that a European revolution could be both good and evil at the same time.[28]

The timing of Bowen's article was unfortunate for him, however, because it appeared amid a dramatic American surge of support for the Hungarians in late 1849. Michigan senator Lewis Cass moved in Congress that the United States suspend diplomatic relations with Austria over the latter's suppression of the Hungarian uprising. Already positioning himself to run for president in 1852, Cass stood to capture Northern support for engineering some kind of official U.S. action on behalf of the Hungarians. Likewise, in Springfield, Illinois, a sympathy demonstration headed by "citizen" Abraham Lincoln resolved, "The immediate acknowledgment of the independence of Hungary by our government is due from American freemen to their struggling brethren, [and] to the general cause of Republican liberty." The Springfield resolution was forwarded to Congress, but congressmen concerned with the cutoff of Austrian markets for American goods defeated Cass's resolution. Domestic politics and economic interests complicated Americans' emotional or ideological support for foreign revolutions.[29]

In 1849 Bowen held the McLean Professorship of Ancient and Modern History at Harvard. His article on Hungary, however, effectively thrust him out of the classroom. He was assailed by critics as a "slanderer of

Hungary," a "college professor of despotism," a "Russian serf," and a "slave of Boston aristocracy." Early in 1851, as American news about Hungary shifted from accounts of the uprising itself to coverage of the flight of the refugee Louis Kossuth, the Harvard Board of Overseers voted to remove Bowen from the McLean chair. It did not help Bowen that many Free Soil politicians sat on the board, or that Harvard was a stronghold of the Unitarian church; many followers of both groups expressed sympathy for the European revolutions (Bowen's Unitarianism took him in a different direction). Approving the removal, the *Boston Commonwealth* asserted that "the public have a right to demand [that] the Professor of History should be imbued with American Principles." Bowen's censorship showed that the European revolutions influenced even the highest halls of American education—in a way that affirmed many Americans' belief at the time that wars of independence couldn't entail ethnic or social dismemberment. Bowen's break with this understanding of revolution in Hungary and America cost him his job.[30]

Francis Bowen's sober assessment of the Hungarian independence movement, and its harsh public reception, moreover, raise questions beyond merely those of intellectual freedom. Americans celebrated the Hungarian uprising at the time because they saw what the Hungarians were pursuing as "revolutionary," and they often did so by memorializing or vicariously reliving the American Revolution. Did the Hungarians' maintenance of an "aristocracy" and subjugation of a minority people, as Bowen alleged, nullify this "revolutionary" status? And if so, did this shortcoming also suggest an incurable shortcoming in the American revolutionary past?

Americans' belief that they were a revolutionary people, although different from Europeans, was perhaps most evident in the large sympathy demonstrations for events in Europe that Americans staged from 1848 to 1851. As Mary Ryan has observed: "Antebellum citizenship was most always exercised in association with one's fellows. . . . The sacred civic act was not a private exercise of conscience or the individual practice of intellect but . . . [happened in] innumerable assemblies in public space." Again, newspapers performed an important function in helping construct a revolutionary public culture. They published stories about the European revolutions, and they publicized and promoted American demonstrations of sympathy for revolution, first by describing the meetings themselves—dignitaries in attendance, descriptions of fireworks, and excerpts of speeches—and second by emphasizing that a "true" or "real" American citizen would by definition wish to join his sympathies with others. Newspapers thus described, or imagined, the civic character of the sympathizers.[31]

The *Richmond Enquirer,* for example, assessed initial news of the 1848 upheavals as "a sublime spectacle to the true American patriot and philanthropist!" Describing a local sympathy gathering, the *Enquirer* declared it "a fitting response from the hearts of Republicans . . . to the workers out of liberal principles throughout the Old World." Likewise, the *New York Tribune* reported: "We have already had French, German, Irish, and Swiss demonstrations [in New York City]. We shall have an American one soon." The *Tribune* gladly reported a few days later that "a meeting of American citizens will be held . . . to express AMERICAN SYMPATHY for the struggle of Liberty in France." In 1849, when U.S. policy makers showed themselves reluctant to recognize the republic declared in Rome, the *New York Herald* editorialized, "Leaders may have no pulse for patriots, but American citizens have their hearts in the right place." Newspapers cultivated civic values by prescribing expressions of American sympathy for events overseas. Only those false to American values would not be engaged in some kind of public expression of revolutionary sympathy.[32]

But did American sympathizers actually celebrate the European revolutions? Actually, no, they did not. What Americans celebrated was that in the United States they had already experienced a revolution and had survived, in fact prospered, to tell about it, as well as to influence other nations with its legacy. Public gatherings in American cities allowed Americans to celebrate the revolutions of Europe in a way that actually affirmed a unique American revolutionary tradition and, through that tradition, a unique national identity.

For example, the "Great Demonstration," as newspapers labeled it, in New York in April 1848 paid tribute to the first news of upheaval in Paris. Thousands of people packed three stands constructed for the demonstration in front of City Hall: the "American Stand" was located in the center, flanked on the right by the "German Stand" and on the left by the "French and Italian Stand." Orators on the American stand delivered speeches, recited poetry, and conducted songs in English. Orators on each European stand performed the same in the native language—German,

Italian, French, or Polish (from the French-Italian stand)—shared by the speaker and audience. Translators made selected speeches universally intelligible. Official and spontaneous renditions echoed the French revolutionary hymn *Le Marseillaise*. "The citizens of all nations clasped hands and shouted for the common cause of liberty. Not once in a century has our city witnessed a sight like this," wrote one local reporter, affirming how a multiplicity of ethnic groups had become unified in their celebration as Americans of events in Europe.[33]

The New York mayor William Brady spoke for many of the celebrants when he suggested American agency in the revolutions. It was no coincidence, Brady declared, that the United States was the progenitor of revolution in the world, "greeting with paternal warmth the birth of the [French] Republic." Moreover, the original American revolutionary identity was not dormant but now characterized the Americans who sympathized with Europe. "[We] applaud all progress of liberty with [our] usual readiness," the mayor affirmed. Through phrases like "paternal warmth" and "usual readiness," Brady connected his listeners with their revolutionary past and conferred or confirmed their own status as legitimately revolutionary American citizens.[34]

Ironically, for Americans to celebrate the 1848 revolutions, they had to distinguish themselves from Europeans. Speakers on the various immigrant stands of the "Great Demonstration," for example, repeatedly suggested how different one side of the Atlantic was from the other. Eleuterio Felice Foresti ("E. Felix," as newspapers identified him), for example, commandeered the French-Italian stand to explain the transatlantic journeys of "liberty" over the centuries: "On this [American] continent, the first steps were taken by Columbus. . . . Italians gave liberty a lasting refuge from the persecutions of tyrants in old Europe, and now the light they kindled is returning to their descendants." Foresti was a former radical in the ranks of the revolutionary Italian Carbonari. After imprisonment in Austria he had been exiled to the United States in 1836. Now an American academic, Foresti explained the European uprisings as a response to the American founding. It was no coincidence, he and other immigrant speakers pointed out, that the French uprising of 1848 had commenced on 22 February, George Washington's birthday, an observation that received "loud and sustained cheering." Indigenous and immigrant Americans alike acclaimed the European revolutions because they seemed to salute the midcentury American republic in its past revolutionary success and to affirm its kinship with the American founding.[35]

Beyond New York other towns and cities including Atlanta, Baltimore, Boston, Cincinnati, Milwaukee, New Orleans, Philadelphia, Richmond, and Washington hosted similar meetings. To be sure, each place added its own idiosyncratic element to its display of revolutionary sympathy. Boston organized "indignation banquets" to show its citizens' displeasure at the old regime's resistance to the revolutions. New Orleans did likewise, preparing "fraternal and patriotic feasts" open to "all persons of whatever political party or nation, to whom worship of liberty is most sacred among all religions." Such events memorialized the "reform banquets" that citizens of Paris had staged early in 1848 to protest food shortages and to confront the monarchy. In Atlanta the city council voted to appropriate several hundred acres of choice farmland to the deposed French monarch Louis Philippe, whose arrival in the United States as a refugee was widely (and falsely) rumored. Louis Philippe was one of many European monarchs, newspapers reported, to whom an American mechanic had sent traveling trunks. All such events cosmetically linked Europe and the United States at the same time as they actually betrayed the differences between European economic desperation and American prosperity.[36]

When revolutionary momentum halted or reversed in France, American interest shifted to the Hungarians, mounting their struggle against Hapsburg rule. Philadelphia saw citizens gather in a fitting location, on "the sacred soil of Independence Square, within sight of the edifice which witnessed the stern resolves of our own patriots," according to the *Philadelphia Public Ledger*. In Independence Square the Hungarian uprising evoked vivid testimonials stressing its parallels with the heroic American past. "There is a propriety in [our] demonstration," noted keynote speaker John W. Forney. Forney was a Democratic newspaper editor and a politician of German descent. His enthusiasm at the Philadelphia demonstration, like that of Mayor Brady in New York, who was running for reelection at the time, and of Lewis Cass in Washington, was no doubt partly motivated by partisan aspirations. But most evident was Forney's concern with "propriety," his desire that the sympathy gathering be correct, thus implicitly helping Americans define themselves as "revolutionary" as much as they explicitly celebrated Europe.[37]

The "propriety" of which Forney spoke derived from the parallels between the Hungarian and the American revolutions. In his address Forney remarked at the similarities between present European and former American military leaders. The Hungarian general Arthur Görgey, for example, was a latter-day Francis Marion, the revolutionary "Swamp Fox" (Americans' prejudice against Görgey as a Benedict Arnold, on the basis of Louis Kossuth's denunciations, hadn't yet taken hold). Polish generals Jozef Bem and Henryk Dembinski, who were assisting the Hungarians, resembled, respectively, Anthony Wayne and Nathaniel Greene of the Continental Army. Kossuth, the most celebrated revolutionary chieftain of all, was the reincarnation of George Washington, Patrick Henry, Charles Cotesworth Pinckney, and Fisher Ames. If ordinary Americans wondered what character had been required of the revolutionary generation of 1776, they need look no further than events in Eastern Europe in 1849—or at least the depictions of these events by American orators like Forney.[38]

Further calling attention to the revolutionary parallels, Forney noted that Austria had denied the Hungarians "the right of representation secured through the ages by a written constitution," despite the Hungarians' intermittent defenses of the Austrian throne from foreign invasion. Moreover, just as British forces had sought alliances with "the fierce savages of our own wilderness" against the colonists, now Austria "has excited among the rude Serbians and Croatians a most bloody rebellion [against Hungary]."[39]

Forney's remarks suggest several characteristics of the Philadelphia gathering. First, his praise for Hungarians and Poles evoked the memory of statesmen and soldiers with backgrounds across sectional boundaries, reflecting a theme of unity not only relevant to the day but also inherent to Americans' sense of their unique revolutionary past. In addition, Forney's descriptions of foreigners, focused on comparisons with famous and obscure American revolutionaries, reveal how Americans typically shared information about overseas events at midcentury. His likening of Serbians and Croatians to American Indians hearkened to the Declaration of Independence, in which Thomas Jefferson alleged that the British monarchy had stirred the "merciless Indian savages" against the colonists. Thus, Forney (like Jefferson) demonized groups with the most ambiguous role in the revolution, ensuring proper American sympathies by making the revolution's meaning as simple as possible to understand.[40]

To be sure, the strength of Forney's speech was not its historical accuracy. For one thing, he misstated Hungary's relationship with Austria: Hungary's pre-1848 constitutional standing in relation to Austria had long been unwritten, closer to the British constitutional tradition than to the American. Moreover, until the retreat of the Ottoman Empire, Hungarians and Austrians had assisted each other against the Turks. Further, before the 1848 revolutions Hapsburg rulers in fact helped Hungarians keep non-Magyar nationalities in line.[41]

But such eastern European history lessons were out of place at the Philadelphia demonstration. Forney's speech had three purposes: to familiarize his listeners with personalities in Europe; to put the achievements of the American founders in a contemporary framework; and, most important, to indicate that the enthusiasm felt by all Philadelphians in attendance had American roots. Philadelphia was the scene for some of the worst clashes between natives and immigrants in the antebellum period. Protestants in the city, for instance, established an "American Republican Party" in 1844 to oppose Irish Catholics, often by force, because, as one nativist put it, "vigilance requires the American example of successful republicanism to guard against attempts by hereditary rulers of Europe to subvert the American government." But people in America, Forney implied, despite their specific or different backgrounds, could unite to salute the American-inspired demise of European monarchy.[42]

Apparent in such public demonstrations of Americans' reaction to the European revolutions, as well as in other forms of expression, was a search for an expression of sympathy sufficiently blending the contemporary radicalism of European revolution with the mystical success of the American independence movement. But the very effort it took to compose a "fitting response" to Europeans' revolutionary challenge—a phrase that appeared frequently in American sympathy gatherings—showed that feelings about the 1848 revolutions were hard to define, or at least complicated. Tension manifested in denigrations of Americans whose opinions about Europe were not "fitting": Horace Greeley was lampooned, Francis Bowen was dismissed, and students who questioned French republicanism were deemed unpatriotic. It was important to Americans that their expressions about the 1848 revolutions be authentic. Initially, this search for authenticity meant that Americans memorialized European celebrities, duplicated what was known about revolutionary clothing or forms of popular entertainment, witnessed arousing if re-created scenes of revolution, advocated the cause of the revolutionaries in academic circles, and joined in demonstrations. But more deeply, Americans' sense of revolutionary authenticity revealed a faith in America's unique national revolutionary past. Throughout the United States expressions of this faith, especially in large cities, involved natives and immigrants alike: it has never been necessary, noted Rush Welter, to live in the United States very long to be able to remember the national beginning. The rise and fall of the 1848 revolutions in American public culture allowed Americans to assert a unified public revolutionary identity amid an uncertain Atlantic and domestic political atmosphere.[43]

3. The Presidential Campaign of 1848
Competing Rhetorics of Revolution

Soon after the upheaval of Paris in February 1848, a coterie of American journalists gathered in Old Fellows' Hall in the national capital. The Washington press wished to issue an "appropriate" statement, to be transmitted to the new French government. Attending the meeting were William Seaton, the publisher of the *Daily National Intelligencer*, a Whig organ; James Robinson, a reporter for the Whig *New York Tribune*, edited by Horace Greeley; the editor Thomas Ritchie of the Democratic *Washington Union*; and Gamaliel Bailey of the antislavery journal the *National Era*, which soon would endorse the new Free Soil Party. Arrangements for the meeting and its resolutions were reported across the country.[1]

The occasion placed William Seaton in an awkward position. The *Intelligencer* had recently ridiculed the popular uprising in Paris. But Seaton was also the mayor of Washington, and it would be embarrassing for a convention of leading American journalists to echo the *Intelligencer*'s cool sentiments about European liberation. Yet it would mock the *Intelligencer* for its publisher now to cheer a violent change of government in the streets of Europe.

The outcome of the Old Fellows' Hall meeting reflected its constituents' partisan differences. The main source of contention was how to salute the prompt actions of the U.S. minister in Paris, Richard Rush. As noted earlier, Rush, without being instructed to do so by the State Department, had extended official U.S. recognition to the revolutionary provisional government of France on 25 February, only three days after the outbreak of violence. Initially, Thomas Ritchie of the *Union*, the official organ of the Polk administration, "offered a resolution thanking Mr. Rush for his cordial and prompt recognition of the new Government of France," which, Ritchie observed, "[had] confirmed the provisional government in power . . . when everything was trembling." The others, however, protested Ritchie's

resolution, declaring that "the sole object [of the meeting] was to congratulate the French people and press, not to offer adulation to our Executive,
or any of [his] favorites." Eighteen forty-eight was a presidential election
year, heightening sensitivities to partisan claims of influence abroad. Ultimately, Ritchie's resolution was rejected, and the press gathering issued a
compromise resolution, tendering the French people congratulations for
respecting "the rights of private property" and recognizing "the rights of
labor." Eventually, many Americans would decide that France could not
properly balance the rights of property and labor. But for now these tenuous good wishes from Washington made their way to Paris.[2]

The disagreement of the Washington press over an alleged American
influence in revolutionary France symbolized a wider partisan conflict in
1848 over how to respond to the news of overseas revolution. The 1848
election is not famous in American history; it is much more obscure than
the elections, say, of 1800, 1860, 1896, 1932, 1968, and 2000. It is not
considered a "critical election," signaling long-term realignment of the existing party system, nor did it mark a change in the parties' ideologies. Its
results were not decided in the courts.[3]

Still, the election generated great interest at the time. It was the first
presidential election in American history in which voters (all male, mostly
white) cast votes on the same day, 7 November. Politics, at least in terms
of voter turnout, was more popular in the mid-nineteenth century than
today: in the 1848 presidential election, nearly 75 percent of the electorate
cast ballots. The two main parties, the Democrats and the Whigs, had well-
funded organizations in most of the states, and the practice of political
"campaigns," wherein candidates traveled around the countryside speaking to public gatherings, had been in place for two decades.[4]

The 1848 election came on the heels of the United States' war with
Mexico, concluded by the Treaty of Guadalupe Hidalgo, on 2 February
1848. This treaty called for U.S. annexation of the northern half of Mexico,
territories that in time would comprise all or parts of seven U.S. states.
Controversy arose over whether the territories would be open to the expansion of slavery. Early in the war a Democratic congressman from Pennsylvania, David Wilmot, had called for a federal ban on slavery in any territory acquired in the war. The Wilmot Proviso never passed both houses
of Congress, but in 1848 it continued to focus both party and emerging
sectional conflicts.

The emergence of a new political party, the Free Soil Party, also raised sectional tensions. Comprised of frustrated Democrats and Whigs, as well as former members of the abolitionist Liberty Party, the Free Soil Party called for passage of the Wilmot Proviso, thus protecting the West for free laborers, mechanical and agricultural. Some Free Soilers broke with the traditional parties out of frustration with their efforts to gain political office, but many believed the existing party system of Democrats and Whigs was not responsive to an emerging liberal movement beyond traditional American politics.[5]

Marvin Meyers once noted: "Party spokesmen were not masters of the principles that they assumed. What emerged from their political talk was not a consistent doctrine . . . but a persuasion: a broad judgment of public affairs informed by common sentiments and beliefs." Meyers was writing about the politics of the presidency of Andrew Jackson, but his statement captures politicians' indiscreet use of the concept of revolution in 1848. The Free Soilers' popular literature often referred to events in Europe, but the party's official platform was silent about transatlantic events. The Democrats emphasized the relevance of the overseas revolutions in their platform but offered little in their campaign literature to back up their platform. Whigs, attempting to obfuscate the troubling issue of slavery's expansion, chose to have no platform at all. As a new party the Free Soil Party claimed the description "revolutionary" perhaps with the most plausibility. Democrats and Whigs also spoke about "revolution," though usually to emphasize only their opponents' counterrevolutionary tendencies.[6]

This chapter argues that politicians and campaign writers resorted to the language of "revolution" in 1848 for two reasons. First, office seekers sought to ennoble their aspirations with the ideals and images of the American Revolution, as well as the contemporary European upheavals. Such themes of revolution could be seen as merely the expected rhetoric of the day: invocations of the American Revolution were customary in antebellum politics. References to contemporary European upheavals reflected simply the international headlines that both office seekers and the electorate were reading in the country's newspapers. Office seekers could gain rapport with voters by simply mentioning the news from Europe.[7]

While surely references to "revolution" often were merely rhetoric, a second reason for their 1848 flourishing is less obvious: politicians, at least of the two main parties, discussed and tried to exploit concepts and images of revolution, especially the revolutions of Europe, precisely because addressing the critical issue of territorial slavery was too risky. Thus, while events in Europe weren't the fundamental campaign issue of 1848, they did provide a means of communication, a way for politicians to test ideas about solutions to the slavery issue without risking everything. Nevertheless, the interplay of debates over the European upheavals with references to American revolutionary ideology produced a campaign that was more than simply obfuscation over slavery. American public figures used a vocabulary of "revolution" not only in hopes of winning the election but also as an expression of what they and, they hoped, the electorate truly believed about the country's revolutionary identity.

As has been shown by other scholars, various domestic factors paved Zachary Taylor's road to the White House in 1848, as well as provoked the formation of the Free Soil Party. Joseph Rayback has described the 1848 campaign as one in which, despite powerful divisive forces, party loyalty "was the largest single factor contributing to the results." This chapter invites a new interpretation of the outcome and significance of the election of 1848. It argues that with the controversy over territorial slavery relegating that issue to furious backstage maneuvering, loyalty to party could mean abandonment of principle. But party loyalty also meant endorsement of a particular interpretation of antebellum Americans' revolutionary identity.[8]

The Free Soil Party came perhaps as close as any group in America to emerging as a contemporary corollary of the 1848 European revolutionaries. Free-labor ideology was not new in 1848, but that year the Free Soil Party held its first convention and nominated a national ticket. The Free Soil platform reflected the Western orientation of the party: "Let the soil of our extensive domains be kept free for the hardy pioneers of our own land, and the oppressed of other lands seeking fields of enterprise in the New World." The Free Soil mission was to protect the American West from the contaminations of slavery for the free Atlantic world.[9]

Thus, the Free Soil platform referred to "revolution" only obliquely, in its appeal to those fleeing urban oppression. But other party communications invoked the European revolutions directly. Those in the Free Soil ranks—former Liberty Party abolitionists, disaffected Democrats of New York and the Northwest, and New England Whigs—together believed that the main parties would acquiesce to the slave states' wishes for access to the new Western territories. Representatives of all these groups, each in his own way, paid homage to the upheavals in Europe as motivation for a free-labor order in America. The vice presidential candidate of the party, Charles Francis Adams, son of the former president, initially disparaged both European and American radicalism, condemning the turbulence of France, and said that talk of third political parties in America was "evil." But those perceptions changed, as Adams sensed the potential similarities between the Old World and the New. In campaign speeches he compared the stand-pat Whig Party to the ousted French monarch Louis Philippe. This comparison is unsurprising, given the campaign season and initial American excitement over the French king's downfall. But privately, Adams also acknowledged a transatlantic perspective. In the summer of 1848 he reconciled the twin rise of French republicanism and Free Soilism, ruminating, "in republics men seem to become machines moved at the will of an idea carried into organization."[10]

Adams's colleague in Massachusetts, Senator Charles Sumner, testified to the historical and transatlantic roots of the Free Soil cause with even more alacrity. Sumner declared Free Soilism "a continuance of the American Revolution" but proclaimed that for its strength it should "pluck fresh coals from the living altars of France." "Let us," Sumner pleaded, "proclaim 'Liberty, Equality, Fraternity.'" This comment suggests how the European revolutions acted as a catalyst for familiar antebellum American odes to the spirit of '76, providing a contemporary example of the possibilities of revolutionary action. At a party convention Sumner expressed the often-quoted epigram that the candidacy of Whig Zachary Taylor had been engineered by a conspiracy of Southwestern and Northeastern Jacobins, the "lords of the lash and the lords of the loom." Sumner chose his words carefully; it is no surprise that he used a metaphor evoking reactionary Europe to characterize scheming American conservatives.[11]

Certain abolitionists also relished the prospect of a new political party as an American equivalent of the 1848 revolutions. The Unitarian minister Theodore Parker wrote, "The revolution in political parties . . . hostile to former doctrines . . . is represented by the words, 'Free Soil.'" He compared Free Soilers' anger to the French people's resentment of Louis Philippe: both "boast[ed] the same origins as the Declaration of Independence." Meanwhile, Gamaliel Bailey, the editor of the *National Era*, compared the Free Soil Party to "French Republicanism" and found it ironic, not flattering, that French insurgents were reported to have requested copies of the Declaration of Independence and the Constitution (they had not). "We do not doubt the example that the United States is exerting a powerful influence on the civilized world," noted the *Era*. "But considering slavery is the cornerstone of the republic, we do not recollect any Old World procession delighting our corps diplomatique by bearing aloft the motto of 'Slavery or Death!'"[12]

A third element of the Free Soil Party in 1848 consisted of New York "Barnburners," former Democrats who now clustered around the Free Soil nominee, Martin Van Buren (thus burning their barn to rid it of rats, i.e., abandoning the Democratic Party rather than attempting to change its unsatisfactory elements). Motivated primarily by hatred of the Polk administration for its stingy patronage awards after the election of 1844, Barnburners sought a third-party movement out of revenge.

Yet Barnburners also spoke of Europe. The New York Free Soiler Samuel Tilden addressed the New York state legislature in the spring of 1848 to hail France's establishment of national labor workshops and workday hour limits. In reply the legislature declared that the "French Republic was a monument to those who established our own government, that what was deemed an experiment has become a model for imitation by nations." Reflecting this transatlantic orientation, a correspondent asked Tilden about "the *Great* question [of] how to sustain our strength at home and make our presence felt abroad." Democratic Free Soilers, in both the public forum of the state legislature and the privacy of the writing desk, testified to their belief that free soilism was international.[13]

Free Soil campaign songs and pamphlets celebrated the party's twin historic and international roots. The "Free Soil Minstrel" began, "Now when the spirit of '76 is abroad, the emotions gush as naturally . . . [as] the lark." "Our Countrymen in Chains" asked, "Shall we scoff at Europe's kings, / When Freedom's fire is dim with us? Shall our own glorious land retain / That curse which Europe scorns to bear?" "The Liberty Rally" pledged, "We'll battle tyrants till they perish, / Fraternity, the tie we cherish— / Freedom to the World!" Another pamphlet more matter-of-factly explained the party's "imperative duty": "First . . . the late events in Europe; second . . . the peculiar facts of our position as a model republic to all nations; third . . . solemn facts connected with legislation of the fathers of this republic." This pamphlet traced the history of the "Free Soil Question" from the year

1774, reflecting how Free Soilers wrestled with how to reconcile America's revolutionary legacy with current events, given apparent evidence that Europe, not America, was in the revolutionary vanguard.[14]

Thus, Free Soil literature pledged twin allegiances, one to the American revolutionary promise of economic autonomy and opportunity, and one to America's global mission to protect liberty previously established. Free Soil materials specifically condemned the burden of unfree labor shackling working-class free men—in both United States and Europe—and implied that antebellum Americans, when necessary, could embrace radical change, not only peaceful continuity. When the Free Soil platform declared that slavery had as little right to be established in the Western territories as monarchy, it confirmed the influence of revolutions abroad on Free Soilers' crusade to disrupt a corrupted transatlantic status quo.[15]

Friends of Free Soil, however, had no monopoly on revolutionary rhetoric in 1848. The platform of the Democratic Party specifically accommodated the European revolutions to fit a domestic agenda: "In view of the sovereignty of the people . . . erecting republics on the ruins of despotism in the Old World . . . a duty is devolved upon the Democratic party to advance 'liberty, equality, and fraternity,' by continuing to resist all monopolies and exclusive legislation." This statement connected events in Europe to the Democrats' proclaimed opposition to government projects favoring often more well-to-do Whigs. The Democratic platform hailed the French revolution for asserting "principles for which their Lafayette and our Washington fought: the inalienable right of the people to make and amend their forms of government in such manner as the welfare of the community may require." These accolades were transmitted to France through the U.S. minister in Paris, Richard Rush.[16]

Such a resolution could help elect the Democratic candidate, Michigan senator Lewis Cass, to the White House. Cass was a hawkish Democratic statesman, gaining party leadership after spearheading Congress's support for the Mexican War. At times a "Young American" advocate of aggressive U.S. foreign policy in the Americas as well as in Europe, Cass had justified war aims against Mexico on the basis of America's "unlimited power of expansion." For Cass Americans, as a people capable of self-government, deserved land acquisition, which would bring national fulfillment. American expansion, or at least the spread of American ideals to other countries, measured America's health.[17]

Cass gained the Democratic nomination largely through his promotion of "popular sovereignty" concerning the question of territorial slavery, an alternative to the Wilmot Proviso, which outraged many Southerners. Cass in 1846 had endorsed the proviso but a year later rejected it as an unconstitutional extension of congressional authority, thus gaining the support of Southern Democrats. "Popular sovereignty"—allowing citizens actually resident in the territories to decide for or against slavery—reflected the Democratic commitment to local governance, but it also allowed Northern Democrats to endorse Cass for not shackling the fate of Western territories to federal law and Southern Democrats to endorse him for not pledging himself to free soil. It shrewdly turned the divisive issue of slavery into the patriotic issue of faith in the will of the local majority, a legacy of the American Revolution that Democrats emphasized.[18]

Thus, the *Richmond Enquirer*, edited by the "Young American" Thomas Ritchie Jr. (the son of Thomas Ritchie of the *Washington Union*), endorsed Cass, although this leading Southern Democratic newspaper focused less on Cass himself and more on disqualifying the Whig candidate Zachary Taylor. The *Enquirer*'s task was delicate, since Taylor had led U.S. forces in the Mexican War, which the newspaper had thoroughly endorsed. In 1845 the *Enquirer* had pronounced American annexation of Texas "the most important event in the progress of human advancement since the Declaration of American Independence," a reflection of how many Democrats perceived the meaning of the American Revolution. As the Declaration symbolized American colonials' revolutionary commitment, the Texas annexation symbolized that same commitment for patriots of Young America: the recurring development of new vistas where people could declare home rule.[19]

Thus, as aggrandizement from Mexico had helped to fulfill the American revolutionary experience, so could American democratic influence manifesting in Europe. The *Enquirer* announced the outbreak of the revolutions in Europe by exclaiming: "American principles are triumphant! . . . The affairs of the old world grow more perplexed, [but] the new world, amidst the fall of dynasties, holds in her hands the first best gifts of good government and civilization." And upheaval in Europe had the Democratic Party to thank in particular: "Never was a time when the Democracy of the Union had so much reason to congratulate itself."[20]

As was the case with several Democratic organs, the *Enquirer* did not immediately condemn revolutionary violence in Europe as long as that violence seemed to lay the groundwork for expansion of the franchise. During the bloody "June Days" of 1848, destitute French laborers rose up violently against the government when it decided to eliminate its public relief, an earlier emergency measure. The *Enquirer* reported accounts from a "highly intelligent correspondent . . . [who] casts entire discredit on . . . reports of the atrocities of the insurgents." Such emphases had been the thrust of both British reports and Whig newspapers in America. The *Enquirer*'s reporter, on the other hand, blamed the letting of "republican blood" on the "savage soldiery" and the "selfish bourgeoisie," vowing that "if universal suffrage be not abolished . . . the working man will triumph yet." It was an article of faith that if revolutionary Europe could achieve the franchise, the Continent would triumph as a kindred spirit to the Democratic Party.[21]

Accompanying the *Enquirer*'s salute to foreign revolutions was its allegation of revolutionary mischief at home if the Whig Party somehow were elected in Washington. After preparing to nominate Henry Clay, a founder of the Whig Party, on a platform opposing acquisition of territory through the Mexican War, Whigs switched to Taylor after many in Congress voted to accept the treaty ending the conflict, fearful that President Polk might use rejection of the treaty to annex even more Mexican lands. A Louisiana slave owner, Taylor placated jittery Southerners for the moment.

To gain the acceptance of Northern Whigs, however, Taylor also pledged that he would not veto the Wilmot Proviso if Congress were to pass it. Thus, Whigs including Horace Greeley, William Seward, and Abraham Lincoln, though sympathetic to the Free Soil cause, consequently argued that theirs was a free soil party, and thus there was no reason for antislavery Whigs to vote for Martin Van Buren. But in Taylor's statement the *Enquirer* saw the makings of a conservative coup. In a column headed "THE JACOBINS AND THE FRIENDS OF THE UNION," the *Enquirer* argued that Whigs intended for Congress to rule unilaterally, without even consulting the president, and would ramrod Southern Democrats with the Wilmot Proviso. The *Enquirer* warned of "a temper [among] Jacobins and demagogue speakers of the Clubs to break down constitutional exercises of our forefathers." The term *Jacobins* evoked the image of the academics and professionals who in the French Revolution of 1789 had, as a minority group, conspired to lead the revolution to its most radical and violent measures. *Jacobinism* was in fact a negative synonym for *democracy* until the 1820s, when the Democratic Party embraced the more positive, modern meaning of the term, although Whigs continued to resurrect *Jacobinism* to criticize Democrats' practices of office rotation and bribery.[22] In 1848 Democrats used the European revolutions to end Whigs' monopolization of the term *Jacobin*, portraying Whigs as antidemocratic elites. Taylor was behaving like a French Jacobin in pledging not to veto congressional antislavery legislation, without "submitting the question to the States and the people," thus violating popular sovereignty.[23]

Whigs were accusing Democrats of Jacobinism at the same time, so the Democrats' invocation of the sinister image of the French Revolution was in part simply retaliation. It was perhaps less plausible to characterize Congress, which after all had a Whig majority, as demagogic than to characterize the Democratic president as such, since he had spearheaded military buildup and territorial conquest. But Democrats were compelled to paint Whigs with the negative brush of revolution, given events in Europe and the revolutionary values upon which the campaign became contested.

The platform of the Whig Party, in contrast to the Democrats' explicit praise for revolutionary Europe, contained no reference to Europe, or for that matter to any other specific issue, so divided was the party over the issue of territorial slavery. Whigs nominated Zachary Taylor as a war hero and because of his complete lack of known political alliances; he had rarely spoken in public as a civilian and had never even voted before 1848. Supporters of Taylor emphasized his resemblance to the great uncontroversial figure in American history, George Washington: a campaign songbook included the titles, "Immortal Washington," "The Lesson That Washington Gave," "Washington's Monument," and "Washington to His Troops." Whig managers kept Taylor's campaign appearances to a minimum.[24]

If they disdained the European revolutions, Whigs joined Democrats in trying to skewer their opposition with charges of revolutionary treachery. Both the candidate Cass and the Polk administration itself provided ample targets. The U.S. minister to France from 1836 to 1842, Cass had savored European culture, taking to writing his official correspondence, even to the State Department, in French—a practice, despite its acceptance among

European diplomats, that Secretary of State John Forsyth told Cass to stop. He had also published a highly laudatory study of King Louis Philippe and his rule, calling him the epitome of "all magistrates, monarchical or republican," and observing that in monarchical France "there [was] great personal freedom." In 1848 Cass changed his tune, cosponsoring a congressional resolution to congratulate French revolutionaries for overthrowing the monarchy. Democratic organs such as the *Albany Argus* tried to assist Cass's epiphany, showing that he actually had *not* gotten along too well with European nobility and insisting that "the wily diplomatists of the Old World were baffled by his bold and frank course."[25]

Whig newspapers nonetheless emphasized Cass's capacity for unprincipled expedience. The *Richmond Whig* noted: "Some years ago [Cass] was most at home among crowns and coronets. . . . Now he is the most radical of radicals . . . making Senate speeches about the new French Republic upon all occasions." Likewise, the *Whig* continued, "eighteen months ago he favored the Wilmot Proviso . . . [but] true to his character he [announced] . . . a revolution was going on in his mind . . . produced, no doubt, by the prospect of obtaining southern votes to sustain Presidential pretensions." The *Whig*'s characterization of Cass's reversal on the proviso as a "revolution" was of course no coincidence. For Whigs revolutions, both real and metaphorical, were dangerous.[26]

Antirevolutionary thinking was even more prominent in the *Daily National Intelligencer.* Founded in 1800, the *Intelligencer* had become the mouthpiece of Whig politics. The long life of the *Intelligencer,* and perhaps its financial setback with the 1846 demise of its monopoly on government printing contracts, shaped its judgment at midcentury that the best course of action for the American republic was maintenance of the status quo.[27]

Such a philosophy informed both the *Intelligencer*'s endorsement of Taylor and its reporting about the 1848 revolutions. The *Intelligencer* condemned the Mexican War, not out of disdain for slavery, as did other Whig papers like the *New York Tribune,* but out of fear of disunion. The Washington newspaper supported various traditional Whig programs—the Bank of the United States, a protective import tariff, and federal financing of internal improvements. Taylor supported none of these, but he was a slaveholder and thus unlikely to provoke Southerners' secession from the party (secession from the country was not the issue it would become later). Thus, the *Intelligencer* endorsed Taylor because he "would bring the country closer to the policy of George Washington than at any time in [the previous] twenty years."[28]

With such reverence for the past, the *Intelligencer* emphasized the dangers of radical change in its coverage of the 1848 revolutions. In an editorial the Washington paper made clear that insurgents in France were poor candidates to achieve a proper revolution: "The movement in France has brought about one of those extreme changes for which that headlong people are remarkable. . . . The Gallic people delight in war, in military glory, and want the braver instincts which [support] law, right, and freedom. We do not deny the right of revolution. . . . But we regard it as a right not to be lightly resorted to by *any* people."[29]

The *Intelligencer* thus outlined a national group revolutionary hierarchy, which Michael Hunt has called a recurring pattern in Americans' perceptions of others, although Hunt, ascribing the pattern to American racial thought, finds that Europeans ranked relatively high in American odds-making of other peoples' capacity to survive the hazards of changing government. All people, in the *Intelligencer*'s view, theoretically have a right to rebel against government. However, not all people should actually exercise that right, especially if they carry with them the baggage of bad history—in the case of the French, the more savage period of their revolution in 1793. The French people had seized their once-and-for-all opportunity and squandered it.[30]

At the same time the *Intelligencer* disparaged foreign revolutions per se, it used the revolutions to critique Democrats who applauded popular rebellion in Europe. "None are so vociferous for 'Republics everywhere, Freedom all the world over!' as that very faction who are fast building up for their own Monarch of the Party a despotic power," it avowed, alluding to the Polk administration. The *Intelligencer* frequently compared Polk to Louis Philippe, alleging that both executives unilaterally made war and treaties and conferred appointments to office by their "sole will" and "unchecked pleasure." Yet Polk's despotism had somehow gained the blessing of the democratic mob, whipped up by "penny newspapers" (so-called because of their working-class affordability and readership) like the *New York Sun* and the *New York Herald*. The *Sun* had defended the American invasion of Mexico as "follow[ing] the open law of nature, and obey[ing] the instincts of animal life," while the *Herald* had argued that foreign revolutions and American expansion taken together indicated "the hand of destiny" in the possible U.S. annexation of Cuba and Canada. As populist "penny newspapers," the *Sun* and the *Herald* were not Democratic organs on principle, but their fiery promotion of national expansion aided Polk's agenda.[31]

Rhetoric about an American instinct toward enacting revolution, however, prompted the *Intelligencer* to charge Democrats with subverting America's real revolutionary heritage. The *Intelligencer* lampooned the turbulence of Paris, using revolutionary images to portray a frightening domestic political scenario: "Suppose the [U.S.] Senate has ratified a Treaty of Peace unacceptable to those fiery spirits whose dreams are all of war and carnage, and a tumultuous body of men in hunting-shirts (blouses) should enter the Senate and seize the Presiding Officer by his venerable locks and hurl him from the chair . . . then proceed to the Representatives' Hall with clubs or paving stones . . . should thence for the President's House and strip the building . . . should then parade the streets bearing some old arm-chair gaudy with gold and crimson, with rabble at their heels." Such descriptions evoked events with which American readers were familiar. The "Treaty of Peace" referred to the recently concluded Treaty of Guadalupe Hidalgo. Presiding over the Senate was Vice President George Mifflin Dallas, whose public accomplishments hardly could provide a basis for his veneration. The eyewitness accounts of the Paris uprising by Americans and others had described the special treatment accorded the throne of Louis Philippe when Parisians ransacked the Tuileries palace: "The people were throwing furniture out of the [palace's] windows" and "carrying the throne of the Tuileries on their shoulders in triumph—singing the Marseilles hymn."[32]

Such images were thus calculated to instill both fear and mirth in the *Intelligencer* readership. Fiery spirits, war, carnage, crimson, and rabble connoted the specter of anarchical violence, while men costumed in hunting-shirts, the vice president ejected from his seat in the U.S. Senate, and hooligans cavorting with gaudy furniture evoked images of buffoon theater. The *Intelligencer* first condemned the Paris revolution, as well as other popular uprisings it might precipitate, and then exploited that negative image of revolution to castigate the Democrats—"the people with the heads of demagogues and the hearts of jacobins."[33]

America was indeed a model, according to the *Intelligencer*, as several

Democratic organs also claimed, but it was a model of antirevolution. Citing Shays's Rebellion, the Whiskey Rebellion, the Nullification Crisis, and the Dorr Rebellion, the *Intelligencer* recalled how these acts of American insurrection had been put down with the "gentleness of authority." This actually wasn't true, as in each case military deployment or its threat had proved necessary to defend the State.[34] But in the *Intelligencer's* cameo history of antirevolution in America, national chemistry, not coercion, had thwarted revolutionary mischief. For the *Intelligencer* revolutionary action—extralegal violence perpetrated against constituted authority—became an event only for commemoration, once a constitution documented what the revolution had achieved and fulfilled and thus exhausted the revolutionary impulse.[35]

Reflecting the divisions within the Whig Party, the *New York Tribune,* the party's leading newspaper, provided a different perspective on Europe and on the 1848 campaign. Its editor, Horace Greeley, described American politics not through their difference from Europe but through their similarity. Writing after the election, Greeley said that the year 1848 saw on both sides of the Atlantic the "replacement of dynasties which had ceased to regard BENEFICENCE as the chief end of government." Dripping irony, Greeley declared, "What Legitimacy and Divine Right were to the governing class in the Old World, Democracy is to the governing class here." Democrats hypocritically had come to believe, like Old Europeans, that true authority was best inherited, rather than earned, and haughtily opposed progress. Greeley's view of transatlantic politics contrasted with those of both Democrats and the *Intelligencer.* Democrats saw themselves as the agents of American redemption of Europe, and the *Intelligencer* denied that European upheavals had anything to do with America.[36]

Greeley and the *Tribune,* in contrast, sought to discover how the lessons of turbulent Europe might assist Americans to fulfill their own revolution's latent promises. Asserting that the Declaration of Independence was "either a pregnant truth or a pernicious falsehood," Greeley saluted Europe, in particular the temporary triumphs of labor in revolutionary France, for capturing the Jeffersonian vision of government provision of economic opportunities for workers to enable their independence. He also was drawn to the ideas of "association" prescribed by the French communist Charles Fourier, whose American disciples had established cooperative "phalanxes" throughout the Northern states in the 1840s. In urbanized Europe improvements to workers' status were limited, but Greeley believed America could be transformed through relocation of urban consumers near agrarian producers in the West.[37]

Greeley was not unfamiliar with the idea of an active state before 1848. As a supporter of the "American System" of Henry Clay, whom the New York editor supported for president in 1848, he had long disdained what he called Democrats' "negative, let-alone, do-nothing" policy toward American labor, slave and free. The same spirit that drove the French republic's initiatives for urban workers, including public works and a shorter workday, was behind the French abolition of slavery in France's West Indian colonies: American circumstances were not so incomparable to European problems and solutions. As Edmund Burke in the eighteenth century had welcomed the American Revolution, hoping its "convulsion would restore the European nations to that liberty by which they were once distinguished," Greeley and the *Tribune* now hoped revolutions across the Atlantic could reanimate America's own earlier revolutionary promises, lately gone astray.[38]

Three distinct interpretations of how America's revolutionary identity should shape national policy thus emerged in the 1848 campaign season. Democrats endorsed an American revolutionary influence driving events in revolutionary Europe, in line with ambitions for an expanding American republic. Conservative Whigs lamented how European revolutionaries were not adhering to American counterrevolutionary doctrine and hoped to preserve that doctrine, along with the republic itself, against disruptive movements at home and abroad. Free Soilers and ardent antislavery Whigs saw events in Europe as a barometer of what, to date, America's revolutionary accomplishment had not encompassed. Electoral choices in 1848 were clear, framed by how the parties calculated and jousted over the meaning and implications of revolution.

If the presidential election had been held in the spring of 1848, when Americans shared an excitement about revolutionary events in Europe, its results might have been different. As it was, voting day, on 7 November, eliminated the influences of earlier states' voting results in later states' polls. But it also meant that electors together could assess a political climate charged by the theme of revolution in light of the demise of the revolutionary movements in Europe, rather than their ascendancy. The labor uprising known as the "Bloody June Days" in Paris had been reported in

American newspapers beginning in mid-July 1848. Such events of counterrevolution separated the Free Soil convention of August 1848, and the
presidential election itself, from the "springtime of the peoples," as the
early months of the year were known, as well as the Democratic and Whig
conventions, held respectively in May and June.

Thus, it became easier to see Free Soilers, who already suffered from the
novelty of their clearly sectional platform, as disruptive or even dangerous
insurrectionists. Critics invoked images of European upheavals to stigma-
tize the new party for opening the country up to European experiments
and violence. The New York attorney George Templeton Strong, for example, lamenting his financial difficulties in the autumn of 1848, smirked,
"I shall turn Socialist, Fourierite, Free Soiler, and Red Republican."[39]

Others found less humor in the Free Soil doctrine. "Are we not all the
children of Washington?" asked a proslavery New York pamphleteer.
"Some of us have derived not only life, but property . . . by slave labor,
and now so maintained." This historical continuity was preferable to European scenes of rapine, where "desperate and ferocious attempts to bring
about a state of things in which they might, by hard toil, obtain a due portion of the fruits of the earth . . . speak volumes as to their state of utter
wretchedness," and "present striking proof of the necessity which some
countries have for slave labor." For this pamphleteer only slavery saved the
United States from anarchy; perhaps its reintroduction in Europe could
stabilize the Old World—an ironic twist on enthusiasm for transatlantic
bridge-building.[40]

Meanwhile, another writer, a pseudonymous "Jacob Leisler," warned
about the creeping centralization of government that the Free Soil movement represented. Based on his choice of pseudonyms, "Leisler" was a
likely a nativist: the original Jacob Leisler was an antipapist in the colony of New York who reacted to the English coronation of William and
Mary in 1688 by declaring himself for Protestantism and representative
government, seizing control of the colony, and forcing the serving pro-
Catholic governor to flee. Three years later a legitimate governor arrived,
and Leisler was arrested and hanged for treason. In 1848 "Leisler" again
warned against European corruption of American political genius. The
American republic was "a Union of political interest . . . found only in
the written compact which created it and sustains it in being." However,
the new French republic had been "formed by a fusion and merger into

one empire of States and Provinces, such as Guienne, Burgundy, Provence, &c.&c., *once* sovereign and potent States." Political change in France had resulted in trivialization of once respectable local governments.

Now the Wilmot Proviso, said "Leisler," foretold corollary centralization and eventual tyranny in the American republic. He urged his "fellow citizens [to] use the talisman bequeathed by the wisdom of the fathers[:] . . . the Federal compact." Recurrence to such original intent, "Leisler" believed, was the only safeguard against "anarchy or military despotism": "If God permit the Free Soil party to control the Congress on the extension of Negro slavery . . . bloody civil war must ensue." "Leisler's" condemnation of the Free Soil Party on account of its advocacy of the Wilmot Proviso seems hyperbolic; both the proviso and free soil doctrine were familiar if controversial issues in 1848. New that year was the prospect, as opponents of the third party feared, of a foreign revolution mutating into a domestic bugaboo, undermining faith that the republic was permanently immune to disorders that humbled other nations.[41]

Likewise, the momentum of transatlantic events raised ultimately fatal questions about Lewis Cass's apparent interest in expanding America's mission abroad. President Polk had conquered Mexico, but would that satisfy another Democratic president? While Cass received the support of German and Irish immigrants hopeful the United States might move toward intervention in the Old World, his assertions of the destined spread of American influence became suspect. Fears arose that Cass, if elected, might embroil the United States in a now chaotic and uncertain Europe. The Whig senator Daniel Webster publicly declared Cass "a man of rash politics . . . committed to policy . . . not in consistency with the . . . security of country"; he was "the most dangerous man" who could become president. Unlike Secretary of State Buchanan, whose election as president in 1856 would benefit from his tenure as a U.S. minister in Europe during the controversial passage of the 1854 Kansas-Nebraska Act, Cass's European sabbatical continued to haunt him. Ultimately, even his own party—and the national electorate—questioned what Cass might do. His "radicalism concerning foreign relations" worried one Democratic organizer in Virginia: "Amid the whirl of revolutions abroad . . . I distrust him."[42]

The outcome of the 1848 election generally has been interpreted as resolving little, given the two main parties' circumvention of the central question of territorial slavery with either an intentionally ambiguous policy or an intentionally unknown candidate. Generally, voters remained loyal to parties in 1848, not sections or regions. Taylor won the popular vote by 5 percent. He was helped in the Electoral College by pulling his home state of Louisiana, Democratic in 1844, to the Whigs. He also benefited from Martin Van Buren's Free Soil showing in a few key Northern states—New York, Massachusetts, and Vermont—which likely doomed Cass.[43]

After the election, meanwhile, the affinity among Free Soilers for the fate of European revolutions continued. In 1849 the Ohio senator Salmon Chase, intent on building Free Soil momentum at the state level, beseeched Charles Sumner, "Can you not, all of you, buckle on your armor, and rousing the people by an eloquence suited to the crisis, achieve a victory for Freedom, which will prove that the world is not wholly given over to reaction—that it will compensate, in some measure, for our defeats in Vermont & Hungary?" Domestic conflicts continued to fester, and revolutionary conflicts continued not only to ebb and flow in Europe but also to inspire the Democratic and Free Soil parties' leadership.[44]

In terms of electoral results, however, Whigs' scorn for the idea that the United States was part of a transatlantic revolutionary community proved triumphant. Horace Greeley, disenchanted with the "slaughterhouse of Whig principles," with which he interpreted Taylor's prodigality, predicted, "The Free States are now ripe for the uprising which *must* come sooner or later." Symbolic of his campaign's successful rhetoric of revolution, Taylor, in his inaugural address, became the first president to refer to George Washington's warning against entangling alliances. In 1848 a nervous white male electorate embraced this message and with it an American reaction against revolution.[45]

4. AMERICAN REFORM
Transatlantic Inspiration

In April 1848 the popular Massachusetts poet and essayist James Russell Lowell composed an antislavery essay entitled "Shall We Ever be Republican?" Lowell answered the question himself, declaring America would never be republican because tolerance of slavery violated moral norms established at the founding of the American republic. "We are afraid," Lowell declared, "of our own principles."[1]

Lowell's answer to the question, "Shall We Ever be Republican?" thus actually would have better answered the question, "Shall We Ever Again be Republican?" For Lowell slavery was wrong because it was incompatible with the American revolutionary principle of equal opportunity shared by anyone submitting to authority established once the United States gained its independence. Lowell pressed for an end to slavery as an enactment of a previously enunciated political and social philosophy of universal rights.

Other antebellum reformers joined Lowell in pressing the United States to enact the defunct philosophical radicalism of the American Revolution toward universal human rights. This was not a new argument by 1848, as historians have shown. But what often has not been recognized is that the European revolutions in 1848, a year that Timothy Messer-Kruse has called "a watershed in the history of American radicalism," both inspired and embarrassed various American reformers. That year American peace advocates, troubled by war with Mexico and the revolutions in Europe, organized a peace conference in Brussels to meet European pacifists and strategize how to persuade governments to ban war. For American advocates of labor, free and slave, and women, the 1848 revolutions punctuated their own country's complacency; gave them, at least momentarily, a common vehicle for their domestic agendas; and changed their strategy or direction toward creating an American revolutionary present. American reformers' reaction to overseas events provides a measure of how much they saw themselves as transnational "citizens of the world" and how they saw the role of the United States in participating in a new transatlantic democratic revolution.[2]

The international and inclusive aspects of American reform predated events of 1848. Quaker antislavery sentiment had arisen on both sides of the Atlantic from the eighteenth century, well before the rise of radical American abolitionism in the 1830s. American antislavery activists took inspiration from the British abolition of slavery in 1833, and British anti-slavery speakers toured the Northern states. Likewise, American abolition-ists went to Europe. Frederick Douglass, an ex-slave, now an abolition-ist editor and lecturer, toured Britain to describe the plight of American slaves. William Lloyd Garrison's newspaper *The Liberator* carried the mottos "Our Country is the World" and "Universal Emancipation." Garrison wrote in 1839 that abolitionism had a "republican character," in that it encouraged "persons of both sexes, and of all classes and complexions—farmers, mechanics, workingmen, 'niggers,' women and all."[3]

Likewise, an international sisterhood had fermented before 1848. American women's rights advocates looked to Europeans of the eigh-teenth century's age of revolutions, including Judith Sargent Murray, Mary Wollstonecraft, and Olympe de Gouges, and to contemporaries including Elizabeth Pease, Anne Knight, Jeanne Deroin, and Pauline Roland. Lucre-tia Mott, Elizabeth Cady Stanton, and Anne Knight first met at the 1840 World Anti-Slavery Convention in London. There, in the wake of male organizers' decision to prohibit women from speaking at the convention—chauvinism also was transatlantic—Knight began a feminist letter-writing campaign to potential sympathizers in Britain, the United States, and France, while Mott and Stanton conceived of the idea of a convention for women that would come to fruition later in the decade at Seneca Falls, New York. Meanwhile, through socialist newspapers and manifestoes ad-vocating Saint-Simonianism, which called for government ownership of property, distribution of production to individuals according to their vo-cation, and social and technological progress through women's participa-tion in all aspects of public life, feminists in America and Europe began to network in the 1820s and to see connections between socialism and the cause of women.[4]

Historians have shown that American laborers and employers, mean-while, largely shared republican values of economic independence and social equality into the 1820s. But in the next two decades, partly due to the immigration of English and German radicals, workers in the United States embraced a more oppositional politics and understanding of industrializing social relations. This change bore some similarities to British and French workers' movements at the time and was partly due to the spread of the ideas of the English socialists John Gray and William Thompson; the utopian reformers Robert Owen and Charles Fourier; and the leader of the National Reform Association (NRA), George Henry Evans. Thompson canvassed working-class voters, although for the Democratic Party, in Philadelphia. Owen established the utopian community of New Harmony, Indiana, and his son Robert Dale Owen helped found a New York Working-Men's Party in 1829. American followers of Fourier, led by Albert Brisbane, encouraged workers to establish associations in an attempt to link socialist and republican traditions, and the National Reform Association called for free public land, limitation of the quantity of land held by any individual, and homestead exemption from debt.[5]

But international events in 1848 in particular presented American reformers with an opportunity to attach data to longstanding ideas about realizing the revolutionary promise of universal rights. American newspapers reported the enactment of universal male suffrage in France; of nearly universal male suffrage in Prussia and in the other German states for elections to the Frankfurt Assembly; and of expanded voting rights, though with property qualifications, in Austria, the Italian states, and Hungary. They also published accounts of the French Second Republic's establishment of nearly three hundred producers' associations formed across numerous Parisian trades, enrolling fifty thousand members and receiving government subsidies.[6] And still other reports announced that both serf labor in central Europe and slave labor among various European colonial possessions was being abolished. In 1848 the German states and Austria ended their systems of serf labor within Europe, and Denmark and, most conspicuously, France abolished slavery in their Caribbean colonies. Such events inspired American reformers to reconsider the nature of their Atlantic linkages and to explore new linkages among previously disparate movements within the United States.[7]

Thus, 1848 in particular saw new alliances take form across traditional organizational boundaries of political participation and race. Theodore Parker, for example, saw the merits of new partisan mobilization against slavery. A Unitarian minister and Transcendentalist, Parker generally called for reform of individual character, rather than institutional overhaul. But in 1848 Parker supported the formation of the Free Soil Party, for him a "revolution in political parties." He observed that as "the occasion of the French Revolution of 1848 was afforded by the attempt of the king to prevent a certain public dinner . . . [so] the occasion . . . of [the] revolution . . . of America is the nomination of a man for the Presidency." Before 1848 Parker had disavowed political engagement on the slavery question because he believed political antislavery compromised the radical abolitionism of William Lloyd Garrison. Now Parker embraced political agitation on the grounds that "one day the motto, 'no more slave territory,' will give place to this, 'no slavery in America.'" A Europe agitated over the boundaries of freedom presented the prospect that American reformers' differences over tactics should be put aside for a larger cause.[8]

Parker also acclaimed the French abolition of colonial slavery, demonstrating how Americans could interpret certain elements of the 1848 revolutions for a domestic agenda. Invited to speak on "The Abolition of Slavery in the French Republic" for the American Anti-Slavery Society in April 1848, Parker used the occasion to illustrate how American development had undermined the principles of the American Revolution. Recalling the French revolutionary motto, "Liberty, Equality, Fraternity," he declared, "Liberty and Equality were American ideas; they were never American facts." But "Liberty [in France] means liberty for all: at one word [the French Republic] set free three hundred thousand souls. [Likewise] Equality means that all are equal before the law. Universal suffrage is at once decreed." Perhaps betraying an uncertainty he shared with many Americans about the socialist implications of the French uprising, Parker didn't dwell on "Fraternity," remarking only that fraternity was "not hinted at in the Declaration of Independence." Nonetheless, France in 1848, owing equally to its slave emancipation and its extension of voting rights, was enacting and extending American revolutionary principles.[9]

The abolitionist and Quaker minister Lucretia Mott also confirmed that the 1848 revolutions suggested the breakdown of social norms in America. Through her affiliation with the Society of Friends, which was open to female ministers, Mott enjoyed unusual opportunities for public speaking. But the French revolution brought an even greater prospect of the retreat of discrimination than her call to the Quaker pulpit. Speaking to the American Anti-Slavery Society in May 1848 on the topic the "Law of Progress," Mott hailed "nations prolific of events," which showed that "the present moment" promised "the ultimate realization of 'peace on earth, and good will to man.'" Remarking on the integration of moral principle and behavior occurring in revolutionary Europe, Mott noted that domestic reform in the United States had intensified, moving from tolerance of hypocrisy to accomplishments in principled action. The temperance movement had moved from encouraging alcohol consumption in moderation to a "language of total abstinence." In religious belief "Protestant reformers of old time [had] said, 'away with your popery,' [but had replaced Catholic authority with] the Protestant priesthood." Now the language of religious reform declared, "Thou shalt judge for thine own self what is right, and God is thy teacher." "Occasionally," Mott said, stating the obvious, even "a woman occupies a place at your pulpits." On the one hand, revolutionary Europe for Mott echoed American reform movements.

On the other hand, Mott noted how European revolutions could help American reform groups converge, as well as show American reformers a more radical vision. She hailed American public sympathy meetings for France, where "not only were Freedom movements hailed by the white people present, but the colored people also came forward. . . . It was an *amalgamation meeting!* Was it by privilege, as women sometimes . . . hold a kind of play meeting? No the white people of that large gathering left their own speakers, to go among the colored crowd, and hear their speaker." Mott used the phrase "amalgamation meeting" with tongue in cheek, her sarcasm suggesting how news of European radicalism dramatized American failure to reform.[10]

Black abolitionists shared Theodore Parker's and Lucretia Mott's understanding that the French revolution's widening of the public sphere offered a challenge to the United States. At an "August First Day" address to commemorate the British abolition of slavery, Henry Johnson declared the day's purpose in 1848 as not only to mark the end of West Indian slavery but also "to rejoice . . . [that France's] acts correspond with her professions. . . . She bids now to become all her former patriots desired." The abolitionist newspaper *Impartial Citizen,* published by the Congregationalist minister Samuel Ringgold Ward, cited the open enrollment policy of the French Second Republic's citizen guard—an institution and element of the 1848 revolutions that fascinated American observers—to critique the race segregation of American Christianity. Frederick Douglass reported in his newspaper *The North Star* a cordial meeting in Paris between a delegation of Negroes and mulattos and the new French government's justice minister, Adolphe Cremieux, who greeted the delegation as "Citizens, friends, brothers!" and, as Douglass emphasized, assured them that "the new Republic will accomplish what the Republic in 1792 proclaimed." The National Negro Convention for 1848 adjourned each of its sessions in Cleveland with three cheers for "Elevation: Liberty, Equality, and Fraternity!" Such festivities demonstrate the different uses of French "revolutionism"—the instantly recognizable French revolutionary motto, on the one hand; a less recognizable detail of the Paris uprising of 1848, on the other—to emphasize the principle of equality that the American revolutionary tradition had enunciated but not accomplished.[11]

This inspiration from Europe prompted Douglass to seek new strategic alliances within the United States, reaching outside traditional boundaries of race and gender. In his British tour of 1845–47 Douglass had insisted on the distinct character of American slavery, different from wage-labor oppression. In an unusual exclamation of "anti-anti-Americanism," as William McFeely puts it, Douglass asked British audiences, "Why does not England do away with forms of slavery at home, before it calls upon the United States to do so?" Douglass at the time felt such imprecise usage of the term *slavery* diminished the Negro slave's anguish. Now in 1848 Douglass conceded: "Whether the immediate struggle be baptized by the Eastern or Western wave of the waters between us, the water is one, and the cause is one, and we are parties to it. . . . Old prejudices are vanishing." Thus, Douglass was motivated to appeal to Northern workers to enlist in the van of transatlantic revolution. In an April 1848 address he singled out the laborers in his audience for recognition of their European sympathies: "I see here the working-men and mechanics [whose] hearts vibrate in sympathy with France. . . . With a consistency that puts our own country to blush, she takes into view the rights of laboring men . . . and has made measures which must bring about the entire overthrow of Slavery in all her dominions." Reversing his earlier position on abstention from party politics, Douglass also endorsed the Free Soil Party in 1848 as a potential friend of abolitionism.[12]

William Lloyd Garrison echoed Douglass's appeal for the sympathies of working-class laborers in the context of European revolution. Garrison's

The Liberator gave extensive coverage to Boston working-class rallies held to salute the French uprising. At one such meeting the "Working Men of Boston" congratulated the "Working Men of France" for escaping "slavish bondage" and "convincing humanity that despotism and slavery are not the natural and necessary conditions of the people." The rally congratulated the French Second Republic for "striking from Labor the curse and odium of slavery." France's public relief for labor and abolition of colonial slavery offered a vision of free white workers and enslaved black workers both benefiting from liberal government. In celebrating the French republic, white Boston workers seemed to abandon their typical shame at suggestions of their racial equality to Negroes but also implicitly denounced their own status as "slaves."[13]

More broadly, American workers did respond to the 1848 revolutions, which erupted amid a depression in America that would last until 1852. In 1847 the NRA had formed an Industrial Congress, which from 1848 to 1851 approved various resolutions of sympathy for European workers and funded American workers' cooperatives with subsidies, in its words, "no less liberal" than those made by the Second Republic to worker associations in Paris. At the New York Industrial Congress, in its inaugural year of 1850, fifty-eight separate trades were represented, and English- and German-language speakers shared the floor, reflecting the arrival in America of German labor "forty-eighters." Among these was the communist Wilhelm Weitling, who founded the *Republik der Arbeiter* newspaper, one of several worker organs established at the time, and endorsed the radical concepts of social security and old-age pensions, and Joseph Weydemeyer, the first "American mouthpiece of Marxian philosophy," who sought to establish a broad German and English working-class alliance in his canvassing of New England, the Great Lakes, and New York.[14]

Perhaps the most prominent native-born labor reformer sympathetic to the 1848 revolutions was the novelist George Lippard, whose novels *The Quaker City*, an exposé of nativism, celebrity scandal, and revenge, and *Washington and His Generals*, which likened George Washington to Jesus Christ, were best-sellers. Lippard's titillations were broad-ranging, from portraying both Catholic and Protestant ministers as gluttons, alcoholics, and sexual predators, to conjuring the myth that on 4 July 1776 the Liberty Bell was rung to proclaim freedom throughout the United States, after fifty-six Founding Fathers had together signed the Declaration. In 1848, spurred by the French revolution, Lippard began to study the works of French socialists Louis Blanc, Fourier, and Ledru Rollin. When he was labeled "a Red," Lippard responded with a satire about a three-headed monster, "Socialist, Red Republican, and Fourierite," desolating New York City. But the protagonist of the story discovers in fact that the monster consists of corrupt newspaper editors, merchants, and church members. When the National Reform Congress met in Philadelphia in June to organize for land reform, homestead exemption, and other rights of labor, Lippard gave the valedictory address, emphasizing the relationship between American and European social problems.[15]

In 1849 Lippard incorporated his interest in European socialism into *Adonai: The Pilgrim of Eternity,* about an early Christian whose spirit travels through time and space, accompanied by both the soul of George Washington and an executioner who sneers at dreams of social reform. When Adonai reaches America in the year 1848, he is horrified that the class divisions of ancient Rome have persisted; meanwhile, the executioner foretells a civil war arising over slavery and the destruction of humans by industrial machines. But reflecting his continuing inspiration by the 1848 revolutions toward labor activism, Lippard also founded the Brotherhood of the Union, a ritualistic, nonsectarian movement for land reform, cooperative unionism, and the emergent practices of unions excluding employers from membership and collective bargaining. Lippard announced the Brotherhood in his newspaper the *Quaker City Weekly* on 29 October 1849, to "battle against the tyrants of the Social System—against corrupt Bankers, against Land Monopolists and against all Monied Oppressors." The Brotherhood combined elements of American mythology and European news. Its central governing unit consisted of a Supreme Circle of fifty-six members, and its chief officers were designated Washington, Jefferson, Franklin, and Wayne. But its acceptance of class animosity, and its advocacy, should peaceful reform fail, of "Labor to go to War . . . with the Rifle, Sword and Knife," paralleled contemporaneous developments across the Atlantic. By 1850 Brotherhood circles had been formed in rural areas in nineteen states.[16]

Internal conflicts and external perceptions of the American labor movement, despite its local manifestation provoking Walt Whitman to call New York City "the most radical city in America," moderated its impact at midcentury. Lippard, disillusioned, died in 1854, aged thirty-one. Workers' cooperatives were less successful in large cities, where ethnic rivalries, the availability of cheap labor, and start-up capital requirements were greater than in rural areas. Catholic churches normally condemned association as a "first step to Socialism," as did such Protestant journals as the *Methodist Christian Advocate,* which warned: "The attempt to improve on the divine law is . . . blasphemous. If men cannot . . . get along as God has arranged and ordained, they can get along in no other way. It is needless to . . . adduce any proof of folly of Fourierism." Many English- and German-speaking workers disdained the Democratic and Whig parties as corrupt, and many native-born laborers sought to exclude foreigners and certain middle-class groups from workers' institutions. No main political party championed land reform, a popular labor cause. Suggesting how the influence of European radical reform tinged the land-reform movement, a Texas congressman declared in 1852: "Show us the constitutional warrant . . . to indulge in that which far exceeds the wildest dream of French socialism. The socialist never demanded that the Government furnish him a farm."[17]

Additionally, while "forty-eighter" Germans rapidly became attracted to the antislavery free soil movement, many English-speaking laborers until the later 1850s avoided the slavery dispute as a "contest between capitalists of the South and the North." Irish American workers tended to oppose abolition as "niggerology." Thus, the labor meeting in Boston that abolitionists hailed in 1848 called for a variety of labor reforms in the United States, including work-hour reductions, free public lands, homestead protection, abolition of the poll tax as a condition for voting, and creation of a federal government department devoted to industrial labor. But absent from the workingmen's resolutions was a demand to end Southern slavery. Over the next century all of these measures would become federal law, but at the mid-nineteenth century none, including abolition, had widespread support. French labor reform, and French abolitionism, affirmed the dignity of American workers' own toils, but did not provoke them enough to declare that black slavery was intolerable; these were issues that remained segmented. White workers' "republican ideology"— their vision of citizen-producers and critique of capitalism—turned out to be racially bound. To cheer the end of another country's colonial slavery was one thing; to work for the end of domestic slavery was another. Working-class reticence signaled the limits of white workers' susceptibility to international antislavery prolabor rhetoric, even in the excitement of the apparent victories of labor across the Atlantic.[18]

Frederick Douglass, however, also reached out to American advocates of women's rights, for whom the year 1848 was perhaps more significant than it was for any other American reform group. Douglass reported in *The North Star* on the proceedings of the Seneca Falls Convention: "Many who have at last made the discovery that the [N]egroes have some rights [like] other members of the human family, have yet to be convinced that women are entitled to any." Douglass recalled that at the World Anti-Slavery Convention of 1840, feeling against female speakers was so strong that "persons abandoned anti-slavery, lest they . . . countenance the heresy that woman, in respect to rights, stands equal with man." Previously, antislavery and the women's rights cause had been separate, even hostile spheres. Now Douglass observed, "Standing upon the watch-tower of human freedom, we cannot be deterred from [approving] any movement, however humble, to elevate the character of any members of the human family."[19]

Organizers of the Seneca Falls Convention shared these sentiments. In July 1848 Lucretia Mott and Elizabeth Cady Stanton, the daughter of a conservative Presbyterian judge but married to an abolitionist, organized this first national women's convention, a watershed for gathering concerns for the "social, civil, and religious condition and rights of woman."[20]

The document produced at Seneca Falls, a "Declaration of Sentiments and Resolutions," drew heavily from the Declaration of Independence to evince its framers' sense that a truly republican society was not practicable without enacting dormant philosophical principles. The older Declaration had asserted a restoration of natural rights, denied by British tyranny. The Declaration of Sentiments, with specific reference to *Blackstone's Commentaries,* asserted a restoration of natural rights, "repeatedly usurped by man toward woman directed at establishment of tyranny over her." Both documents asserted not new rights, but the recovery of old ones.[21]

The most radical resolution of the Seneca Falls convention was its demand for women's suffrage. Elizabeth Cady Stanton pushed the suffrage resolution despite opposition from other delegates, men and women, including Lucretia Mott, who, as a Quaker, believed a suffrage resolution would overshadow other concerns such as the rights of free blacks and Indians, women's rights to property, and antislavery. Women's suffrage was so radical a demand in 1848 that it could pose a threat to the credibility of the women's movement as well as other reforms.[22]

Mott may also have been aware of stories in American newspapers ridiculing the emerging Atlantic feminist movement. The *Wisconsin Argus* told of "Old Maids of Paris" who, "among the processions of different classes to the Hôtel de Ville . . . promenaded along the quai in virtuous order, and respectfully demanded that the arrangements for marriage should be looked into, that every honest woman might receive, at least, her minimum of a husband." The *United States Democratic Review* moaned: "One of the most horrible features of the late insurrection is the brutal conduct of the women connected with it. So it will ever be with woman when she unsexes herself; she attains a pitch of cruelty and brutality which man cannot even emulate." The *New Orleans Picayune* and the *New York Herald* ran stories of women's atrocities committed during the June Days uprising. The *Herald* explicitly connected these atrocities with women's activism in America and Europe, editorializing: "The work of revolution is no longer confined to the Old World, nor to the masculine gender. The flag of independence has been hoisted, for the second time, on this side of the Atlantic, and a solemn league and covenant has just been entered into by a Convention of women at Seneca Falls. . . . We confess it would go to our hearts to see them putting on the panoply of war, and mixing in scenes like those at which, it is said, the fair sex in Paris lately took prominent part." Such reactions illustrate the attitudes against which antebellum feminists struggled. Further, as attested by the *Herald*'s patronizing remark—"the flag of independence has been hoisted, for the second time, on this side of the Atlantic"—even detractors understood the claim of women's rights as an appeal to an American revolutionary consciousness, awakened by Europe.[23]

Why did Stanton, despite others' reluctance, demand the right of suffrage at this time? In her memoirs she does not indicate why she chose the occasion of Seneca Falls 1848 to insist on the suffrage plank, and no detailed transcript exists of the convention's debate over women's right to vote. In a letter to British abolitionist Elizabeth Pease she had mused privately, in the early 1840s, about the possibility of the "organization of a third [political] party" to advocate women's rights. But circumstances surrounding the Seneca Falls gathering made the theme of "the sacred right to the elective franchise," in Stanton's words, popular in the summer of 1848, qualifying it for public declaration. The movers of the Seneca Falls Convention were cosmopolitan and opportunistic enough to apply ideas from international affairs to the immediate business of women's rights. Lucretia Mott visited Seneca Indians in the summer of 1848 and observed, "They too are learning somewhat from the political agitations abroad, and . . . are imitating the movements of France and all Europe in seeking a larger liberty." "The spirit of freedom," Mott said, "is arousing the world."[24]

Europe in 1848 made the issue of the franchise, and women's aggressive entry into the public sphere, particularly sensitive in America and stirred Stanton to strike for suffrage then. European news brought images of women taking part in actual revolutionary struggles. They sewed new national flags and dressed in national colors. Hungarian women fought both in disguise and in the open, one observed wielding a musket in Vienna, counseling male cohorts to hold their fire until the enemy drew near. In France women formed clubs, built barricades, and wielded weapons. In Germany they fought in the cities against government troops and attended workers' congresses and lobbied government for the reorganization of labor. Across Europe feminists published journals, pamphlets, and petitions. To much ridicule and without success, the French feminist Pauline Roland attempted to vote in 1848, and a year later Jeanne Deroin would run for legislative election. Gender and national boundaries both blurred in the transatlantic tide of 1848.[25]

With the triumph of regimes in France, Austria, and Prussia hostile to feminism in the 1850s, some European feminists were imprisoned, and others fled to America, where—partly, and paradoxically, because of the disappearance of a wide-ranging agenda of international radicalism—the demand for the vote became the core issue of the women's movement. In 1848 Emma Willard, the director of the seminary that educated Stanton, sent a public letter to the French government appealing for women's suffrage. At a women's rights convention in Worcester in 1851, the Unitarian minister William Henry Channing called attention to Roland's attempt to vote. An address, the "Enfranchisement of Women," by the British feminist Harriet Taylor Mills, which ended, "the example of America will be followed on this side of the Atlantic," became a best-selling tract among American feminists.

Thus, the American feminist example drew on both the transatlantic turbulence of the age and the legacy of American revolutionary principles. At Seneca Falls Stanton emphasized that women's rights usurped by men "have been baptized in blood" and that they were the same rights as held by those whose contest was "rocking to their foundations the kingdoms of the Old World." Likewise, in 1852 the abolitionist Jane Elizabeth Jones compared the prospect of women's suffrage to "the progress of lightning [and] the waves of the sea" and called every listener to "keep her hand on her sword and her banner unfurled." In 1854 Stanton would argue: "The thinking minds of all nations call for change. There is a deep-lying struggle in the whole fabric of society, a boundless, grinding collision of the New with the Old." Stanton spoke in international terms of a conflict between political tradition and innovation. She cautioned Americans, "When [they] shall rebuke the disobedience of their forefathers it will be time for us to bow down to men's interpretation of the social laws . . . by being deaf and dumb." The Declaration of Sentiments' invocation of the Declaration of Independence, as well as American feminists' emphasis on gaining the right to vote, were no accidents. The inspiration of the European revolutions provided a necessary context for American feminists to reconstitute an old American revolutionary promise of political rights.[26]

While most American reformers took inspiration from revolutionary Europe from a distance, two other Americans who shared hopes of a transformed America, William Wells Brown and Margaret Fuller, observed revolutionary Europe and its aftermath firsthand. Brown traveled to France in 1849 to attend an international peace conference. Afterward, partly to escape the U.S. fugitive slave law of 1850, he remained in Britain as an antislavery lecturer until 1854, when British supporters bought his freedom from his former American owner. Fuller began her European tour in 1846 as a correspondent for the *New York Tribune*, traveling in Britain and France before settling in Italy until 1850.

Both Brown and Fuller are known for their writings concerning the plight of nonwhite males in the early American republic. Brown, like Frederick Douglass, drew upon his experiences as a former slave. His autobiography, the *Narrative of William Wells Brown*, launched his career as a lecturer for the American Anti-Slavery Society, and his *Clotel*, the first published African American novel, describes a slave child's attempts to escape from her white father-owner, who, in the novel's first edition, published in London, is Thomas Jefferson. Meanwhile, in *Woman in the*

Nineteenth Century, which became a manifesto for the early women's rights movement, Fuller called for women's entry into the intellectual and public spheres of society and for recognition of the feminine qualities of the human ideal to which both women and men ought to aspire. While Brown described his personal experience as a slave to compelling effect, Fuller used slavery as a device, analogizing its horrors to the unfair conventional relations between the sexes. Brown's and Fuller's reactions to their first-hand experiences in Europe were actually similar to the reactions of reformers at home, strengthening their determination that the legacy of the American Revolution was not merely arrogant self-assurance; they thus differed from many other American expatriates. But, especially witnessing the defeat of the European revolutions, they became more aware than their compatriots at home and abroad of the possibility that recovery of the Revolution's legacy of upheaval might require violence.[27]

William Wells Brown was one of several hundred delegates who descended on Paris for the peace conference of 1849, one of a series of gatherings in European cities from 1848 to 1853. American peace societies had begun to be established in America and Britain in 1815, and the American Peace Society was founded in 1828 to create pacific public opinion through the distribution of peace tracts, the periodical *Advocate of Peace,* government petitions, and conferences to abolish war and provide a peaceful substitute for settling national differences. Although the 1849 conference had no legal standing, its constituency was impressive: Victor Hugo was president, and in attendance were Richard Cobden, the British advocate of free trade, and Elihu Burritt, a Connecticut blacksmith and philanthropist. Disturbed by the Irish potato famine and the U.S.-Mexican war, in 1846 Burritt had founded the League of International Brotherhood, thirty thousand members committing to lobby for total renunciation of war, including refusal of military service and "any voluntary support or sanction to the preparation for or prosecution of any war." League members vowed to associate "with all persons, of whatever country, condition, or color, who have signed, or shall hereafter sign the pledge." Inspired by the French revolution of 1848, Burritt organized a peace conference in Brussels that year to manifest his beliefs in Christianity and an American global reform mission. Embracing the biblical verse of Acts 18:26, "[God] hath made of one blood all nations of men," Burritt declared, "It is reserved to crown the destiny of America, that she shall be the great peacemaker in the brotherhood of nations." The peace movement, until interrupted by the Crimean War and the onset of sectional violence in the United States, advocated international arbitration, general disarmament, codification of international law, a congress of nations, and an international court.[28]

Brown wrote briefly about the Paris peace conference of 1849 in his travel narrative, *An American Fugitive in Europe*. Literary scholars have found this work significant mainly because of Brown's intention to show his literary equivalence to his white American compatriots. But Brown's view of Europe also formed a basis for his critique of the United States, which differentiated him from his white colleagues. For example, upon his arrival in the Liverpool customs house, he described officials' morbid fascination with a female slave's "iron collar," which Brown had brought with him in his luggage. Such a "democratic instrument," wrote Brown, "became the center of attraction." Where other travelers often waxed nostalgic about the comforts of American democracy upon enduring annoying searches by European customs agents, Brown used the occasion to remind readers of the racial limits of American democracy.[29]

Brown did praise American over European conditions in one significant instance, however. He ridiculed the Paris peace conference as "mere child's play" on account of its reticence concerning the dictator Louis Napoleon, who, during the conference, despite paradoxically providing conspicuous hospitality for American and British delegates, including hosting the conference at Versailles, sent a French army into Italy to crush the upstart republic of Rome. "Not a word was said in reference to [the invasion]," lamented Brown. "The fact is, the Congress was *gagged*. They put padlocks upon their own mouths, and handed the keys to the government." The conference's avoidance of controversy made him wish "for a New England [abolitionist] atmosphere with Wendell Phillips as the speaker . . . !" The peace conference's silence concerning France's blatant violation of pacifist international relations perhaps reminded Brown of the hypocrisy of Americans' revolutionary rhetoric. To this former slave his compatriots' odes to the Declaration of Independence, the Constitution, and the revolutionary heroes of yore rang empty, for "the time has come when nations are judged by the acts of the present, instead of the past. And so it must be with America." Brown meditated briefly on the defeat of the 1848 revolution in France, observing that by the time of his visit the streets of Paris yielded up only "the stillness of death—nothing save here and there a *gens d'arme* . . . going his rounds in silence." Brown shared other Americans' smugness about Europeans' partial or flawed attempts to accomplish revolution. He used a paralyzed Europe not to salute American revolutionary success, however, but to reaffirm his commitment to overthrowing the American slave regime—evidence that the American Revolution itself had failed.[30]

While Brown arrived in France after its 1848 revolution had come and gone, Margaret Fuller's time abroad coincided with the rise and fall of the European revolutionary impulse. Fuller, like Brown, used Europe to enhance her status as an American intellectual. But more so than for Brown, who, as an agent of the "Underground Railroad," was already committed to subversive activities, Europe agitated Fuller's interest in revolutionary action, bringing her from the intellectual sidelines, as a Transcendentalist and feminist, into the partisan fray. In Europe Fuller recognized a link between reform causes she had considered disparate in America: the rights of women and laborers, and the cause of antislavery, again an example of how the 1848 revolutions helped broaden and unify the perspective of various American reformers. Fuller also recognized and wrote publicly about the potential similarity between a Europe in upheaval and an unregenerate America. Fuller became less the American spectator in Europe and more the radical expatriate.

When Fuller first left the United States, she ironically envisioned the voyage as a sabbatical from her liberal agenda in America. She foresaw that Europe would not "modify [her] mind and character much, but only add to [her] stores of knowledge," and confided that "the more treasures of true life accumulate, the less am I inclined to do anything with them." Fuller's interest in visiting Europe stemmed from her education in classical literature and German romanticism and from her focus as literary editor for the *New York Tribune* on European writers and themes, reflecting Ralph Waldo Emerson's 1837 call for an "American scholar" to produce work equivalent to superior European literature. Like many other American travelers at the time, Fuller crossed the Atlantic in search of cosmopolitan enlightenment, not ideological trial or public activism.[31]

Yet via her "Things and Thoughts in Europe" articles for the *Tribune,* Fuller became recognized as an important journalist, supplying a unique firsthand view of the Roman republic and an alternative perspective to the British view of Europe, upon which American newspapers often otherwise relied. Her presence in Rome during the 1848 revolutions as one of America's first war correspondents ironically made her writing more widely read by mainstream American society and as such magnified the possible impact of her radical consciousness.

Fuller began her European tour in 1846 in Britain, where she immediately noticed the social casualties and extremes of wealth precipitated by that country's early industrialization. She hailed the splendor of London's theaters and gentlemen's clubs but juxtaposed these images with meditations on the masses who drank and bathed in polluted city water and the sexual exclusion of London's posh gentlemen's clubs. "Poverty in England," she wrote, "has terrors of which I never dreamed at home." Such reporting satisfied Fuller's vocational requirements as a practical Yankee and her personal interest as a social critic, two styles American travel writers often employed. But Fuller did not then thank the stars that no such problems had infested her halcyon homeland. Instead, she made the less obvious point that their development in America might be warded off by a solution with roots in Europe—the utopian communities prescribed by the French socialist Charles Fourier. "Can any man," she asked, "who has seen these things, blame the Associationists for their attempt to prevent such misery and wickedness in our land?"[32]

In Britain Fuller seemed little inclined toward political action, however. She evinced no awareness or sympathy for Chartism, earlier a widespread working-class program, and while she visited Manchester, she did not visit Friedrich Engels, despite having earlier reviewed his *Condition of the Working Class in England*. She did meet the exiled Italian nationalist Giuseppe Mazzini, who rejected class warfare, and she lectured at his school in London, calling for an international exchange of British mechanical ability and honor, German industry and intellect, and Italian love of poetry and art. She delighted in such speaking opportunities, writing, "Habits of conversation [here are] so superior to those of Americans, I am able to come out a great deal more than I can at home." Such national stereotyping and sense of personal validation showed Fuller's resemblance, at the time, to other American tourists.[33]

Late in 1846 Fuller left London for Paris, where she met intellectuals who complicated her desire "only to add to her stores of knowledge." She visited Victor Considerant, the editor of the socialist newspaper *La Democratie pacifique* and a disciple of Charles Fourier who later would establish a utopian community in Texas. Considerant agreed to send Fuller copies of his newspaper, upon which she relied for news while in Italy. She also met the exotic George Sand, who was living openly out of wedlock with the composer Frederic Chopin and organizing poor relief through proceeds from her novel writing. In America Fuller had defended Sand's ideas of female intellect and the rights of the masses, calling Sand "a warning and a leader." Her meeting Sand in person reconfirmed the French woman's eminence. Fuller wrote that Sand "has bravely acted out her nature. . . . She takes on weight in society like a man, for the weight of her thoughts."[34]

Fuller remained in France only until February 1847, a full year before the outbreak of the revolution in Paris. She enjoyed the city's fine arts, but perhaps because of her poor spoken French, she found French people, in memorable words, "slippery" and admitted to a sense of provincialism in the City of Lights, referring to herself as a "Columbian ignoramus." Fuller did note rumblings of disquiet over government censorship of radical pamphlets and the irony of a government-sponsored Mardi Gras festival amid unemployment and famine. In France as in Britain, Fuller's stories to America decried European social inequality and peculiarities of national character—again similar to the accounts of other American travelers. And despite the radical company she kept, contemplation of utopian reform, not will for violent revolution, was the image Fuller carried to Italy.[35]

Fuller reported her first sight of Italy with the remark, "I have at last found my Italy . . . so [capable] of pure, exalting passion . . . the fulfill-ment of a hope!" Fuller's sense of Italy as a refuge for contemplation was typical of American artists, especially literary women. But once revolution erupted, Fuller's Italy became a different kind of refuge, a place where moral action emerged from historical obscurity, offering a vision for eq-uitable conditions accomplishable through violence. She arrived in Italy at the high tide of the reforms of Pope Pius IX and witnessed the forma-tion, across class boundaries, of male citizen militia units in Florence and Rome in connection with the Italian uprising against Hapsburg authority. Drawing on her American background, she observed that these militias were crucial for democratic progress. Her praise for male-only citizen mi-litias was surprising, given her perennial insistence on women's action. She had come, however, to regard revolutionary deeds by Italians, male and female, as virtuous action on behalf of "The Mother of Nations," as she referred to Italy. Fuller described such citizen militancy as the "spirit of true religion"—a kind of muscular Christianity, which, she asserted, had "won for . . . my Country [the United States] . . . all thou canst call thy own . . . [:] the assertion, though thou hast not been true to it, that all men have equal rights, derived from God." The Italian mobilization of religion and nationalism, awakening Italians from their long impotence, electrified Fuller. The same forces, she believed, had once inspired and legitimized the American revolutionary republic—perhaps they could do so once more.[36]

Soon after Pope Pius IX repudiated the Italian liberation movement against Austria, Italians overthrew him, and Romans assassinated his chief minister. Fuller applauded both events in her newspaper column and also used the *Tribune* to appeal for American assistance to the Romans, asking readers to organize the purchase and delivery of artillery for defense against foreign invasion. Fuller speculated that she would christen American cannons with names like "the AMERICA, the COLUMBO, and the WASHINGTON," to ensure that the world could make no mistake about American revolutionary sympathies. Like her Young American compatriots, Fuller called for American intervention in Europe. But she saw such intervention as a medicine that would treat a dying American revolutionary consciousness, not a confirmation of its current health. Beyond her newspaper writing Fuller also took charge of a field hospital administering care to fallen soldiers defending Rome against French occupation. Recoiling from the carnage there, she cried: "I found myself inferior in courage to the occasion. . . . To sympathize with the poor mothers who had nursed these men, only to see them all lopped and gashed. . . . I forgot the great ideas." Such an admission shows Fuller's change from the time when she predicted that in Europe she would "only add to [her] stores of knowledge"—her move from academic critic to vigilante apologist and republican mother.[37]

In the process Fuller also became an apologist for transatlantic revolution and began to link the Italian liberation movement with antislavery in allegedly peaceful America. Before her European departure Fuller had shied away from the movement to abolish slavery, on the grounds that it was too distant from her passion to change perceptions of women. Fuller's position resembled that of American associationists, as described by Carl Guarneri: "[A] focus on reconstructing Civilization fostered the idea that slavery was a derivative, secondary social problem."[38]

But in Rome Fuller, like William Wells Brown, exclaimed: "How it pleases me here to think of the Abolitionists! [Their cause is] worth living and dying for[,] to free a great nation from such a threatening plague." Fuller's perception of feminized martyrdom in Italy prodded her to see American slavery and European despotism as emanating from the same system of transatlantic oppression: for her patriarchal power, not liberal democracy, knitted the Atlantic world together. Antislavery and feminism therefore were not mutually exclusive causes but twin forms of resistance to a transatlantic evil. Fuller decided that in their claims of tranquil democracy, advocates of American exceptionalism failed to heed international signs.[39]

Thus engaged, Fuller did her best to impugn both skepticism about Italian independence and skepticism about American slave liberation. Fuller was in contact with other Americans in Italy, some of whom expressed confidence in and supported Italian republicanism. Thomas Crawford, the sculptor of the *Progress of Civilization* pediment and the *Armed Freedom* statue on the U.S. Capitol, was a long-term resident of Rome. Crawford joined the Roman civic guard, formed after the overthrow of the pope, provoking other American expatriates to question his loyalty to the United States. The defiant Crawford appeared in public in his military uniform, replying that "he had property at stake in Rome, and that [even] if he had not, to be the defender of liberty there would not alienate him from his own country." Likewise, Hiram Powers, of Florence, gained a commission from the U.S. government to sculpt a piece that he initially named *Liberty*. Inspired by scenes in a nearby piazza, where Florentines erected liberty trees and liberty poles and called for the city to unite with the republicans of Rome, Powers crowned the sculpture with a "liberty cap," the ancient symbol of slave emancipation made popular by partisans of the eighteenth-century French Revolution. "'Very radical,' you will say," Powers wrote a correspondent in December 1848, "but it suits the times."[40]

In the *Tribune,* however, Fuller decried the more cynical attitudes of other Americans toward the Roman republic, on the basis, as one observer told her, that Romans "were not like *our* people." Fuller found such smug American expatriates revolting, for "they talk about the degenerate state of Italy as they do about that of our slaves at home. They affirm that, because men are degraded by bad institutions, they are not fit for better." For many Americans it was dangerous for "degenerate" peoples, abroad or within the United States, to consider revolution. The majority of Americans, as Protestants, held Italians in particular suspicion on account of their Catholicism. The Presbyterian philanthropist Theodore Dwight, for example, published an account of the Roman republic that could only attribute the Romans' foundation of a secular republic to their apparent conversion to Protestantism! Similarly, many white Americans shared Thomas Jefferson's reluctant view that "blacks . . . are inferior to the whites in the endowments both of body and mind" and therefore incapable "in the faculties of reason" assumed essential to independence of mind and civic responsibility. In Fuller's day only the most radical of white abolitionists sought complete racial equality in America.[41]

Fuller shared the anti-Catholicism of some Americans, writing, "How any one can remain a Catholic—I mean who has ever been aroused to think . . . I cannot conceive," and, "The revolution in Italy is now radical, nor can it stop till Italy become independent and united as a republic. Protestant she already is." But she did not share their racial prejudice. She praised Frederick Douglass's autobiography as "an excellent piece of writing, and on that score to be prized as a specimen of the powers of the Black Race, which Prejudice persists in disputing."[42]

Likewise, she also did not believe that Italians' capacity for revolutionary virtue was fatally flawed. Decrying American newspapers' reliance on the reports from Italy of the arch-conservative *Times* of London, "a paper . . . violently opposed to the cause of freedom," she recalled the irony of a line from a schoolbook: "Ay, down to the dust with them, slaves as they are."[43] For her Italians had proven their right to freedom simply by offering revolutionary resistance to Hapsburg and Bourbon authorities. Similar to the attitude held by the radical New Left of the 1960s, Fuller believed actions were the guarantees and preconditions of ideas. Revolutionary behavior itself was redemptive, forming national character, not merely reflecting it.[44]

For Fuller Americans had once become revolutionary by acting against odds; she advocated her homeland's return to its radical roots. Many abolitionists who envisioned the ending of slavery as the final act of the American Revolution shared such a view. Fuller still did not see herself as an antislavery activist: in her private correspondence, for instance, she did not reach out to abolitionist acquaintances, promising to join the antislavery crusade upon her return home. But the logic of her thought was that American slaves, should they, like Italian patriots, arise and accomplish a dramatic political act—violent liberation—would thereby prove themselves worthy of republican citizenship.

Besides a slave uprising, or abolition of slavery, for Fuller redemption of the United States was accomplishable by an international noble act, especially by providing diplomatic assistance to the Roman republic. Advocating support for "popular sovereignty" in Europe, she called for U.S. diplomatic recognition of the Roman republic, pointing out, "The only dignified ground for our Government, the only legitimate ground for any Republican Government, is to recognize for any nation the Government chosen by itself." She wryly mused that she might ask to be appointed U.S. minister to Rome herself, except "woman's day has not come yet." Unfortunately for Fuller, no such actions had emerged by the time she left Italy in May 1850, as U.S. officials in Washington did not share her zeal for Roman revolutionary redemption or its American corollary concerning the liberation of women and slaves.[45]

In the winter of 1849–50 Fuller prepared to return to America. She continued her observations of Europe, though she turned from analysis of the present to predictions of the future. Sounding like a prophet, she boldly asserted, "The next revolution will be uncompromising, [and] all forms of arbitrary lordship must be driven out." Her omission to specify where such a revolution would take place suggests her sense that the United States was not different from Europe. Failing to undertake necessary democratic reform, the United States was likely subject to the troubles of the "failed" Old World.[46]

Yet also, surprisingly, given her criticisms of American conservatism, Fuller's last written words anticipated a new long-term linkage between the two sides of the northern Atlantic, one eclipsing the crusty chords of patriarchy. Earlier she had declared, "I am no bigoted Republican," but she now predicted, "For what has happened in these sad days, the entirety of Europe, at the end of this century, will be under [a] Republican form of Government." In this prophecy Fuller at once emphasized the virtues of possible global republicanism and rejected the notion that such a transformation depended exclusively on the American example. She did not realize it, but these would be among her last public words, as she, along with a young Italian nobleman whom she had married and their infant child, drowned when the ship carrying them wrecked and sank near the New York coast.[47]

In Fuller's last days and after her death, her American associates became horrified at her radical turn. Elizabeth Barrett Browning, in Florence with Fuller, wrote home that Fuller had become "one of the out & out *reds*." The compilers of her memoirs—Ralph Waldo Emerson, among others—caught between honoring their friendship with her and disavowing her political opinions, were silent about her final commentaries from Europe. A letter written by Lucy Henry, of Charlotte County, Virginia, suggests opinion of Fuller among ordinary Americans near the time of her death. Henry wrote John Bigelow, the editor of the *New York Evening Post*, a rival of the *Tribune*, to ask advice about subscription information. She explained that her interest in the *Evening Post* had begun once she realized that "[Horace] Greeley is a socialist; [and] . . . Miss [Margaret] Fuller's papers are the most heinous articles I ever read." Henry's comment illustrates both Fuller's controversy and her wide, if scandalized, readership at the end of her life.[48]

Fuller in the twilight of her European odyssey, however, still did not articulate a vision of a socialist state of the kind many Americans disparaged as too European for American conditions. Instead, she envisioned changes both more reassuring and more foreboding than the onset of pan-Atlantic socialism. Her prediction of a Europe free of monarchy resembled the aspirations of exuberant "Young Americans" at home who foresaw signs of American destiny manifesting on both sides of the Atlantic. But the prophetic tone and substance in her last dispatches concerning a new American revolution mimicked the increasingly desperate rhetoric of abolitionists, to whom she was closer at the end of her life, especially in their emerging openness to violence, than she was to European liberals and even former revolutionaries, many of whom were abandoning violent revolutionary tactics. In Europe Fuller became a clarion, like other American reformers, for a dynamic, not only historic, American republicanism.[49]

Thus, revolutionary Europe was important for American reformers for various reasons. It taunted them, as potentially radical American republicans, that the equality promised by the American Revolution had not been achieved. It challenged them to think more broadly in urging the

American republic to enact, not to commemorate or abandon, its own revolutionary promises toward groups out of power and demarcated boundaries of domestic mobilization beyond which some groups at the time would not go. And finally, revolutionary Europe, not despite its flaws but because of them, demonstrated that complacency—failure to reform—was transatlantic and thus implicitly challenged the notion of American exceptionalism.

5. The Conservative Christian Alliance

In 1850 John Hughes, the archbishop of New York City, wrote about an exchange with "an esteemed Protestant Friend." "We Protestants," declared Hughes's counterpart, "are going to take Pius IX from you, and then what will your Church do without a Pope?" Hughes replied, "If you take the Pope from us, what will your Church do without an Antichrist?" This exchange captures the issues on which American Protestant and Catholic spokesmen focused when they beheld turbulent Europe. What did revolutions against political and religious authority in Europe mean for Christians in the United States? This chapter describes how outspoken, ardently Christian Americans answered that question and shows what American religious reactions to European upheaval revealed about the United States.[1]

By 1848 church ministers and religious scholars in the United States, Protestant and Catholic alike, had endured some seventy-five years of challenges to traditional church authority. The American and French revolutions of the eighteenth century had unleashed a host of popular spiritual movements whose impact, in Nathan Hatch's words, was the "democratization of American Christianity." Just as American and French patriots had toppled monarchies, so could American citizens challenge educated clergy's sanction of methods of worship and interpretation of Scripture. A *History of All the Religious Denominations in the United States* appeared in 1848. Reflecting the multiplicity of American forms of worship, it described the distinctive elements of fifty-three different Christian denominations! While evangelical Protestants and Catholics constituted the mainstream of American religion, other faiths grew also. Unitarianism flourished in New England, attracting intellectuals repelled by what they considered evangelical dogmatism and preference for emotion over reason in their path to salvation. Quakerism, practiced across the country, emphasized the equality of all people in their capacity for realizing God's "Inner Light" within themselves and communicating it to others. Mormons followed the Bible but also the Book of Mormon, which their founder, Joseph Smith, said the angel Maroni had revealed to him, detailing God's special dealings with prehistoric settlers in America and long-lost tribes of Israel and directing the foundation of a New Jerusalem in America. Millerites, named for their founder, the Baptist preacher William Miller, believed Christ's return was imminent, setting a succession of dates in the 1840s, calculated through extensive scriptural typology, on which they gathered for vigils to await the Advent. Common people especially relished the unique opportunity that the American republic provided for "a fair prospect for a beginning," a "declaration of independence of the kingdom of Jesus." Violent clashes occurred intermittently between advocates of theocracy such as Smith and protectors of popular sovereignty, but among mainstream Protestants and minority sects alike, the religious upheaval of the early republic seemed providential, and millennial prophecies abounded that God would soon build his kingdom on American soil.[2]

American Catholicism also underwent a democratizing experience in the first part of the nineteenth century, called "trusteeism," in which lay Catholics challenged bishopric authority. Some Catholics, especially immigrants from Germany, called for accommodating the European ecclesiastical to American republican structures, specifically popular election of clergy and lay management of church property. Most Catholics from Ireland, however, supported the power of the bishops, and central authority survived the challenges of democratization in the Catholic Church more than it did in the Protestant establishment. Overall, Protestants tended to embrace the republican virtue of freedom; Catholics tended to embrace the republican virtue of respect for law and authority. But Catholics shared with Protestants the belief that the United States would witness a great religious upheaval. Indeed, in 1850 John Hughes predicted that given their religious liberty, "in less than half a century the majority of [American] inhabitants would be Catholics."[3]

Similarly, Protestant and Catholic Church spokesmen together benefited from a virtual explosion of mass communication in the antebellum period. The religious press, some of whose journals and newspapers enjoyed the largest circulation of any serial publications in the world at the time, printed full texts of sermons and tracts. As leaders of expanding, self-conscious constituencies, Protestant and Catholic apologists apprehended that their voices could carry nationwide.[4]

One important, if paradoxical, way advocates of Protestantism and Catholicism frequently used their influence was to inveigh against each other's faith. In the open American society religious leaders felt that laypeople should not only adopt the tenets of the Protestant or Catholic faith but also condemn the faith they did not choose. Although religious pluralism indeed existed, many religious apologists did not embrace its virtues. These hard-driven spokesmen claimed that the country should be all Protestant or all Catholic, not a safe haven for both. And to pursue this task at midcentury, both groups adopted the language and images of European revolution.

Religious apologists, however, invoked Europe to tarnish their opponents with revolutionary images, not to embrace revolution as a positive metaphor for their own faith. Similar to Democrats and Whigs, American Protestants and Catholics disparaged each other by portraying the other's sinister revolutionary premises: "revolution" was a negative image, not a positive one. Archbishop Hughes declared: "The Protestant system essentially casts off all authority. The first exigency of condition in Protestantism [is] to PULL DOWN." In contrast, Hughes asserted, "What is the Catholic doctrine with regard to the right of revolution? The Catholic Church does not authorize the principle."[5]

To Protestant thinking, however, Catholicism did portend upheaval, accomplished not by popular revolution but by conspiratorial coup executed upon unaware Protestant republicans. As the publication *Pope or President?* declared, "The hand of popery, secretly mov[es], misdirecting or holding in check the rights of the people." At the outset of the 1848 revolutions, an English immigrant in Rochester, New York, wrote home that he hoped England would be seized by a revolution, not to overthrow the monarchy but to provide justification for "hang[ing] every Irishman . . . all the world over," thus staunching the flow of Irish immigration to America. Zealous Protestants believed that since Catholics were accustomed to slavish obedience to monarchs and the pope, left unwatched they would infiltrate American society and undermine its democratic freedoms.[6]

Yet despite Protestant and Catholic efforts to distinguish their doctrines via events in revolutionary Europe, those events ultimately revealed the similar views of the two groups regarding social upheaval in the United States, a phenomenon counter to the traditional opposition of the faiths. Thus, antebellum American religious and political culture, which historians typically approach from a denominational perspective on the assumption that evangelical Protestant and Catholic Christian experiences invariably were different, should be reconsidered. Antagonism between the two faiths was often the rule, but international events such as the 1848 revolutions could align conservative Protestants and Catholics ideologically, even as they continued their doctrinal sparring. The European upheavals helped reveal a unique condition of American Christian religious culture in the late 1840s and early 1850s, shared across lines of denominational faith.[7]

Antebellum Protestant ministers and writers bore witness to an American revolutionary identity, as well as a Christian identity, when they remarked on the turbulence of midcentury Europe. Protestants emphasized the linkage between American millennial destiny and the Protestant Reformation of the sixteenth century. The Reformation had replaced the doctrine of the Catholic Church as the mediator between the individual and God, and salvation through faith and works, with the doctrine of personal piety and private repentance, and salvation through God's grace alone, along with an emphasis on local rather than centralized authority. All American Protestant groups adhered to these basic tenets. As such, the Reformation was deemed the source for all subsequent social and political change and thus the great precursor of contemporary events in Europe. The *Methodist Quarterly Review* quickly placed the events of 1848 in historical context: "In the checking of the Reformation in France, Germany, and Italy, the dragon's teeth were sown. The volcano burst forth in the English revolutions of 1648 and 1688, and the American Revolution of 1776, all resulting from the great revolution, . . . the Reformation. . . . [In 1848] the harvest has begun."[8]

Over the course of the antebellum period, many American ministers remonstrated about the prospect of a papal overthrow—before 1849 an unfulfilled hope—to promote denominational allegiance and, to Protestant thought at the time, to hasten postmillennial bliss: the thousand-year reign of Christ on earth, manifested by prosperity and peace, after which time he would take his followers to heaven and culminate world history. The 1848 revolutions seemed a fulfillment of prophecies of Catholic demise. Protestants in 1848 could point to actual revolutionary events as perhaps the final chapters of God's will being done. Encouraging missionaries to go west, the Congregationalist Edward Norris Kirk declared: "We dwell in peace, while Europe is in commotion. This [the United States] is truly a chosen soil for the seed of the kingdom." Kirk's idea of the United States as a chosen place aligned with what ardent Protestants had preached and prayed for since the time of Jonathan Edwards, the most important eighteenth-century cleric to envision an American utopia destined to witness Christ's return. The 1848 revolutions seemed to confirm that Europe had failed to embrace the Protestant Revolution, whose core precept, American Protestants believed, was the separation of ecclesiastical authority from secular government. Though disestablishment had occurred slowly in the United States, the last state to abolish established religion, Massachusetts, had done so by 1833. Four centuries after the Reformation, the papacy still retained its temporal authority, reinforced by Catholic heads of state across central and southern Europe. American Protestants foresaw God punishing the Continent for these shortfalls, while sparing the United States.[9]

For several reasons, moreover, Europe became an object of intense scrutiny for signs of the end times. Biblical scripture that Protestants understood to refer to Europe underlay their enthusiastic assessments of a possible apocalypse. Considered "the repository of all wisdom, the arbiter of all disputes, the very revelation of the mind and will of God Himself," the Bible informed and framed Protestants' interpretations of events across the Atlantic. Bible readers intent on a Second Coming of Christ took a keen interest in events in Europe, and observers of events in Europe naturally resorted to the Bible for answers. The book of Daniel prophesied the rise of "a vile person," who "shall gain power with a small force of people," as well as the overthrow of despotic kingdoms—the enemy of true (i.e., Protestant) Christianity—in preparation for the millennial coming of the Kingdom of God. The book of Revelation described an angel ascending "from the east," hastening the earth's punishment for its sin and the consummation of history. Asia, the Near East, and Africa, as well as Europe, could all be considered east of the United States, of course, but European politics and religion were most familiar to American Protestants.[10]

Thus, beginning with the bloodthirsty days of the French Revolution of the eighteenth century, Europe's wars and revolutions had struck American Protestants as signs of the end times, the pouring out of divine wrath described in Revelation 16. In 1815 a New Jersey minister preached that Orthodox Russia and Anglican England, like Catholic France, were children of the "[papal] Roman Whore." All of the partisans in the Napoleonic Wars were ripe for messianic destruction. During the French revolution of 1830, the *Southern Religious Telegraph,* a Baptist journal, told readers that the state of Europe would always interest "those who pray 'thy kingdom come.'" Already before 1848, therefore, when Protestant leaders assessed European upheavals amputated from the primordial Reformation and thus the American founding, they associated revolutionary behavior with impending apocalypse, not progressive reform.[11]

But 1848 earned its own meaning as prophecy fulfillment among zealous Presbyterians, Baptists, and Methodists. Alexander Taggart McGill, a Presbyterian minister and church historian at Western Theological Seminary in Pittsburgh, noted, "Commentators have designated this year for the overthrow of him who exalteth himself above all that is called God." A numerologist, McGill painstakingly demonstrated that the number 1848 could be prophetically and mathematically associated with a seventh-century pope's historic blasphemy.[12] The *Baptist Banner* performed a similar calculation, deriving the number 666, the "number of the beast" in Revelation 13:18, by assigning numerical values to the Latin translations of French monarch Louis Philippe (LVDOVICVS) and "Pius IX, the false priest" (PIVS NONVS SACERDOS FALSVS). The *Banner* was satisfied that the European revolutions "are but preparatory to the millennial reign of Christ." Likewise, the *Methodist Quarterly Review* condemned the French revolutionary motto "liberty, equality, fraternity" as a "fanatical and infidel" appropriation of the teachings of Jesus. And a Methodist minister in Virginia warned his communicants in 1848: "These are the latter days of the earth. . . . Mankind are shortly to see the fulfillment of the great purpose of the Gospel."[13]

Despite 1848's seeming fulfillment of prophecy, however, and contrary to reactions to the French Revolution of 1789, many American Protestant ministers and writers did not interpret the European revolutions as a blessing on America. Instead, they greeted turmoil in Europe, and the prospect of a papal overthrow, with anxiety, speaking more often of the revolutions as a sign of Atlantic punishment than American progress—which is surprising, given their historical alacrity for the downfall of European religious and political institutions and the apparent alignment of turbulent European events with biblical prophecy.

In fact, European turbulence gave expression to Protestant church leaders' midcentury apprehensions over American domestic developments. Echoing the confidence of Edward Norris Kirk, noted above, the Congregationalist minister Horace Bushnell had little doubt of the American mission to inspire European upheavals. In 1848 Bushnell preached, "Dynasties subverted . . . enlarged liberty of conscience [in short] everything beneficent in European affairs, is produced by institutions of the United States." Yet Bushnell could only lament American domestic conditions. In the same sermon he observed flagging religious discipline, uncontrolled westward migration, a heavy foreign population, poor education, the Mexican War, "creeping [Catholic] Romanism," and emerging division over slavery. Bushnell anguished over such an American society, in his words a "bowie-knife style civilization." As a minister to two "nonevangelical" groups, Unitarians and orthodox Calvinists, Bushnell was less zealous about a millennial apocalypse, and less virulently anti-Catholic, than were more evangelical clergy. He believed progress was gradual, to be achieved by a covenanted community, not immediate, grasped at through a few humans' rebellion or sudden epiphany. Thus, his apprehensions about signs of a sinful American society conflicted with his profession that a superior American ideology had inspired European upheaval.[14]

Others shared Bushnell's turmoil. The Presbyterian scholar James Henley Thornwell, of South Carolina, condemned not only social ills but also the remedies proposed by church reformers as signs of rampant "human instrumentality . . . , which he who reads the Bible must feel to be shocking." Thornwell, the president of South Carolina College (now the University of South Carolina), had founded the influential *Southern Presbyterian Review*. Like other clergymen of the day, both North and South, he believed God was behind human history, orchestrating eventual progress. Meanwhile, people should accept the status quo, guarding against the dissipation of human morality on one hand and attempts to radically alter the status quo on the other. Thornwell reflected the widespread condemnation by Southern clergy of illicit economic aspirations and attitudes infesting antebellum America, a condemnation reaching its apogee after the mid-1840s. Thornwell and his brethren censured not only notions of economic "go-aheadedness" but also Americans' apparent openness toward surging transatlantic social change.[15]

Thus, this Southern Presbyterian frowned upon all manner of nineteenth-century diversions, including drinking, novel reading, horse racing, and the theater. Dancing in particular was a form of licentiousness, said Thornwell, "an insult to God who has made us beings of intellectual dignity." Thornwell's distaste for dancing wasn't surprising, except that he and others attributed "radical dancing," as it was called, to foreign, anti-Christian influences from Europe. "The year 1848 seems to be famous for dancing, playing, [and] singing carnal songs," the Baptist Banner complained about the festive atmosphere of American social life during that revolutionary year. Injecting nativist suspiciousness into its commentary, the Christian Magazine of the South noted that "those figures and waltzes are most admired which have been introduced from France and Spain. [They] provoke universal scandal for their licentiousness." The South Carolinian Benjamin Morgan Palmer preached against "Christian children" receiving dancing lessons from "vagrants who have been graduated in the soup houses and kitchens of Paris." Palmer cited Moses's scorn for dancing, recorded in Exodus 32:19: "As soon as he came unto the camp, he saw the calf, and the dancing: and Moses' anger waxed hot, and he cast the tables out of his hands, and broke them beneath the mount." In hindsight exotic dancing posed little danger to the overthrow of American civilization. But at midcentury such foolery represented a world coming apart.[16]

Surprisingly, clergymen such as James Henley Thornwell, though they condemned social evils like dancing, shunned efforts to reform them. The mid-nineteenth century, an age of "perfectionism," saw the birth of a host of reform movements, including movements to promote Sunday school, Bible distribution, antidueling, temperance, and antislavery. But injunctions to "be perfect" troubled Thornwell, because, as he preached, the "Gospel does not propose to make our present state a perfect one— to make our earth a heaven." Moreover, most reform organizations grew outside the traditional church and thus were scorned by Calvinist clerics who argued that human inventions were unnecessary to accomplish "the legitimate action of the Church . . . which Christ has established." Antebellum temperance societies, for example, flourished in rural areas both North and South, but Thornwell decried them as "secular enterprises . . . having no connection whatever with the kingdom of God."[17]

Likewise, but even more dangerous, abolitionism was an application of liberal religious interpretation to a secular institution. To many Southern as well as Northern Christian church leaders, abolitionists were alien agitators, representing the most threatening of the "infidel commotions," "fantastical ultraisms," and "ferocious Jacobinism," rooted in the French Revolution of 1789. These evils seemed to have crossed the Atlantic by midcentury, conspiring with radical antislavery against the fragile American republican experiment and, moreover, making antislavery seem anti-American.[18]

Thornwell had a personal stake in muffling abolitionist cries against the peculiar institution: like many Southern clerics he himself was a slave owner. But aside from that, he determined that antislavery was part of a giant division of society, confirmed by the 1848 revolutions in Europe. "The agitations which are convulsing the kingdoms of Europe," he wrote, "the mad speculations of philosophers, the excesses of unchecked democracy, are working out some of the most difficult problems of political and social science; and when the tumult shall have subsided . . . it will be found that the very principles upon which we have been accustomed to justify Southern Slavery are the principles of regulated liberty . . . that we have been supporting representative, republican government against the despotism of the masses on the one hand, and the supremacy of a single will on the other." For Thornwell slavery provided an assurance that Americans were not prone to the "heaving billows" of unrest that engulfed Europe. There was no difference between an American agitator and a European one: the parties were "not merely Abolitionists and Slaveholders, they [were] Atheists, Socialists, Communists, Red Republicans, [and] Jacobins on the one side, [opposed by] friends of order and regulated freedom on the other." American abolitionism was but the domestic import of European revolutionism; through antiabolitionism the United States could retain its peculiar, more Christian character. In his views of threats to civilizational order as innocuous (to us) as dancing and as ominous as abolitionism, Thornwell conceived of a "foreign" enemy. American society could not produce disruptions in the national fabric; therefore they must come from abroad.[19]

In Pennsylvania John Williamson Nevin shared Southern clerics' concern over the threat to order at home and abroad; religious anti-European conservatism was hardly sectional. A formally educated German Reformed theologian, Nevin saw the church as indispensable to bringing faith to the believer and emphasized that parishioners seeking independence from ecclesiastical instruction were not only social revolutionaries but rebels against Christ. Early in 1849 Nevin declared that "the most dangerous foe is not the Church of Rome," but "the numberless popes who would enslave Protestants once more to human authority in the form of mere private judgment." Nevin, for example, considered Charles Grandison Finney, the leading evangelist of the antebellum period, a "quack" for cultivating "transient excitement" among religious converts, rather than faithful systematic instruction.[20]

Nevin grew especially alarmed at excitement over the Hungarian revolutionary Louis Kossuth, whose anti-Catholic pronouncements during his American tour in 1852 initially endeared him to many Protestants. Nevin perceived that Kossuth sought to tie American republicanism to European socialism—a feat easier now, Nevin remarked sarcastically, than it had been in the past, when both sides of the Atlantic seemed eager to establish a "brotherhood of nations" espousing "liberty and human rights." Kossuth was a menace, determined Nevin, the "veritable Antichrist of the age." Nevin was less antagonistic to Roman Catholics than other Protestants were, writing in 1853, "I find it more and more difficult . . . to [support] any opinion . . . in contradiction to . . . the Catholic Church." But he shared their understanding that radical democracy in its various transatlantic forms—the despotism of mass opinion, the demagoguery of charismatic individuals, and the agitation for immediate change—too hastily disturbed the social order. These theologian's warnings against lay Americans' growing antiauthoritarianism highlighted the tenuous position of educated clergy during a time when American Protestantism was becoming "democratized," a process that European struggles for liberty exacerbated.[21]

Such commentaries reveal several elements of the Protestant perception, and reception, of the European revolutions. Rebukes of parishioner lifestyles, including both dangerous reform movements and self-indulgent dissipation, reflected an increasing tension between church leaders and the lay majority. The European revolutions captured Americans' imagination, becoming a source of cultural radicalism expressed in ways of dress, forms of entertainment, and popular literature. Protestant leaders' rebukes offered an oblique comment on the extent of such cultural radicalism. Lay American citizens were agitated by European events, but less interested in their theological implications.

Thus, when the prophecy of Catholic demise seemed on the verge of fulfillment in 1848, Protestant apologists could not declare victory. Reluctantly, they saw events abroad as God's warning about American backsliding. As the French revolution degenerated into grisly bloodletting in the summer of 1848, James Henley Thornwell sensed the philistine cry of popular sovereignty engulfing the entire transatlantic world: "France is now blundering until redemption becomes hopeless . . . [while] the tendency of things in this country [the United States] is to corrupt a *representative* government into a *democratic* government . . . . As . . . the only safe guide is . . . in the prophetic Scriptures, I have begun with increased zeal the study of a book, which has heretofore been to me . . . a sealed volume: the Apocalypse of John. . . . God is riding on the whirlwind . . . and out of the chaos and tumult of nations, He will surely evolve His own grand purposes." The European revolutions became a providential reminder of former religious vigor and the potential for future calamity—and undermined Protestants' belief in American millennial destiny.[22]

Like Protestants, American Catholics frequently assessed the 1848 revolutions in terms of the fate of Pius IX, elected by the College of Cardinals in 1846. Before the 1848 upheavals Pius had gained high praise in the United States for his liberal reforms—freeing political prisoners, employing a civic guard comprised of Roman citizens, and creating a kind of citizen-advisory council for his papal administration. Perhaps the pope was a republican? Popular literature explained his good deeds to the American public. Citizens in Philadelphia convened a mass meeting in January 1848 to "express cordial approval of the liberal policy of Pope Pius IX in administration of the temporal government of Italy." The Louisiana state legislature passed an official resolution of praise. Both endorsements were sent to Rome.[23]

Yet Pius's reforms did not keep up with the pace of revolution in Europe. Pius refused the people's demand that he join the northern Italian states in fighting against Austria and ordered the papal troops to defend the Vatican, not to assist the liberation of Italy. But succumbing to popular pressure, Pius fled the Vatican in November 1848 and remained in exile until April 1850, when the Roman Republic had been bombarded and the city occupied by a French army.

American Catholics defended Pius's increasingly reactionary role in the European revolutions and condemned Protestants' jubilation at his downfall. But Catholic apologists shared Protestant leaders' sense that a radical Europe was subversive; moreover, they wished to avoid stirring up anti-Catholic nationalism in the United States, a majority Protestant nation. Thus, in other ways their reaction was similar to that of Protestants.[24]

The *Catholic Herald,* published in Philadelphia, illustrated Catholic objectives early in the coverage of the European revolutions. "We have arrived at a strange time," the *Herald* noted cautiously in a May 1848 editorial titled "THE CHURCH AND THE REVOLUTIONS." "Europe is threatened . . . all over its surface with an eruption of democracy, republicanism, and the levelling of ranks." The *Herald* chose its metaphor subtly, using the image of revolutionary eruption to characterize recent developments in America as well as in Europe: "From the very caverns and bowels of the earth beneath our feet, from unwashed laborers and artisans . . . come invaders of an old civilization and social state. The democracy of this day are . . . rude, violent, [and] untaught." Ironically, the *Herald's* invocation of "an old civilization" referred to the American republic, threatened with new working-class Goths and Vandals—immigrants and urban laborers, fleeing severe European conditions. Omitting to note that many "unwashed laborers and artisans" were Catholic immigrants, this Catholic newspaper expressed a nativist attitude, normally characteristic of the zealously Protestant press. The 1848 revolutions created the image of an ethnically mongrelized America, crowded by European refugees and radicals intent to level society and in the process to bring down ultramontane Catholicism.[25]

Interestingly, when news arrived of more radical upheavals in Europe, the *Herald* reversed opinion about the impact of Europe on American democracy. In June 1848 the "June Days" in Paris raised the specter of working-class socialism paralyzing the government. The American Catholic press emphasized the June Days' assault on Catholicism in France. "Hundreds of priests were murdered by the democrats, simply because they were priests," reported the *Boston Pilot.*[26] This was an exaggeration, but street insurgents did murder the archbishop of Paris when he ventured atop a barricade to negotiate a truce. Not surprisingly, the *Herald* condemned the Paris uprising and proclaimed the archbishop a martyr. But beyond this the *Herald* now decreed: "Since the [American] War of Independence the social and political condition of the people has been advancing. . . . In this country we understand . . . social reform. . . . [We] are, therefore, successful in such experiments. . . . Let France take a lesson from us!" The explosion of class violence in France was foreign to the alleged steady progress of Americans' tradition as a legacy of their own revolution, a tradition this Catholic organ—but also, it implicitly insisted, this American organ—meant to embrace.[27]

The *Catholic Herald* expressed the views of locally read Catholic news sources. By comparison, assessments of the 1848 revolutions by the itinerant intellectual Orestes Brownson and the ecclesiastic John Hughes were widely circulated. Brownson was the more unorthodox of the two, Hughes the voice of the Catholic establishment. But both rendered similarly harsh judgments of events in Europe and used these events as a foil in their struggle against American Protestantism.

Although by 1848 he was an ardent Catholic, Brownson in his life and writings reflected the dynamism of American antebellum religious and political culture. His denominational affiliations had passed from Methodism to Universalism to Presbyterianism, then back to Universalism, in which he was ordained a minister. Brownson became pastor of a rural New Hampshire Unitarian church and then went to Boston in the mid-1830s to form the Society for Christian Union and Progress, to help Boston's working classes. He founded the *Boston Quarterly Review* in 1838, and his controversial "Essay on the Laboring Classes" soon appeared, in which he described wage labor as exploitation worse than slavery, comparable to European serfdom, because it did not offer even the minimum solaces of paternal slave keeping. Brownson also called for government control of business. Critics assailed him as a socialist, an American Robespierre. Brownson at the time did not shirk such labels, envisioning the second coming of the French Revolution, "one of the most glorious events in human history," to establish a truly Christian democracy.[28]

However, Brownson grew disillusioned with politics and less experimental in his thinking after the Whig presidential victory in 1840, which he felt revealed popular naivete. He grew suspicious of the ordinary person's capacity for self-fulfillment and thus rejected Unitarians, "transcendentalists, humanitarians, and naturalists . . . [who] take as their rule of morals the maxim . . . 'follow one's own inclinations and tendencies.'" Like many Protestant theologians Brownson came to see democratic and even humanitarian reform, accomplished without the guidance of the established church, as "worship of the human soul," as he described Unitarianism to William Henry Channing, its leading minister.[29]

In 1844 Brownson entered the Catholic Church, persuaded that people's moral condition could exist only under the authority of the unsplintered Church and the uncontrovertible State. With the 1848 revolutions Brownson had the occasion to apply his religious transformation to the defense of the beleaguered Catholic papacy and to expound on his thinking about an American revolutionary identity.

In defiance of early American sympathies for revolutionary Europe, Brownson declared, "People, we know, are prejudiced against the doctrine [of] the divine right of government; but it is because . . . they identify liberty with democracy." Brownson, like other Americans, conceived of democracy largely as the right of universal male suffrage. Others rejoiced over apparent democratic steps in Europe—for example, the push for male universal suffrage in France and the democratic elections to the Frankfurt Assembly—and assumed achievement of the franchise a great objective of revolutionary Europe. Brownson argued, however, that the franchise was not a right seized or even earned, but "a municipal grant," bestowed by the grace of the ruling authority. Like his Protestant counterparts Brownson believed that democracy, unless it did not imply "sovereignty of the popular will," represented "Jacobinical" madness. *Jacobinism* had entered American political rhetoric in the late eighteenth century, originally suggesting rule by a mob but by the mid-nineteenth century reversed to suggest rule by cabal. Amid the 1848 revolutions religious commentators, Protestant and Catholic alike, also invoked the term, but cautioned against "Jacobinism" in its older sense. Revolutionary Europe revealed not the virtue but the danger of "popular sovereignty."[30]

Though following a tortuous path, Brownson ultimately came to defend the American political system. Reversing his earlier attitude, in the late 1840s he warned against the prospect of spreading socialism, which he, like many Americans, came to believe animated the revolutions in France and Germany. Brownson even believed that socialism was thriving in Italy. He associated socialism with apocalyptic dangers: "All possible heresies are here actualized in one universal heresy, on which the age . . . erects a counterfeit Catholicity for the reception and worship of Antichrist as soon as he shall appear in person."[31]

Likewise, Brownson was surprisingly sensitive, given his conservatism, to being labeled a "monarchist": "It is gravely argued, if you deny the popular origin and right of government, you are a monarchist or an aristocrat.

We deny the conclusion." He asserted, "[Although] we do not embrace . . . the democratic doctrine of the country . . . we are republicans, because republicanism [in the United States] is the established order." Recalling the American Revolution, Brownson asserted that it "was no revolution. . . . There was no subversion of the state, no destruction of the existing constitution." Meanwhile, he "cheerfully conceded the prosperity which has followed the separation." Brownson shared a refrain common among American observers, lay and clerical: that the United States had experienced a somewhat perfunctory war of independence, giving rise to a calm, provincial republican prosperity. Thus, Brownson saw Catholic conservatism not only as a bulwark against radical Protestantism and secularism. He also came to see its embrace by the United States as the only sustainable means of protection against the arrival of the "universal Red Republicanism or revolutionism of the Old World."[32]

Unlike the itinerant Brownson, whose bombastic style and multiple conversions many considered eccentric, John Hughes was something of an official Catholic spokesman in America at midcentury. Hughes's life and writings captured the conservative idiosyncrasies of a religious prelate and the struggle of a Catholic immigrant in the antebellum republic. Hughes had immigrated in 1817 and received theological training in Baltimore. As a Philadelphia priest he provoked Protestant warnings against Catholic proselytizing when he drew attention to the Irish emancipation bill of 1829, which allowed Irish Catholics to hold public office in Britain. In 1839 he toured Europe, receiving funds for his American bishopric from Pope Gregory VII and the Austrian Leopoldine Society and meeting Daniel O'Connell, the champion of Irish emancipation, in London. Interestingly, Hughes used his meeting with O'Connell not to praise O'Connell for delivering Irish liberty but to chastise the champion of Ireland for his meddling against slavery, which Hughes insisted was an American tradition "for which the present generation is by no means responsible." Hughes was instrumental in preventing sectarian violence in New York, although he was threatened with assassination and saw his property destroyed by nativist insurgents in the early 1840s. He became the archbishop of New York City in 1850.[33]

Unlike Brownson, Hughes never was very interested in politics or politicians, except to preach against their presumptuousness. He voted only once, for the Whig Henry Clay in 1832, and refused his only potential political office, an 1847 offer from President James Polk of an ambassadorship to Mexico. (In contrast, the suggestion that Orestes Brownson be offered an academic position at Harvard was scoffed at by the university's administration.) Hughes saw the 1848 revolutions as a marker of a general civilizational breakdown of social mores and institutions. He indicted numerous parties as purveyors of the dangerous "theory that the people have the right to select their own authority": "poets, printers, advocates of Communism, or Fourierism, or Socialism," as well as Mormons, Millerites, and "women assembling now in Congresses and clamoring for woman's rights; claiming to be Christians, but forgetting their dignity." Here Hughes indicted not only reform movements but nontraditional churches. Although some Quakers, Unitarians, and Mormons shared Hughes's hostility to rapid change in politics and society, and especially to acts of civil disobedience, many prominent practitioners of these faiths embraced both American reform and the 1848 revolutions. These included the Quaker Lucretia Mott; the Unitarians—or at least the former Unitarians—Horace Greeley, Margaret Fuller (whose calls in the *New York Tribune* for American support for the Roman republic especially drew Hughes's wrath), Theodore Parker, Thomas Wentworth Higginson, and Ralph Waldo Emerson; and various high-ranking Mormons, who celebrated the establishment of the republic in Rome not only because it "prepare[d] the way for the kingdom of Heaven to be established on earth" but also because of the Roman republic's granting of rights to Jews. The spread of Jewish civil rights in Europe would lead, Mormons believed, to their restoration in Palestine, in accordance with Mormon millennial doctrine. Such an eclectic coterie of religious and political freethinkers, to Hughes, sought to merge humanity and authority, inviting divine punishment: "God will mark by an angel unseen the working of his providence, and you will see how . . . wicked designs to govern the world shall be brought to nought." Like Brownson, as well as conservative Protestants, Hughes prophesied doom for European revolutionaries and their American sympathizers.[34]

To combat such an onslaught, Hughes offered a subtle argument that ultimately showed the compatibility of Catholic belief and American revolutionary experience. First he explained the position of Roman Catholicism toward revolutions. Catholic citizens, he maintained, revered constituted authorities and honored the dignity of power "from a principle of conscience [in] the safety of society": "If you ask us Catholics our reason for submitting to authority, we answer that in the exercise of reason, we have concluded that God has appointed a Church to be the depository of his truth, to the end of the world. What can be more rational than to submit our reason to the guidance that God himself has appointed?" Hughes here joined John Williamson Nevin in condemning the rational, independent-thinking creeds of Transcendentalism and Unitarianism flourishing in New England at the time. Hughes also displayed an old American prejudice against dogmatic reason, championed by Thomas Paine. Americans at first had celebrated Paine's writings for helping forge a revolutionary movement across the colonies. But during the French Revolution Paine was condemned for his antireligious *Age of Reason*. Hughes critiqued the 1848 upheavals as a Catholic authority, but his view also suggested the persistence of an old American revolutionary premise: that revolutions should leave religious institutions intact—if not champion Christianity itself.[35]

Hughes also described more explicitly what he believed to be the American revolutionary experience. To make his point, Hughes first turned to the revolutionary situations in Rome and France prevailing by late 1849. In Rome the republic had surrendered to an invading French army. Pope Pius's fortunes had turned, and his return to the Vatican from exile, escorted by troops from France, Spain, Austria, and Naples, was under way. The fleeting achievement of the Roman republic, to Hughes, indicated not the Romans' capacity for creating enlightened popular government, but their condition as "children—so unworthy of His Holiness [Pius] but so greatly needing his care."[36]

In France, meanwhile, Louis Napoleon, elected the president of the Second Republic by popular vote in December 1848, moved toward transforming the government into a dictatorship. By June 1850 he had instituted a three-year residency requirement for voting, stripping the suffrage from radical refugees, and installed Catholic ecclesiastics to oversee the French national school system. His coup in December 1851 dissolved the national assembly and reversed the republic's fledgling attempts at liberal reform.

Hughes used all of this to mock earlier transatlantic hopes for the success of the 1848 revolutions: "The world boasts of the wonderful exploits, heroism, and what not, of this European revolution. [But] the results have not corresponded with the anticipation." Hughes belittled the conditions that had spurred the French people to rebel and contrasted the freedom existing in France before and after the 1848 uprising: "[In 1848], the reason for the revolution in France, was that French citizens were not permitted to assemble at banquets in such numbers as they thought proper. Now, under a popular government, created by a successful revolution, I am sure they would not be permitted to have similar banquets; they are denied even the miserable privilege of complaint." For Hughes revolutionary change led inevitably back to conditions prevailing before the revolution; momentum could not be halted exactly halfway around the arc, at the bliss naive revolutionaries promised.

Yet Hughes, like other American ecclesiastics, cited the American Revolution as an exception to this principle: "The revolutions in Europe bear but few grounds of comparison with that of America." The events of 1776, Hughes maintained, did not "turn upon the spontaneous whim of the people to overthrow one form of government in order to substitute another." Those events instead had effected change by vindicating the deliberations of "a fair majority of the reasoning part of the community." Established government, like established religion, was sacrosanct, and rapid change, not evolving from the grave opinions of a select portion of the community, was inevitably flawed. The American Revolution, in Hughes's view, was organic, successful, and therefore truly revolutionary, paradoxically because it did not assert new rights; did not occur suddenly; and did not intend the replacement of political, social, or religious authority.[37]

Thus, for Hughes Catholicism and the American revolutionary experience together stood in novel opposition to the current chaos of Europe. The implied overlap of the two historical experiences, one a religious institution, the other the national past, implied their compatibility: Catholicism reinforced Americans' heritage, and vice versa. Catholic apologists and communicants could move, at least ideologically, toward the middle of American political and religious culture.

The mid-nineteenth century confronted American Christian leaders with the specter and evidence of far-reaching revolutionary change. Many lay observers on both sides of the Atlantic explained "revolution" as a reflection of the irresistible triumph of human agency over historical barriers of imperial hegemony, aristocracy, corruption, and ignorance. Technological and medical breakthroughs of the day—the steam engine, the telegraph, and chloroform, for example—were lauded as "miracles" in the popular press, although these were considered miracles made possible by the nascent industrial age, not divine intervention.[38]

Reinforcing scientific phenomena, Karl Marx's *Communist Manifesto* appeared in late February 1848 on the eve of the revolutions. The *Manifesto* did not influence the course of events then as it would in Russia in 1917, and it was not published in the United States until 1871. But the *Manifesto* reflected a widespread transatlantic sense that history could be scientifically shown to be matching technological progress, marching inexorably toward the triumph of secular humanism, without the possibility of divine intervention stopping it.[39]

Because of their skepticism about human agency and their faith in the possibility of divine intervention, leading Protestants and Catholics in America rejected the notion of an "inevitable" popular revolution and its implication of mechanically progressive history. On the other hand, they also perceived that biblically forecasted events of an apocalypse were lining up amid European turbulence. But Protestant leaders could not be altogether jubilant. An apparently degenerating American society suggested that Europe and the United States were becoming depraved together. Catholics, of course, opposed the subversion of Catholic authority and thus reveled when the revolutions met with defeat, especially the succumbing of the secular republic declared in Rome.

Both groups, however, took recourse in the American Revolution as a successful revolution, a revolution that was remembered to have championed not only republicanism but also people's allegiance to God and the church. This argument was an early episode of the "Americanist Controversy" that emerged in the late nineteenth century between the papacy and American Catholic leaders over their efforts to accommodate Catholic traditions to institutions in the United States. In the shorter term the argument served Catholic authorities intent on countering Protestant nativist violence against "un-American" Catholic immigrants, by aligning the Church with the most conservative American ideologues. The mythical American revolutionary past was a foil used to condemn the atheistic ways of European revolutionaries, as well as their alleged antebellum American coconspirators.[40]

Ominous signs at midcentury suggested that if God meant ultimately to redeem the nation for his glorious purposes, in the near term it would have to survive stark trials only he could permit to occur. During the Mexican War waves of tropical diseases swept through the American ranks, killing eleven thousand. A cholera epidemic hit New York City in 1849. In July 1850 acute gastroenteritis sent President Taylor to his grave, joining William Henry Harrison, who had died of pneumonia contracted during his inaugural, as the second sitting chief executive to fall within a decade. Ministers across the country interpreted these occurrences as portentous outpourings of God's retribution for various sins: national belligerence, or perhaps apathy; frenetic mass elections; lack of political leadership. Perhaps the taking of the nation's highest officer twice within a decade was a latter-day crucifixion, a sacrifice of one individual for the sins of the community. Domestic and international events seemed to be converging. The response of many American Christian apologists—using the American revolutionary past as a conservative standard to mark American difference from Europe—ultimately rendered them little different from secular American commentators, instead bringing them together in a conservative alliance.[41]

6. SECESSION OR REVOLUTION?
The South and the Crisis of 1850

In 1850, perhaps gazing at Europe, William Henry Trescot, a South Carolina lawyer and future U.S. diplomat, asked, "What is the position of the South . . . as a slaveholding people?" At the time some promoters of slavery in America were considering separation from a country increasingly resistant to the institution's aggrandizement. Of any American group, Southerners with ties to slavery were most likely to become uneasy over news of the European upheavals. Whether "revolution" meant greater liberty or greater license, the concept suggested a destruction or change to the existing order. This change did not bode well for Southern society, whose slavery orientation created a conservative outlook that assumed the maintenance of an inherited order. This chapter answers William Trescot's question: how did Southern slavery and European revolution interact during the critical years of the mid-nineteenth century, when fragmentation of the Union seemed a real possibility for the first time in a generation?[1]

Many Southerners joined their fellow Americans in initially celebrating news of the European upheavals. Sympathy rituals and gatherings in Southern cities echoed the enthusiasm evinced in the large urban areas of the Northeast and the emerging towns of the West. News from Europe arrived on the heels of triumphant news of the victories in Mexico won by the American armies, a majority of whose troops were from the Southern states. It was easy for Southerners' enthusiasm about nearby foreign events to spill over into enthusiasm for the revolutions across the Atlantic, especially under the impression, shared with the rest of the Union, that an American spirit animated overseas events.

Some forms of Southern enthusiasm for Europe were idiosyncratic. With the exception of New Orleans, whose German population attended such revolutionary dramas as *Wilhelm Tell* and *Robert Blum's Tod* ("Robert Blum's Death": a tribute to the member of the Frankfurt Assembly who was executed in Vienna), few if any theater productions illustrating revolution debuted in Southern cities, in contrast to productions that appeared in Northern cities like New York City and Boston. But this was not surprising. Southern theater patrons had a long-standing aversion to works with political themes, owing to sensitivity over any issue that might reflect on slavery. Temperance reform, strong in the South in the 1840s, had the effect of weakening interest in the theater late in the decade for its association with drunkenness, and this reticence carried over into the revolutionary days of 1848 and afterward.[2]

Southerners, however, did respond to events in Europe in other ways that resembled the expressions of Americans outside the region. Citizens in Richmond, Baltimore, Louisville, Charleston, St. Louis, and New Orleans organized torchlight processions. Atlanta, like many cities along the Atlantic seaboard, anticipated the rumored arrival of the deposed King Louis Philippe by voting him "several hundred acres of excellent land." Surely the French ruler would jump at the chance to grow Georgia cotton! New Orleans, with a sizeable German population alongside its Irish, French, Spanish, and Italian populations, hosted numerous "Reform Banquets," modeled, albeit remotely, on the protests that launched the Paris uprising in February 1848. At one such bacchanal "three dark-eyed Creole girls impersonated Liberty, Charity, and Pity. With . . . fascinating smiles [they] collected a handsome contribution *con amore* for those wounded in Paris." Though the personal hardship of revolutionary Europeans was not the element that Southerners most tried to emulate, they were sympathetic nonetheless.[3]

The European upheavals also found brief favor among Southern intellectuals. Francis Lieber, a Prussian immigrant, became too excited to hold his classes at South Carolina College over news that "Germany too is rising." William Gilmore Simms, the most popular Southern writer of his day, joined Edward Duyckinck, the New York literary leader of the "Young America" movement, in urging indigenous, nationalistic literature, cleaved from European themes. In the spring of 1848, however, Simms rejoiced over European developments, which he saw linked to the presidential campaign of Zachary Taylor, a man uncorrupted by ties to either the Democratic or the Whig party (though ultimately he led the Whigs to the White House in 1848). Simms interpreted the European revolutions of 1848 and Taylor's candidacy as twin crests of a favorable democratic tide that would sweep away the creaking monarchies of Europe and the morally bankrupt American two-party system.[4]

As elsewhere in America, however, Southerners' enthusiasm for revolutionary Europe soon waned. In the spring of 1848 the French Second Republic attempted to extend the revolution from political change to social overhaul, instituting guarantees of work, shorter workdays, and public relief projects (the *ateliers nationaux*). Although Northerners also worried about a socialist government and society emerging in France, Southerners especially suspected the prospect.[5] Such a threat made it easier for Southerners to identify events in Europe with disdained Northern "-isms." "We must go crazy with sympathy because the Parisian mob . . . have undertaken to establish . . . a pure democracy which I regard as impracticable," lamented David Outlaw, a North Carolina Whig congressman. Likewise, William Henry Trescot criticized the "hasty welcome" given by the U.S. Senate in 1848 to the "socialist" government in Paris, seeing it as a sign of the Northern states' enthusiasm for "revolutionary restlessness." The news from Europe exacerbated Southern suspicions of Northern shenanigans.[6]

The emancipation of slaves in the French West Indian colonies by the Second Republic confirmed for many Southerners the evil attending the European revolutions. The *Savannah Republican* regarded slave emancipation as a "cruel absurdity." The anonymous "J.," writing in the *Southern Quarterly Review*, predicted that the West Indian emancipation would precipitate another "St. Domingo," a reference to the race rioting and bloody violence of the Haitian slave revolution of 1791–1804. Together with signs of budding socialism, emancipation demonstrated that fanatics were running the young French republic.[7]

Fanaticism seemed to be moving closer to home, moreover, in the form of the Northern Free Soil movement. Before the late 1840s the proslavery regime had taken comfort in the way that slavery served to "exclu[de] a populace made up of the dregs of Europe." In 1850 only one in twenty free Southerners was not native-born.[8]

But now Free Soilers were not content to harangue defenders of slavery from a distance. "The free soil movement is extending and barnburners are to be found . . . in Maryland and Virginia," David Outlaw observed. Southern leaders saw a Southern corollary to the Northern Free Soil movement, potentially hostile to slavery, developing among foreign-born workingmen in the South, refugees of an Old World dominated by a landlord class. British artisans and mechanics, sometimes uniting with enslaved blacks, agitated against proslavery authorities in Southern cities in the late 1840s. Beginning late in 1848 German refugees brought radical ideas to the South, organizing Free German Societies (the *Turnverein*). The so-called Turners opposed tyranny of all sorts. Some Turner ideas, such as popular referenda as a basis for U.S. constitutional amendments, abolition of the presidency, and government ownership of railroads, were far-fetched. However, others, including calls for the restriction of slavery, were more realistic and dangerous. "The issue of Free Labour against Slave Labour will soon be made in the South," warned a correspondent of South Carolina senator John C. Calhoun. By the end of the 1840s the threat to Southern society appeared close at hand.[9]

To slavery advocates Free Soilers were seeking to strangle the South by violating fundamental American principles of protection of property—the right to possess slaves and to carry them into the West. Southern liberty was at risk no less than it had been in 1776, said an Alabama congressman: "The power to dictate what sort of property the State may allow a citizen to own and work—whether oxen, horses, or Negroes . . . is . . . tyrannical." Domestic and international forces, both considered alien, threatened Southern property rights.[10]

To defend against this perceived alliance of Northern Free Soilers and foreign radicals, Southern ideologues joined Americans elsewhere in espousing a peculiar American revolutionary heritage that established ideological distance between antebellum America and its enemies. They distinguished the United States from Europe by emphasizing the American Revolution's minimal social upheaval and violence, the material prosperity enjoyed by Americans both before and after the conflict, the safeguarding of Christian values, and the American Revolution's success compared to the Europeans' apparent inability to achieve similar results. All of these factors set the American revolutionary identity apart from the European experience.

Thus spurred by the specter of a new international revolution against slavery and social order, Southerners portrayed the South as the originator and inheritor of distinct American revolutionary principles. The jurist Beverly Tucker distinguished between old (Anglo-Saxon) revolutions, including the American independence movement, which sought "to vindicate the rights of property," and new (Continental) ones, which "assail[ed]" such rights. The French people were "slow to understand" that the only justifiable upheavals were those ensuring the government protected existing rights. Upheavals impelling government to confer new rights were illegitimate. Tucker affirmed the South as the grand sanctifier of property—and, therefore, the most resolute protector of an inviolable American revolutionary way. Likewise, William Stiles, returned from duty as the U.S. minister in Austria, distinguished between the 1848 revolutions and the American Revolution by emphasizing that where the former was a struggle over "human rights," the latter strove only for "the right of local self-government." For Stiles slavery, as an inherited social institution, was not at stake for American revolutionaries. In the same vein William Gilmore Simms published a partisan account, "South Carolina in the Revolution," to encourage the South to "reassert her history" and to "furnish an argument, much needed, to our [Southern] politicians." Simms's narratives of the American Revolution have been rightly seen as a veiled reaction to abolitionist tracts. But Simms was also part of a Southern coterie of jurists, politicians, historians, and novelists who rendered the American revolutionary past a guideline for resisting innovation.[11]

Actually, in their attitude toward revolutions, Southerners resembled the Catholic Church. Of course, sometimes the voices of apologists for Catholicism and of apologists for slavery were the same. In scolding Daniel O'Connell for his critiques of American slavery, Archbishop John Hughes insisted that slavery was a tradition "for which the present generation is by no means responsible"—an argument frequently voiced by Southern defenders of the institution. Bishop Francis Gartland of Savannah, writing to Ireland to recruit priests, warned a Dublin seminary not to send clerics "manifesting more wisdom than their Church, by their intemperate and untimely zeal for the freedom of the slave population. All that we have to do is mite their souls [so that] whether bond or free they may be saved." Gartland's conservatism reflected the worldview of ultramontane Catholics and antiabolitionist Southerners alike. Both groups embraced hierarchy and shared fears of social disorder; for them transatlantic liberal individualism violated the morality of organic communities and the claim of constancy. Thus, preached Archbishop Martin Spalding of Baltimore, unhinged European revolutionaries sounded "demoniacal shout[s] of liberty" in both 1789 and 1848. But the American Revolution was admirable, said Archbishop John Hughes of New York, for how the patriots had achieved their independence through the deliberative decision of "a fair majority of the reasoning part of the community." The best revolutions were gradual and logical affairs — and the European versions failed on both these counts.[12]

Twin emphases on what might be called a "gradual majority" also linked Southerners' defense of slavery and the response of the Catholic Church to the European upheavals. Archbishop Hughes's deliberative "fair majority," though not exactly the same concept, resembled the "concurrent majority" envisioned by John C. Calhoun in *Disquisition on Government*, completed shortly before his death in 1849. The *Disquisition* demonstrates a Southern mindset grappling with a tumultuous transatlantic world, Calhoun envisioning an increasingly sectionalized America represented ultimately by two presidents, North and South, each with a constitutional veto. The concurrence of all interest groups regarding vital public matters, not simply a popular majority, much less a revolutionary uprising, would be necessary to change the status quo. Southern ideologues like Calhoun joined Catholic authorities in defining a "good" revolution by its gradualism and its preservation of private property. These criteria set impossible standards for the upheavals in Europe.[13]

Southerners also emphasized another characteristic of American revolutionary experience: the resilient supremacy of local government. Developments in France in 1848 revealed that the French had mistakenly allowed their national government to become too sophisticated, eroding the provinces' authority. In an analysis of French democracy, the *Southern Quarterly Review* noted the absence of states' rights from the French system. States' rights were "the grand conservative feature in our system," the article stated, "the one most important of all advantages" of American republicanism. Even the location of the national government in Paris jeopardized the French political system. "France's safety," wrote William Gilmore Simms, "will depend . . . upon a removal from Paris of the seat of government." Paris was the center of European attraction and the "seat of sciences, fashion, and pleasure," opined the *Southern Quarterly Review.* Such attributes detracted from good government, fostering vanity among Parisians, whose concern for provincial interests would dwindle, presumably, in the midst of such decadence. Central government would be better set in a crude and, therefore, functional place like Washington, D.C.[14]

Americans North and South in fact shared sensitivity to the weakening of provincial power by central authority. Local government lay at the heart of the argument for the authority of "popular sovereignty" over territorial slavery, an argument that many Northerners embraced. Thus, one New York journal described France as "above all other countries of the globe a centralization, . . . its heart and head . . . Paris." Another decried the country's "sad system," where "forty thousand communes" were "chained by the commune of Paris." A third alleged, "Centralization has always been the stumbling block for freedom in France." Contrasting American stability with French tumult, this journal ironically pointed to U.S. origins in "a number of colonies, and wide extent of country, creating sectional interests and consequently sectional feelings." Many Northerners echoed Southerners' embrace of local authority at midcentury as an important distinction between the American revolutionary tradition and the European one.[15]

While Southern observers focused on revolutionary France, they did distinguish between events in Paris and revolutionary developments elsewhere in Europe. The Hungarian Louis Kossuth received a chilly reception when he toured the South in 1852. Before his arrival, however, Southerners expressed their sympathies for Hungary in rallies in New Orleans and Atlanta, and each citizen in Little Rock resolved in 1849 to contribute ten cents a month to the achievement of European liberty. Mississippi senator Henry Foote sponsored legislation to grant federal lands to Hungarian refugees on condition of their permanent settlement and naturalization as citizens. Foote declared that those who believed that the South "would react with cold indifference toward the establishment of free institutions in Hungary . . . know very little of the lofty characteristics which belong to the slave-holding population of the Union." If French revolution making drew scorn, Hungary's cause provoked sympathy.[16]

In praising Hungary, however, Southern literati could sometimes not muffle domestic tensions. In 1849 the Hungarian revolution against the Hapsburg Empire spilled over into an ethnic suppression of Croats and Serbs living within Hungary. But the Southern Literary Messenger showed a sense of fraternity with the Magyars—even at one point using the vocabulary of the simmering American dispute over slavery to characterize overseas conditions. The Messenger opined, "The [Hungarians are] fully aware of their dangerous position. . . . Hated by the Slaves, isolated among the nations of the earth, they were left alone . . . to resist the conspiracy against them." The spelling of the modern word *Slav* as *Slave* reflected the origin of both words in Western Europeans' practice of enslaving the Slavic peoples of Central Europe in the Middle Ages. While the *Messenger's* rendition was consistent with the grammar of other American periodicals, the tone and contextual language in which the Southern journal's sympathy for the Hungarians' plight was expressed made it seem like a bleak Southern self-assessment.[17]

Elsewhere, likewise, the *Messenger* saluted Hungarian patriots' resistance to Austrian efforts to "centralize" them and defended the Hungarians against their condemnation by the *North American Review,* a conservative journal published in Boston. "Articles in the [*Review*] have . . . proclaimed . . . the contest . . . as a design to reduce all other races to the domination of the Magyars," the *Messenger* noted, but this Southern journal saw the purpose of the Hungarian uprising as "equality of rights before the law and equal privileges for all classes." Such a commentary shows how Southern partisans could use European events to deflect antagonistic rhetoric fired by a domestic enemy. In this case the *Messenger* subtly reinterpreted the Hungarian conflict. According to the *North American Review,* the Hungarians were creating racial domination, a characterization dangerous to protectors of slavery. But the *Messenger* portrayed the conflict in terms of class, more conducive to condemning Northern oppression of Southern liberty to maintain slavery. Hungarians, in this way, were engaged in struggles that slavery-abiding Southerners saw themselves facing. This element of Southerners' perspective was unique.[18]

Only slightly less than in Hungary, struggles in the German states drew Southern interest. Southerners were optimistic about the German capacity for both revolution and constitution framing. For the *Southern Quarterly Review,* "free institutions . . . succeed [only] with certain classes of men. . . . [We] gravely question the success of democratical government among any present European nation, save the Anglo-Saxon and the German." John C. Calhoun also praised the German states—surprising given his overall somber view of the human condition. Calhoun led opposition to Congress's resolution of congratulations to the revolutionary regime in France, citing the "composition of the people" as a strike against the French capacity for republican government. He characterized the French situation as European "Dorrism," referring to Rhode Island's constitutional rebellion of the early 1840s. In the spring of 1848 Calhoun wrote: "I regard this life very much as a struggle against evil. . . . I am not surprised that the powers of Europe so much dread changes. They are right; reform will lead to anarchy, [to] revolution and finally to a worse state of things than now exists, through the most erroneous opinions now entertained both in Europe and this country." Yet despite such a philosophy, Calhoun was enthusiastic about the prospects of midcentury revolutions in Germany. "I have more hope for Germany than France," he admitted. "Her old institutions . . . furnish an excellent foundation on which to erect a federal constitutional Government." The revolutionary Frankfurt Assembly impressed him, although its slow deliberations over the framework of a new German empire ultimately contributed to its demise. Calhoun wrote, "If the [German states] do not attempt too much . . . [such as a] federal Republic like ours[,] . . . [their] old institutions" could "do much to strengthen them." Calhoun even sent written instructions to the Prussian minister-resident at Washington on how to implement republican and federal political philosophy.[19]

Why did Southerners support the liberation of Hungary and the German states, while doubting the French upheaval? Neither Germans nor Hungarians were promoting socialist utopias, nor did they maintain West Indian plantations, where slave emancipation was looming. Moreover, neither group had a preexisting revolutionary identity that had gone sour. Like American patriots of old, contemporary Hungarian and German freedom fighters existed at a distance from antebellum America and lacked the stain of revolutionary failure.

In March 1849 the Frankfurt Assembly, after meeting for nearly a year to create an all-German constitutional republic, abandoned its plans and asked Frederick William, King of Prussia, to rule a liberal German empire. But Frederick William refused the invitation, embarrassing the assembly and thwarting nascent German democracy. Under threat of arrest the assembly relocated from Frankfurt to Stuttgart, where, when they arrived, delegates suffered the indignation of being locked out of their arranged meeting place. Ironically, the Frankfurt Assembly acted as if it were following John Calhoun's advice too well: accomplishing little by May 1849, its delegates dispersed for good.[20]

But radical political conventions were taking place on both sides of the Atlantic at the time. In response to what they understood as an emerging threat to slavery, Southern extremists met in 1850 to openly consider secession from the Union. Like the members of the beleaguered Frankfurt Assembly, secessionists hoped to frame a movement to create a distinct nation.

Proslavery Southerners' worries grew dramatically as the presidency of Zachary Taylor unfolded. Despite his slaveholding and his Southern roots, Taylor displayed national, not sectional, allegiance, declaring in late 1849 that if legislation to prohibit territorial slavery passed Congress he would not stop it from becoming federal law. The territories of New Mexico and California began preparations to enter the Union with state constitutions that prohibited slavery. Antislavery delegates to the constitutional convention of California went so far as to proclaim, "The eyes of all Europe are now directed toward California." Horace Mann, an educational reformer and U.S. senator from Massachusetts, bluntly told Southern congressmen that the civilized world was against the South.[21]

Dismayed Southerners reacted angrily to domestic and international threats to the established order, a dramatic reversal of their attitude during the "springtime of the peoples" in 1848. Then, for example, the *Richmond Enquirer* had envisioned the American Revolution being extended to Europe, celebrating how "American principles are triumphant" in the Old World. Two years later the *Enquirer* was again espousing an American revolutionary consciousness, but one needing sectional protection, not one poised for being launched overseas. Now the *Enquirer* asserted that the South was called to protect what the "Union of the old thirteen states" had achieved: the right to an "undisturbed enjoyment of slave property."[22]

Mississippi state leaders convened to endorse state sovereignty, condemn congressional restrictions on territorial slavery, and call all slaveholding states to a great convention to devise resistance to antislavery aggressions. The convention, set for Nashville in June 1850, would be the first time that Southern political leaders would meet explicitly to consider a sectional separation. The Tennesseean Cave Johnson noted that among those headed for Nashville "a settled determination [manifested] with the extreme men . . . to dissolve the Union." The situation seemed critical, even to international observers. The American representative in Naples reported that Italian newspapers were taking bets on the imminent dissolution of the United States.[23]

Meanwhile, in early 1850 Congress tried to diffuse the mounting crisis. Kentucky senator Henry Clay introduced a series of resolutions offering offsetting concessions to the antislavery and proslavery forces, which eventually resulted in the 1850 Compromise, abolishing the slave trade in Washington, D.C.; admitting California to the Union as a free state; passing a strict federal law to ease the capture and return of runaway slaves; providing that the residents of the New Mexico and Utah territories be allowed to determine whether to accept slavery; and resolving a boundary dispute between New Mexico and Texas. Several factors led to the passage of the 1850 Compromise after nine months of debate: Clay's and Daniel Webster's eloquence prodded Congress to move toward conciliation; President Taylor's death in the summer of 1850 removed a dogmatic voice; Calhoun's death during the debate provided Southern advocates more flexibility; and Illinois senator Stephen Douglas's parliamentary skills pushed the compromise toward its passage after Clay gave up.[24]

The specter of bloody revolution also haunted the Senate's attempts to prevent sectional conflict. Those who favored compromise measures used the prospect of violent interstate conflict to argue in support of Clay's proposals. Calhoun warned that soon only military force would remain to hold the country together, should agitation on the slavery issue continue. Clay averred that if Northerners interfered with slavery where it existed, "my voice would be for war." The prospect of sectional conflict, a war, Clay said, "in which all mankind would be against us; in which our own history itself would be against us," prodded legislators to search for ways to avoid the violence of sectional civil uprising, the specter of the United States replicating scenes of European revolution and reaction. While domestic factors exerted the greatest influence on American statesmen to work out their positions on the 1850 Compromise, international events also played a role.[25]

Various congressional speakers on both sides of the slavery question invoked the revolutions of 1848 and the counterrevolutions of 1850 to bolster their case. Albert Gallatin Brown of Mississippi warned the North to respect Southern rights or risk the troubles facing the imperial powers in Europe: "Picture to yourselves Hungary, resisting the powers of Austria and Russia; and if Hungary, which had never tasted liberty, could make such stout resistance, what may you not anticipate from eight millions of southrons made desperate by your aggression?" Brown portrayed Southerners and Hungarian insurgents not as radicals, but as defensive patriots suffering under imperialism.[26]

By contrast, Northern senators opposed to a Southern independence movement emphasized the differences between American and European circumstances. William Seward of New York scoffed at Southerners' threats that such a violent upheaval might happen in America. He cited local government as a buffer against revolution: "The constituent members of this democracy . . . are not the citizens of a metropolis like Paris, or of a region subjected to the influences of a metropolis like France; but they are husbandmen, dispersed over this broad land." Thus, Seward echoed the above-noted American critiques of the cosmopolitan influence of European capitals as an inducement to revolution. Protagonists in the slavery debate took inspiration and evidence from revolutionary Europe. Sometimes they likened domestic scenes to transatlantic corollaries. Other times they reasserted exceptional American conditions arising from the nation's revolutionary founding. Their sense of transatlantic community at the mid-nineteenth century was selective and complicated.[27]

The great Northern advocate of the 1850 Compromise, Daniel Webster of Massachusetts, took threats of Southern belligerence more seriously than Seward did. Webster saw violence over slavery as a real possibility and endorsed Henry Clay's proposed strengthening of the fugitive slave laws, facilitating eventual passage of the compromise. "I hear with anguish the word secession," said Webster. "There can be no such thing as peaceable secession. . . . That disruption must produce such a war as I will not describe." Webster feared that Southern radicals had convinced themselves that secession by the American colonies from the British Empire in 1776 had occurred as a matter of natural course, with little violence necessary. And he feared that the lessons of European revolution had not been heeded: "No monarchical throne presses these states together. . . . To break up! to break up this great Government! to dismember this great country! to astonish Europe with an act of folly . . . ! No, sir! no, sir!"[28]

Indeed, Webster, serving as secretary of state in 1850, instigated a minor diplomatic crisis between the United States and Austria, probably in order to inspire the national unity he insisted was in existence. In March 1850 the *United States Congressional Globe* published the instructions given by President Zachary Taylor to A. Dudley Mann, a U.S. tobacco agent in Germany, to investigate whether conditions in Hungary's struggle for independence from Austria warranted U.S. recognition of Hungarian sovereignty. Upon learning about the Mann mission, Chevalier Johann Georg

Hülsemann, the Austrian minister to the United States, lodged an official protest, citing American ignorance of foreign affairs and inquiring how the United States could be concerned with Hungarian independence, when it enslaved millions of African Americans—an embarrassing point for anyone who hoped for American liberal influence across the Atlantic. Hülsemann also threatened that if the United States persisted in interfering with European political affairs, it would risk commercial retaliation. That Europe might somehow become off-limits to American cotton was the kind of threat that infuriated conservative Southerners (and Northerners) dependent on political continuity in the Atlantic, not mettlesome radical democracy building, such as the Taylor administration had dabbled in by sending out Mann to investigate.[29]

Webster chose to rebuke the Austrian sharply, using words rarely found in an official diplomatic transmission: "The power of this [American] republic is spread over a region one of the richest and most fertile on the globe. . . . In comparison . . . the possessions of the House of Hapsburg are but a patch of the earth's surface." To the Austrian's warning that American involvement in Europe would meet with commercial retaliation, Webster snorted, "As to . . . this hypothetical retaliation, the Government and people of the United States are quite willing to take their chances and abide their destiny."[30]

Elsewhere in his letter, however, Webster was less combative. He explained that the United States "claim[s] no right to participate in the struggles of foreign powers to promote . . . popular constitutions and National Independence." Yet "circumstances . . . have made [Americans] . . . representatives of purely popular principles of Government." Thus, they "could not . . . [obscure] . . . from mankind . . . the causes" of their current global position. "The successful [American] example of free government . . . contemplated . . . in other countries," Webster explained, was the "necessary consequence of the American Revolution." Webster thus joined with other Americans in their collective use of the European revolutions to commemorate the great American upheaval. Webster's defiance of the House of Hapsburg turned out to be more a defensive fortification than an attack.[31]

In fact, Webster's defiant "Hülsemann Letter," as Kenneth Shewmaker has shown, as much as it reflected Americans' desire to set an international example, was calculated to rally an American public recently fractured,

North and South, by the path to the 1850 Compromise. Privately, Webster wrote, he hoped his letter would unite Americans. Stephen Douglas supported him by seeing to it that thousands of copies of Webster's publicly "leaked" retort were printed for national circulation.[32]

Webster's diplomatic bravado, and Austria's role in resisting an American sectional crisis, were necessary because in 1850 some Americans were talking of secession in earnest. As the debate on Henry Clay's omnibus compromise drifted into June 1850, and Webster made his plea for peace and insulted Chevalier Hülsemann, representatives of nine Southern states arrived in Nashville to deliberate about the course of the South and to engage in a "cool calculation [of] the advantages . . . of a Southern Confederacy." The Nashville delegates, 175 at a June convention, and 59 at a subsequent meeting in November, were hardly typical Southerners: they were political elites, mostly slave owners, and some "fire-eaters"— persistent advocates of Southern independence as a weapon against democratic change that was seemingly taking on international proportions. The two conventions had a strange status: though called to contemplate disunion, most of the delegates had been elected by state legislatures or congressional districts and therefore had legal if not federal sanction. Many of the convention delegates' views on secession were radical only because eventually they would prove to be ahead of most Southerners' opinions, not different from them. How did these potential American revolutionaries understand "revolution" in 1850?[33]

The Nashville Convention began in June with a reiteration of the grievances of the South: the region was under threat of external revolutionary forces, residing across the Mason-Dixon Line and across the Atlantic. Judge George Goldthwaite of Alabama stated what he assumed all of the Nashville delegates already knew: "It could not be disguised that the civilized world was leagued abroad against us. Revolutionary France [has] . . . set free three hundred thousand slaves . . . and other nations of Europe [have done] the same also." Concurrently, the Northern states had voted to restrict slavery to its present limits. Abolitionists, "who, a few years [ago], were mobbed, now [have their] views adopted in pulpits and in the . . . schools." Under these desperate conditions Goldthwaite urged action: "Suppose [secession] produced not only war, but famine and destruction. Suppose the fertile fields were deluged in blood! Is that any reason why we should ignominiously submit and put off the evil day?" Goldthwaite urged secession as a matter of both expediency and principle. He was for revolution.[34]

Other Nashville delegates declared for secession not as an act of honorable desperation, but for its economic promise. Several imagined the South ruining depleted Northern manufacturers and forging powerful trade relations with a Europe too eager for cotton to allow Northern aggression to interrupt Atlantic trade. The South Carolinian Langdon Cheves envisioned a Southern republic blessed by favorable soil and climate as "one of the most splendid empires in which the sun ever shone." Beverly Tucker of Virginia envisioned a Europe "determined to oppose . . . any war that might disturb her commerce . . . on which her very existence depends."[35]

Southerners outside the convention echoed these views. William Henry Trescot envisioned the South as "the guardian of the world's commerce," commanding a powerful exchange of cotton and manufactured goods through the Gulf of Mexico. A pamphlet from the Southern Rights Association calculated that some twelve million people's livelihood, in both America and Europe, depended on the "cotton raised by the slaves of the Southern States." Surely, said a South Carolina legislator, "should there be war all the nations of Europe would desire to preserve their commercial intercourse" with this life-giving system in the South, thus defying abolitionists who wished "a revolution in the affairs of the civilized world."[36]

Such comments reveal the ironic radical Southern proslavery agenda in the early 1850s, especially with regard to Europe. Foreign revolutionaries and their Northern minions who threatened to overthrow Southern civilization enraged secession advocates. At the same time they were keenly interested in establishing an autonomous partnership between the South and the trading and manufacturing concerns of Europe, uninterrupted by political agitation. Europe's appeal during the 1848 revolutions, demonstrated by the activities of visiting financiers like William Corcoran, thus lay not in its revolutionary experiments with social reform, but in the maintenance of its economic status quo. This commercial interest probably helped to diffuse the sectional crisis by draining interest from disruptive politics.

Developments on both sides of the Atlantic seemed to validate such conservatism. In Congress measures to reconcile the issue of territorial slavery were sent to the full Senate in May 1850, and in September President Millard Fillmore signed the various compromise bills into federal law. Such reconciliation measures deflected many would-be secessionists' hunger for disruption. Meanwhile, Louis Napoleon in France moved toward curtailing the liberal regime of the Second Republic. In direct violation of the French Constitution of 1848, Napoleon imposed a three-year residence requirement for suffrage, disenfranchising some three million voters and reserving the franchise for a minority of the French people, largely legitimists seeking to re-create the authoritarian stability of the July Monarchy.[37]

American opinion divided over Napoleon's action, some newspapers bemoaning the rise of European "despotism" and "absolutism," others praising the return of Old World stability. The journal the *Living Age* lamented that "universal suffrage [in France] proved so far a mockery that the only thing the people seemed disposed to vote for . . . was their own subjection to a new master." This New York journal's pejorative comment on the elective franchise was encouragement to Southerners suspicious of democratic institutions. The Tennessean Henry Clay Yeatman visited an island where Louis Napoleon exiled opponents of his dictatorship. Yeatman ridiculed these political prisoners as the "so called democrats of 1848." William Trescot lamented the "strange zeal" of slaveholders "to be good democrats," thus "betray[ing] the South." James Henry Hammond indicted "Democratic republics in which universal suffrage and offices are open to all" as the "the worst of all forms of Government." "Democracy," perhaps only slightly less than "socialism," was a controversial concept in the mid-nineteenth-century Atlantic world. Paradoxically, authoritarianism in Europe at the time helped pull the troubled American democracy from the brink of fragmentation.[38]

Southern radicals subsequently revealed a reluctance to move toward secession, once they saw the prospect of reconciliation in Congress and the disastrous consequences of revolutions overseas. Delegates gathered again in Nashville in November 1850 to consider their options. They plainly were less restive in light of transatlantic setbacks to democratic reform: the reassertion of authoritarian government in Europe and the passage of a harsh national fugitive-slave law—what Michael Rogin has aptly deemed an "American 1848."[39] Delegates to the second Nashville Convention, joining the governor of Alabama, state conventions in Georgia and Mississippi, and the *Richmond Enquirer*, moved from plans to secede to philosophical justifications of the right to secede, at the same time declaring that the existing situation did not justify actual recourse to such a drastic measure. It is symbolic that Andrew Jackson Donelson, the U.S. minister in Germany at the time of the Frankfurt Assembly's dispersal, having been recalled by the Whig administration, influenced the second Nashville Convention toward its moderate position. Donelson could bear witness to what had happened to German ideologues lingering too long over a radical agenda. Moreover, while in Germany Donelson had written Secretary of State James Buchanan about the prospect that all of Europe might be republicanized—"provided that the United States does not fall apart." Such was the strength of Americans' belief at the time that the European revolutions depended on the legacy of American revolutionary success, which, at the time, for Donelson, secession would have undermined.[40]

As the secession debate continued into 1851, Southerners both for and against secession uniformly renounced any discussion of Southern revolution, so negative had the transatlantic image of that concept become. Advocates of the right to secede, largely Southern Democrats, distinguished between secession and revolution. Secession was a theoretically prescribed, peaceful remedy, thoroughly grounded in American political practice. Revolution, on the other hand, was violent and, moreover, reminiscent of recent scenes in Europe; it was foreign to the American experience. A Louisiana newspaper described secession as the peaceable withdrawal of one party from a contractual partnership, once that party decides that the partnership is no longer of benefit: "He takes his portion of the stock, makes his bow, and retires. This is Secession." In contrast, revolution was a much more hostile form of severance: "If [the party] should seize a musket, rush into the establishment . . . that would be Revolution." The idea that secession was constitutional, but revolution was not, emerged in secessionists' 1850 efforts to distinguish their undertaking from what they perceived as European fanaticism.[41]

The planter Langdon Cheves developed this point in a slightly different way. He persistently warned of the threat international forces posed to the South and favored secession as a way to avoid the even bleaker prospect of a South destroyed by domestic violence. Cheves argued that while supporters of "free soil" wished for the moment only to "pen [slavery] up within restricted limits," fanaticism "has no stopping place." He predicted that antislavery efforts would eventually trigger a race revolution, resembling "the sufferings, the massacre and the banishment, in poverty and misery, of the white proprietors of Hayti," which for a half century had been a nightmare for American planters. French mismanagement of slavery in the Caribbean had allowed the Haitian situation to explode and provided encouragement to American opponents of the peculiar institution. Interestingly, in Nashville, Cheves raised the model of Haiti to promote preemptive secession, in effect denouncing one form of unacceptable and un-American revolution—racial upheaval—in order to promote another one more grounded in American orthodoxy—political exodus.[42]

Opponents of Southern secession, mainly Whigs, denied the possibility of peaceable exodus from the Union. The South Carolina cotton-gin maker William Gregg opposed the Nashville conventions as distractions from a more viable path toward the independence of industrial development and autarky. Typically keen to demonstrate how manufacturing could bolster slavery's economic power, Gregg referred to the European revolutions to show how slavery made industrial development safe for owners of Southern capital: where "labor and capital [assume] an antagonistical position . . . in all other countries . . . here it cannot be the case; capital will always be able to control labor, even in manufactures with whites, for blacks can always be resorted to in case of need." Southern industrialists such as Gregg enlisted the specter of European class warfare to call for a delay in secession, allowing the South's peculiar advantages in developing a class-free industrial base to be exploited.[43]

Other opponents were less calculating, maintaining that secession was wrong precisely because it was nothing short of revolution. Alexander Stephens of Georgia warned hotheads to "beware of revolution—refer to France. . . . The right of secession is . . . a right of revolution, and . . . no just cause for the exercise of such right exists." A Whig newspaper in Georgia argued that the right of secession "must be . . . a revolutionary sentiment leading to the destruction of the government." Whig journals in Washington, D.C., and Tennessee affirmed that there was no difference between secession and revolution and that seceding would mean bloody civil war. Although Southern Democrats and Whigs differed over secession, most agreed that revolution was an unacceptably dangerous alternative to present troubled conditions.[44]

By 1851 Southerners saw the failed upheavals of Europe as examples of thorough authoritarian triumph over virtuous but disorganized advocates of revolutionary republicanism and local government. John Townsend complained that the cooling of secession ardor elsewhere had made it suicidal to establish "The Little Nation of South Carolina," if there was any lesson to be learned in the plight of Venice, which was "at this very moment, under the iron heel of Austrian soldiery." The Venetian republic had been established in March 1848, temporarily independent of Hapsburg control, but without collateral resistance the Venetians capitulated after eighteen months. For this reason "revolutions ought not to be made too easily," declared the Southern Rights Association of South Carolina. "Witness France, where revolutions have become the bloody toy of the multitude; who fight for they know not what; spurning today the idol of yesterday, and calling for revolution as they would for a parade, or 'un spectacle.'"[45]

In 1851 Secretary of State Daniel Webster described Louis Napoleon's coup as a "catastrophe which . . . may weaken the faith of mankind in the permanency and solidity of popular institutions." Webster correctly assessed proslavery Southerners' response to such a "catastrophe." The counterrevolutions in Europe impressed upon Southern radicals that a popular uprising would lead not to independence, but to greater submission to a repressive regime. Such an uprising, according to De Bow's Review, would shove Southerners down the ill-fated path just taken by European revolutionaries. De Bow's asked what the South would gain should it become independent. Southerners, like the Europeans of 1848, would be "a people who revolutionize their government, [only to] depose one tyrant to become subject to another."[46]

Ultimately, Southern secessionists at midcentury mimicked the delegates to the Frankfurt Assembly, not only in their independence convention but also in their failure to act. Pinning their hopes on a burgeoning spirit of nationalism to join together disparate local causes, they could not overcome fears of radical action and convince many others to join them. Amid the crisis of 1850, the example of revolutionary Europe augmented domestic events and helped deter the Southern impulse toward secession from the United States. Specifically, the fear of anarchical upheaval presented by France was more persuasive than the prospect of popular liberation offered by Hungary. With this view Southerners decided not to undertake a disruptive act that at the time appeared to them un-American

FRANCE IS TRANQUIL!!

FIGURE 5. Reproduced in American magazines, this *Punch* image of Louis Napoleon's destruction of the French Republic suggested to some Americans the fate of peoples attempting ill-conceived revolution. Others would embrace the irony of the cartoon's message of tranquility achieved through authoritarianism. (Library of Congress)

and foolhardy, a violation, not a fulfillment, of the conservative tradition of the American Revolution. Such a cautious outlook on revolution demonstrates that proslavery partisans in the South were unexceptional, their outlook on the transatlantic world reflecting, not refuting, that of the rest of the nation.

7. Louis Kossuth and the Campaign of 1852

Americans erupted in a final frenzy over revolutionary Europe in early 1852, despite, or because of, the recent setback experienced by Louis Kossuth, the dashing Hungarian revolutionary. Kossuth had come to the United States late in 1851 to raise support for renewing the Hungarian independence struggle against Austria. He arrived via Turkey and Britain, each of which granted him temporary asylum from Hapsburg officials who wished to kill him. Reacting to accounts in American newspapers of the enthusiastic British reception of the Hungarian, Senator Henry Foote of Mississippi arranged for an American warship to bring Kossuth across the Atlantic.[1]

Reputed to have taught himself English by reading Shakespeare and the Bible while in an Austrian prison, Kossuth at first did not disappoint Americans eager to see an articulate, romantic, Christian revolutionary firsthand. When he met Americans and first heard "Yankee Doodle," he remarked that it reminded him of an *esarda*, a popular Hungarian dancing song. He spoke the language of revolutionary peoples in 1848: in addition to speaking in eloquent English, he also gave addresses in French, Italian, and German. Americans got a first taste of his stirring rhetoric by reading newspaper stories of his addresses in England, such as at Birmingham:

> [I] lay before the Parliament of Hungary the . . . terrible alternative which our fearful destiny left to us . . . to present the neck of the nation to the deadly stroke aimed [by Austria and Russia] at its very life or . . . manfully to fight the battle of legitimate defense. Scarcely had I spoken the words . . . when the spirit of freedom moved . . . and nearly four hundred representatives rose . . . and lifting their right arm towards God, solemnly swore, "We grant it, freedom or death!" There they stood . . . awaiting what further words might fall from my lips. . . . A burning

tear fell from my eye, and a sigh of adoration to the Almighty God flut-
tered from my lips, and bowing low before the majesty of my people,
as I bow now before you . . . I left the tribune . . . speechless, mute
(M. Kossuth paused a moment. . . .) Pardon me . . . gentlemen . . . the
shadows of our martyrs . . . pass before my eyes, and I hear the millions
of my nation once more shout, "Freedom or death!"

Kossuth was "rather taller than we had supposed," according to the *New
York Tribune*, yet his blue eyes, prominent forehead, and "oriental features
. . . distinctly marked by suffering" conveyed an intriguing mix of exoticism and humility. Kossuth wore a beard, which became a source for many
American men's emulation and women's enchantment. Moreover, he was
a defeated revolutionary seeking answers in America. Kossuth captured
American attention like no foreigner had since the Marquis de Lafayette
visited in 1824.[2]

Yet Kossuth's and Lafayette's visits provoked profoundly different reactions. Americans roundly exalted the Frenchman, but many found the
Hungarian's appeal deeply troubling. Thus, instead of Lafayette's 1824 tour,
an even better historical analogue of Kossuth's mid-nineteenth-century
visit is the 1793 visit of Edmond Charles "Citizen" Genêt, a representative
of the Girondin regime that established republican rule in France after the
revolution had toppled Louis XVI. As French minister to the United States,
Genêt had two charges. First, he was to involve America in the French
mission to spread universal liberty, specifically by recruiting Americans
to arouse the peoples of Florida and Canada against their colonial rule by
Spain and Britain and thus distract those powers. Second, he was to negotiate a commercial treaty with the United States, to the exclusion of British
interests. Genêt quickly began commissioning the outfitting of French pri-
vateers, manned largely by American sailors, to prey on British ships and
to conduct expeditions into Spanish Florida. When he arrived at Charleston, and on his ensuing overland trip to Philadelphia, the national capital,
Americans treated Genêt to thundering welcomes all along the way.[3]

Genêt wrote to the French foreign affairs minister that American citizens and local officials were embracing him and his cause with "perpetual
fetes," which, he apparently assumed, indicated impending official American support for France. But no such support developed. The Washington
administration treated Genêt coolly. Two weeks after he arrived in the

United States, Washington proclaimed the country "friendly and impartial toward the belligerent powers" and warned U.S. citizens that their government would not come to their aid should they be apprehended assisting any European power or trading in war contraband. Genêt threatened to take his cause directly to the American people, over the head of the government, at which point the United States formally requested his recall to France. Genêt failed to realize that his warm reception could have hidden meanings. First, local demonstrations of sympathy were frequently organized by political supporters of Thomas Jefferson, who was known both to detest Britain and to suspect the Federalist Washington administration of trying to undermine republican government. Therefore, the enthusiasm that Genêt generated exerted pressure on Federalists to justify conservative or centralizing policies. Second, expressions of public sympathy obscured the fact that Americans could both love Genêt and remain officially neutral. Overall, the Genêt affair helped define the first formation of American political partisanship. It also backfired, in terms of Genêt's objectives, by provoking a long-lived statement of American political and military neutrality toward Europe.[4]

Like his predecessor Genêt, Louis Kossuth saw his celebrity and foreign exoticism lapse precipitously during his American tour. He eluded different American partisans' attempts to invest his celebrity in their cause and proved disturbingly interested, like Margaret Fuller, in calling for Americans to prove their alleged revolutionary mettle by lending direct assistance to his country in its quest for freedom—a reversal of historical American diplomatic and military practice. Kossuth saw his star fade rapidly, although Americans' response to Kossuth was less politically partisan and more sectional in its organization than the response to Genêt had been.

Kossuth spent eight months in the United States, from December 1851 to July 1852, traveling from New York to Washington, west to Cincinnati, south to New Orleans, east to Charleston, then returning north to New England before leaving New York for Europe. Enthusiasm for Kossuth was greatest in the North and the West. He often met with indifference, or even hostility, in the South. While reactions along Kossuth's route reveal a regional pattern of American opinions, they collectively demonstrate that Americans ultimately rejected the Hungarian's appeals for support in the belief that he meant to wrest the republic away from American revolutionary values.

New York City welcomed Kossuth to the United States as a revolutionary hero, saluting him with popular expressions ranging from the banal
to the bizarre. In November 1851, shortly before the arrival of the "The
Exile," as New York newspapers referred to Kossuth, his persona made its
way onto the theater stage. *Kossuth's Kum* ("Kossuth's Come") debuted at
Brougham's Lyceum in New York and subsequently was performed in cities on Kossuth's Western tour. Likewise, New York's National Theater presented *The Hungarians and Their Struggle for Independence*. The title of this
patriotic production could also have applied to *Kossuth's Kum*. The latter, a
satire, actually featured no character in the role of Kossuth, because it debuted while the Hungarian was still at sea, and perhaps Americans did not
quite know what he looked like. But *Kossuth's Kum* did offer the thoroughly
familiar American characters of buffoon city aldermen and brave military
officers. American theaters were quick to fit Kossuth into the mold of familiar cultural images, portraying the intriguing Hungarian revolutionary
as an American archetype.[5]

New York City's welcome of Kossuth set the tone for the Magyar champion's reception across the North. The Hungarian and his retinue arrived
at Staten Island on 5 December and then were ferried to Manhattan.
Cannon and rifle salutes fired from shore created a din as they crossed
New York harbor. At the Battery Kossuth was welcomed by the New York
mayor, accompanied by the Richmond Guards, the same corps that had received and attended Lafayette on his American tour. At the Battery's Castle
Garden Kossuth began a speech, but he was cut off by well-wishers who
threatened to trample him. When one enthusiast began snipping at Kossuth's hair, he and his band escaped up Broadway Avenue, surrounded by
the Richmond Guards, suddenly pressed into action.

The Broadway welcome of Kossuth presented "a scene such as the world
seldom beholds," as the *New York Times* described it. Perhaps one hundred
thousand people (a fifth of the city's residents) lined the avenue. Bunting
in the shape of an oversized Hungarian tricolor and the traditional revolutionary liberty cap covered a rostrum in front of City Hall, where Kossuth
spoke briefly. Hotels, stores, and saloons displayed the flags of the aborted
Hungarian republic, the United States, Britain, and Turkey. Press accounts
noted the name and address of commercial establishments contributing
to the day's iconography—and the same information for abstaining establishments. New York vendors shamelessly hawked "'Kossuth khabans,'

'Kossuth boots,' 'Kossuth gloves,' 'Kossuth cigars,' 'Kossuth punch,' 'Kossuth' everything from fabrics of silk to gross articles of food." Selling revolution was good business.[6]

The parade itself demonstrated New Yorkers' dual celebration of the European present and the American past. In front of Kossuth were military regiments, comprised conspicuously of immigrant as well as native-born volunteers. The Irish Volunteers, the La Fayette Fusiliers, the German Hussars, and the Washington Guard—"in old style with blue and buff coats, high boots, and powdered wigs and tails"—provided a martial flavor. The second division included Kossuth and assorted political celebrities, from the U.S. district attorney to the city port collector and county coroner, as well as veterans of the American Revolution and the War of 1812. The third division included firemen's companies, German "Turners"—refugees from gymnastics associations that had been banned in Germany because they were a front for radical politics—and representatives of local unions: omnibus proprietors, journeymen tailors, and butchers. A banner proclaiming "The Sons of Liberty" hung from the lead carriage of this working-class entourage. Preceded in the parade by civic guards hearkening to past military achievements, and followed by urban labor groups claiming the mantle of America's first revolutionary ringleaders, Louis Kossuth evoked the image of past, unified revolutionary valor.

Ironically, but perhaps predictably, amid the New York "Magyar mania epidemic," as the lawyer George Templeton Strong described it, a small group of radicals rejected Kossuth. Before Kossuth's arrival in America, abolitionists had joined other Americans who lauded the Hungarian as an American savior. But they reversed course once he arrived and they realized his lack of antislavery commitment. In the 1850s opposition to slavery, if not abolitionism, would build throughout the North, moving from radical carping to mainstream opinion. That movement makes what happened between Louis Kossuth and the abolitionists especially significant. The encounter between the European radical and his American counterparts eventually amounted to an aborted alliance, a transatlantic cause that did not gain momentum. Most poignantly for abolitionists, their Kossuth encounter illustrated the incongruities between foreign revolutionary symbols and radical domestic goals.[7]

During Hungary's fight for independence against Austria and Russia and Kossuth's subsequent flight westward, abolitionist sentiments had

Figure 6. When Kossuth rode up Broadway, 6 December 1851. Oil painting by Sándor Bodó, from a contemporary lithograph. Americans roundly acclaimed Louis Kossuth before and upon his arrival in the United States, but many grew suspicious of the Hungarian thereafter. (Courtesy of the Library of the Debrecen Reformed College [Debreceni Református Kollégium Nagykönyvtára], Debrecen, Hungary)

echoed other Americans' paeans to the underdog Magyar struggle. *Burritt's Christian Citizen* demonstrated the abolitionists' sense of kinship with Kossuth: "His history is one of determined consistency and self-sacrifice. He is the William Lloyd Garrison of Hungarian liberty." The real William Lloyd Garrison granted that while Kossuth was too warlike to closely resemble Jesus Christ, he "ha[d] suffered everything but death, and [stood] to offer up his life at any moment. . . . He is . . . earnest in purpose, and self-sacrificing in action."[8]

Meanwhile, the Fugitive Slave Law, passed as part of the 1850 Compromise, empowered federal marshals to capture escaped slaves in free states and even to enlist local citizens to enforce its provisions. To many Northerners, and all abolitionists, the law revealed the federal government's complicity in the spread of slave power and a suggestion that the U.S. regime was capable of atrocities analogous to those of European reactionaries. Harriet Beecher Stowe raised the chaos of Europe as a warning to disdainful Americans in writing *Uncle Tom's Cabin.* Other abolitionists portrayed Louis Kossuth's flight to America as a symbol of all refugees' persecution. Frederick Douglass directed readers of his newspaper to "help the American Kossuths." Antislavery propagandists labeled the hunting of fugitive slaves "Austrianism," conducted by "Haynaus," in reference to the Austrian military governor of Hungary whose punishment of captured rebels was so cruel that England, France, and even Russia called for moderation. The antislavery *National Era* newspaper compared the hazardous experiences of Northerners traveling in the South to those of Americans finding themselves in Austria. Black abolitionists in Ohio called "the Russian serf, the Hungarian peasant, [the] American slave and all other oppressed people [to] unite against tyrants."[9]

In a second part of their resolution, these Ohioans also specifically promised Kossuth "the same aid our fathers gave in the American revolution at the battle of New Orleans, and [gave] to [Simón] Bolívar for Columbian independence." What support the Ohioans had in mind is not clear, nor was their recall of history precisely accurate. Some four hundred free blacks had helped Andrew Jackson defeat British forces at the famous battle of New Orleans in 1815. While New Orleans was frequently hailed in the nineteenth century as the symbolic last battle of the American war of independence against Britain, the abolitionists' proclamation to Kossuth suggested some confusion between the American Revolution and the War of 1812. Moreover, no abolitionists, black or white, went filibustering in Eastern Europe; likewise, North Americans had been ambivalent about Bolívar and the Spanish American wars for independence, over the question of whether Latin Americans could achieve stable self-rule. Still, while the Ohio abolitionists seemed poor historians, their invocation of armed struggle, at home and in support of liberation movements abroad, presented a variation on mainstream invocations of America's revolutionary past.[10]

Yet Kossuth's favor waned among abolitionists almost as soon as he reached American shores. In Britain he had offered public congratulations for the emancipation of colonial slaves in the West Indies, giving American abolitionists hope he would forthrightly denounce American slavery. But

America, Kossuth must have realized, had nothing like the British antislavery consensus. Nor, among potential American benefactors for Hungarian freedom, did abolitionists have the deepest coffers of funds: the wealthiest Americans were large slaveholders in the South. Thus, when an African American committee at a New York hotel confronted Kossuth within a month of his arrival in the city, demanding that he pledge himself for or against slavery, Kossuth refused to do so, triggering a backlash. Lucretia Mott, Frederick Douglass, and Wendell Phillips—a wealthy Bostonian turned antislavery radical—asked how Hungarians could expect American support when they were indifferent about the bondage of slavery. Abolitionists now castigated Kossuth for drawing a line between his interests and theirs, for disengaging from matters of high (i.e., American antislavery) principle. Once abolitionists realized they could not count on Kossuth to support their cause, they excoriated him as a hypocrite.[11]

Abolitionist frustration with Kossuth was captured in William Lloyd Garrison's February 1852 *Letter to Louis Kossuth concerning Freedom and Slavery in the United States,* published and distributed by the American Anti-Slavery Society. Garrison composed the *Letter,* over a hundred pages long, in a familiar abolitionist format, coupling together for dramatic effect odes to American freedom and facts about American slavery. In the *Letter* Garrison juxtaposed excerpts from Kossuth's speeches lauding America as an asylum of liberty and various American newspaper advertisements for slave runaways, "that a candid world may see, at a glance, the prodigality of your [Kossuth's] flattery!" In contrast, an issue of the *Liberator* from December 1851—on the eve of Kossuth's arrival—had juxtaposed the same runaway clippings with excerpts of praise for Kossuth's heroic espousal of liberty in Europe. Earlier the *Liberator* had highlighted Kossuth's bravery to condemn slavery; now it used his pandering to American conservatives for the same purpose. Kossuth was proving expendable, and the reversal of the abolitionists' attitude toward him suggested how they, like other Americans, would belittle European liberal democracy at the time.[12]

Garrison also renounced his earlier praise of Kossuth's Christian magnanimity. Succumbing to New Yorkers' adoration, Kossuth had remarked, "Humble as I am, God, the Almighty, has selected me to represent the cause of humanity before you." Garrison, in an improbable confederation with religious conservatives, pounced on this show of vanity, hurling at Kossuth God's admonitions to the prophets Ezekiel and Micah to speak the truth to "the rebellious house," who "lean upon the Lord and say. . . . No evil can come upon us!" For Garrison Kossuth's messianic words were a disguise, cloaking petty nationalism in the garb of a humanitarian plea.[13]

In concluding the Letter, Garrison turned to the American Revolution to point out Kossuth's imperfections. Although it was more out of disgust with Kossuth than empathy with the American founders, Garrison expressed a rather hardnosed insight into the mythology of revolutions: "WASHINGTON, JEFFERSON, AND PATRICK HENRY [risked] life, character and property to overthrow British oppression, as you have done in attempting to throw off Austrian usurpation. . . . As to what you have suffered for Hungary, it proves how great has been your devotion to the interests of your own countrymen; it proves nothing more. Local patriotism, courageous and self-sacrificing . . . is no anomaly in human history." Like others who cheered the Hungarian struggle, Garrison linked the Hungarian independence struggle and the former American uprising. Yet he ridiculed the idealism of each struggle, rather than praising it, thus betraying the poignant lessons that abolitionists had learned from premature efforts to exploit Kossuth and the European revolutionary cause for the antislavery struggle at home. Abolitionists had expected revolutionaries in Europe, crossing the Atlantic, to attack American slavery as well. Yet that exercise could succeed only if a particular European's revolutionary agenda could surpass the American Revolution by being universally relevant—an impossible expectation of the usefulness even of the American Revolution.[14] Hungarians' desire for independence from a despotic government was the same and only goal that many antebellum Americans believed parochial American revolutionaries had held in the eighteenth century. This goal was unsatisfactory to cosmopolitan American abolitionists.[15]

Still, because most Americans were not abolitionists, Kossuth, despite his failure to appease the abolitionist lobby, left New York City buoyant after his tumultuous welcome and several well-received speeches in lecture halls and churches. He traveled to Philadelphia, the republic's second-largest city, to continue his fund-raising for Hungarian war relief. Philadelphians welcomed Kossuth with parades and gifts, including a gold medal containing a miniature of George Washington and a lock of the patriarch's hair. But some Philadelphians shared more than merely adoring reminiscences about the American past. Adolescent students addressed Kossuth in

January 1852 with thirty-eight essays, written specifically for Philadelphia's welcoming ceremony. These essays reflect the fact that the upheavals in Europe had quickly become part of American students' school curriculum, intertwining with educational and civic practice. They also show how deep-rooted Americans' sense of the propriety of their own revolutionary inheritance was at the time.[16]

The Philadelphia students' essays read somewhat like an exuberant U.S. Citizenship and Immigration Services civics questionnaire. Miss Annie Reed's essay queried the Hungarian celebrity: "When you first landed on our soil you perhaps wondered at our progress as a nation, and asked, 'whence all this unity? Why is it that anarchy and despotism cannot obtain a foothold in Columbia's happy land?'" Miss Reed affirmed the lesson in which many American students of revolution, young and old, took comfort: "Kossuth, you behold your answer here. We are an educated people. Visit but the smallest village, and you will find there the cause of our happiness, groups of smiling children wending their way to the place where their minds are trained to love liberty." Liberty learned, not liberty seized, distinguished the American nation.[17]

Other essays repeated the image of America as a refuge of freedom, properly nurtured. "By the virtues of our Mothers," declared Master John L. Painter, aged thirteen, "we are taught from infancy to lisp our detestation of tyranny. . . . Welcome to the protecting shade of the star spangled banner." Painter's colleague Master Malcolm A. MacNeil, also thirteen, sounded the most coeducational theme of the day: "The same spirit which prompted America's daughters to raise floral triumphal arches to receive Washington, and to throw themselves upon the 'protection' of him who had been the 'defender' of their mothers, still burns within their breasts, and now they unite with us in welcoming him who would fain have proved himself a Washington to Hungary. . . . Be assured, sir, the schoolboy is not alone."[18]

Nineteen of the thirty-eight essays, in fact, compared Kossuth to George Washington, a nearly instantaneous identification many Americans in fact made between the two men. In New York hotels and saloons were adorned for Kossuth's regal procession with portraits of him and Washington, along with portraits of Lafayette, Sultan Abdulmecid, and the British Lion. When Kossuth later visited Boston, workmen erected a banner over the state capitol declaring "Washington and Kossuth, the Occident and the Orient."[19]

But a contrast also emerged in the comparison between Washington and Kossuth. Washington was the father of a national progeny who were literally and figuratively nursed on liberty. The American commitment to liberty owed as much to collective character as to safe delivery by Washington. As the minister William Ellery Channing had declared earlier in the century, "There was too much greatness in the American people to admit [an] overshadowing greatness of leaders." Washington, then, reflected greatness, but he himself was not great. In contrast, both external enemy and internal character burdened Kossuth, and it was the latter that doomed his crusade. Even Kossuth himself—perhaps not realizing that his praise might inspire Americans toward protecting their peculiar virtue, rather than spreading it abroad—asked, "Who is your hero? . . . Instead of one mortal man's renowned name I find . . . an immortal being's name, and that is, *the people*." Hungary's revolutionary failure—a result of collective ineptitude, not Kossuth's own shortcomings—strengthened Americans' sense that their revolutionary identity was not only great but exceptional.[20]

After his welcome in the Northeastern states, Kossuth traveled to Washington, D.C. The national capital at that time was in a state of repose, resting between the struggle that had been necessary to piece together the delicate 1850 Compromise and the upcoming presidential campaign in the summer of 1852. States seemed to be complying with the most controversial element of the compromise, the Fugitive Slave Law. The administration of Millard Fillmore lumbered along, and the capital was ripe for excitement. Kossuth fit the bill. As was the case in 1850, when Secretary of State Daniel Webster first sought to exploit the Hungarian cause to move American attention away from the fractious compromise, Kossuth provided an opportunity for national leaders to finesse sectional harmony, an important element of his reception in Washington.

Kossuth was received in the highest offices of the U.S. government. President Fillmore received him at the White House. Like Lafayette he addressed the U.S. House of Representatives and was received by the House and the Senate as those bodies' official guest. His strongest advocates in Congress, Senator Lewis Cass of Michigan and Senator William Seward of New York, led a resolution to grant to Kossuth and his followers land in Iowa, calling it "New Buda." At banquets Washington luminaries applauded the Hungarian's cause and made financial contributions.[21]

But could Washington offer Kossuth more than memorials and private support? The Austrian minister in Washington, Chevalier Johann Georg Hülsemann, sensed trouble. At one Washington affair Webster, still the secretary of state, toasted Kossuth and predicted the arrival of Hungarian independence because of the irresistibility of favorable public opinion, coupled with the sheer cost to the Austrian government of indefinitely policing a resentful Hungary. When Hülsemann learned of Webster's comments, he grew furious. Webster explained, not convincingly, that he had spoken only as a private citizen, but the Austrian nonetheless broke off his country's relations with the United States for over a year—notwithstanding Webster's omission to provide any material or military support for Hungarian liberation.[22]

The too-subtle reticence of Webster became more obvious when Kossuth ventured to see the feeble Senator Henry Clay, exhausted after his efforts to patch together the 1850 Compromise. Kossuth believed that if Clay could be persuaded, the nation might listen. Clay had vigorously advocated U.S. support for Greek liberation from the Ottoman Empire in the 1820s. But in a forerunner to the reception he would receive in the South, Kossuth found the Kentuckian dismayed at his attempts to pull the United States into European affairs. A few weeks from death, Clay pulled Kossuth close to him to reveal the prevailing opinion of Washington policy makers over the example of the United States. Clay rasped: "If we should involve ourselves in the tangled web of European politics . . . and in that struggle Hungary should go down, and we with her, where then would be the last hope of friends of freedom . . . ? Far better is it that . . . we should keep our lamp burning on this western shore than to hazard its utter extinction . . . amid the ruins of fallen or falling republics in Europe." Washington officials were eager to welcome revolutionary celebrities for their wooing words about American virtue but were unwilling to share or spread that virtue at the risk of losing it in a faraway conflict—especially given the emerging sectional conflict at midcentury.[23]

Resilient despite his mixed Washington reception, Kossuth departed for the West. Recent European immigrants, especially many Germans, had settled in the region. As suggested by the number of effigies of German princes burned in Milwaukee, immigrants in large part made the West's response to Kossuth more fervent than in any other part of the country, including vigorous support for American intervention in Europe.[24]

Westerners' pugnacity showed in their national representation and at the local level. Amid a U.S. House of Representatives debate on whether to receive Kossuth on the House floor, congressmen from Ohio, Indiana, Illinois, and Iowa were adamant that the United States militarily assist Hungary. In Pittsburgh, at the time a Western city, a spokesman denounced Russia for supporting Austria in subjugating Hungary and demanded that the Fillmore administration "use all diplomatic means with Emperor Nicholas. But if they fail, write your commands with the point of a sword, and seal them with a cannon's mouth." Another speaker interpreted George Washington's farewell message to mean that the United States should keep out of entangling alliances but should ally with suffering humanity, wherever it might be: "Were Washington alive today . . . he would rush to assist the oppressed, wherever they are." Leading citizens in Springfield, Illinois, including the attorney Abraham Lincoln, drew up resolutions of sympathy and invited Kossuth to their city, Lincoln's stance consistent with his 1848 speech in Congress, when he had argued for Hungarian self-determination. "Any people anywhere," he had observed, "have the right to rise up, and shake off the existing government, and form a new one that suits them better." The Ohio general assembly resolved to loan Kossuth all of the state's rifles and war munitions, "to be returned in good order upon the achievement of Hungarian liberty." Ohio citizens augmented their legislature's loan with a gift of five hundred muskets, in response to a local pamphlet that betrayed Americans' perceptions, at the time, of the difference between Europe and their own country: "Send in the guns—they are not needed here, but they soon will be greatly needed over there."[25]

All along the route of Kossuth's tour of the North and West, well-wishers poured donations into the coffers of the benighted cause of Hungarian freedom. In addition to the arms of Ohio, Kossuth received rifles from the Connecticut factory of Eli Whitney, the son of the inventor of the cotton gin, who declared his confidence "that the present acquired reputation of this rifle will not suffer in the hands of your brave countrymen." Kossuth's receipt of actual weapons was unusual, as most Americans simply donated money or other more arcane items to his war chest. It is uncertain how much money Kossuth actually raised in the United States, probably seventy-five thousand to one hundred thousand dollars (roughly two million dollars today). Many funds came from admission charges for Kossuth's speeches, such as the exorbitant five-dollar fee gathered by Henry Ward

Beecher from the parishioners of his church in Brooklyn and by the Young Men's Lyceum of Cincinnati. Contributions also came from groups. Miners in Pittsburgh gave a week's worth of wages to the Hungarian cause, some six thousand dollars. The women of Pittsburgh established the first "Ladies Association for the Friends of Hungary"; raised one thousand dollars; and helped establish branch societies, called "Women of the West" clubs, throughout the country. "Women of the West" clubs led the U.S. women's movement in support for Kossuth, a significant aspect of American women's networking with radical European ideologies and revolutionaries that had emerged in 1848. Back east the Central Hungarian Committee, organized by "Young Americans" John L. O'Sullivan and Theodore Sedgwick, sold "Hungary bonds," redeemable upon Kossuth's return home to govern an independent Hungary. Local organizers used these bond certificates as admission tickets to Kossuth's wildly popular speeches, which proved dangerous when bond sales exceeded speaking-hall capacities. In Boston patrons squeezing into Faneuil Hall were trampled or passed out in the early-summer heat.[26]

Less flamboyant were the smaller contributions many Americans made to Kossuth's cause. The *New York Tribune* profiled New York donors whose contributions totaled $11,500 during the first week of Kossuth's visit. These included "A Gentleman, $5; A Workingman, $10; A Lady, $20; German newspaper printers, $30; the Mechanic's Union Association, $100; a Sunday school donation, $12.60; Dr. Lilenthal, Rabbi, $20; Valentine's stereotypers, $70; Daughter of a Revolutionary officer of 1776, $20." Fifty-five Connecticut cigar makers gave a dollar each to Kossuth, enclosing a gallant note explaining that "we trust in but a few days you will receive it and establish Republicanism."[27]

As it turned out, even before they left for Hungary in June 1852, Kossuth and his band had spent most of the money they received from American well-wishers on hotels, meals, and even the glittery rallies cities staged to welcome the Hungarian—embarrassingly, municipal officials sometimes asked the Hungarians to pay for their own festivals. In addition to currency, Kossuth also received deeds to land, gold rings, bullets from the battles of Bunker Hill and New Orleans, and locks of hair belonging to George Washington and Thomas Jefferson. Reflecting the joining of religious pluralism with transatlantic republicanism possible in the United States at midcentury, the Jewish community of Washington, D.C., gave

Kossuth a painting depicting Moses, Washington, and Kossuth himself. Kossuth, a bona fide revolutionary, was thus the beneficiary of Americans' curiosity about revolution, a curiosity they could satisfy with both financial and more idiosyncratic forms of philanthropy.

Perhaps Americans' most long-lived memorials involved not direct material contributions to his cause, but the place names they changed to honor the traveling Magyar and the new facial features American men began to sport in the wake of his visit. The Hungarian leader saw towns in New Hampshire, Pennsylvania, Indiana, Ohio, and even Mississippi take his name as their own. Iowans created Kossuth County, with Kossuth Center as the county seat, as well as the town of Kossuth in Des Moines County. A planter in Washington County, Maine, named his home Kossuth Plantation.[28]

And reflecting Kossuth's handsome features and his romantic influence on men and women alike, a large number of American men, largely without precedent in the nation's history, began to wear beards. Before the mid-nineteenth century beards were largely regarded as eccentric, but after 1840 observers in Europe, noting facial hair among bohemian artists and political troublemakers, declared a full beard a sign of being "democratic." Remarking on the Hungarian's magnetism, an Indiana journalist wrote that "since Kossuth's arrival in this country . . . we do not recollect ever having seen so many whiskerandos in Indianapolis as during the past week." In such imitations of Louis Kossuth's name and appearance, Americans found a means to symbolically support popular foreign struggles.[29]

Western settlers' alacrity regarding American intervention in Europe reflected their sense that the West embodied quintessentially non-European values: primitivism, raw opportunity, and self-reliance, for example—attributes decried by moral reformers like Lyman Beecher in the East, but that Westerners envisioned Hungarians suddenly manifesting. The West, moreover, was not as caught up in the tension of the slavery debate as were Easterners and Washington politicians, although this exemption would soon change.

Yet unless the West staged a revolution and seceded from the Union to declare an alliance with Hungary, Washington politicians and Southern conservatives would in large part determine the fate of calls for U.S. intervention. In the spring of 1852 the U.S. Senate debated a resolution, prepared by William Seward, designed to warn Austria and Russia of the consequences of further repression of the Hungarian freedom movement. The resolution declared that the United States would not allow "acts of national injustice, oppression, and usurpation, whenever or wherever they may occur." Foretelling greater U.S. foreign interventionism in generations to come, Seward argued: "I have heard frequently that we can promote the cause of freedom and humanity only by our own example. . . . But what should that example be but that of performing not one national duty only, but all national duties. Not those due to ourselves only, but those which are due to other nations and to all mankind."[30]

Opponents of the resolution saw Seward's argument for the idealistic use of force on behalf of less fortunate foreigners as a search for monsters to destroy. Senator James Jones of Tennessee offered a response typical of the era's hard-boiled Southern mindset: "Because I love this Union . . . I am against Utopian schemes, modern doctrines of progress, manifest destiny, [and] higher or lower law. Why should we go abroad? Have we not enough to do at home?" Senator Jacob Miller of New Jersey denounced U.S. interventionism because it would "Europeanize America," not further "Americanize Europe," as he implied had been the effect of previous U.S. isolationism. By March of 1852 arguments for intervention lost momentum, at the national and local levels. Seward's strongly worded resolution was never put to a Senate vote. Technology—radio, television, the Internet—that could have broadcast Kossuth's campaign and nourished Westerners' enthusiasm did not exist. As Kossuth chugged away from Cincinnati, where an estimated one hundred thousand people had lined the railroad tracks when he entered the "Queen City" (a monarchical nickname over which he chided Cincinnatians to great effect), and headed toward the South, his greatest support weakened and faded from view.[31]

Moving south of the Ohio River, Kossuth was bringing his appeal to the region whose congressional representation had been most apprehensive about the Magyar's appeals. For example, in the House votes on Henry Foote's resolution to send a U.S. ship to bring Kossuth to America, Southerners as a group had voted 65–41 against, whereas Northerners had voted 176–27 in favor. In the resolution Foote had declared that Southerners would show sympathy with Hungary's cause despite the attempts of those seeking to "violate constitutional principles by profess[ing] a peculiar sort of abolition sympathy for the heroic defenders of freedom upon Hungarian soil." He was referring to attempts by abolitionists, especially his Senate antagonist John Hale of New Hampshire, to exploit the Hungarian issue to press the case of American emancipation. The Senate on three occasions had debated resolutions to express sympathy for the 1848 revolutions. Each time Hale had offered amendments broadening the legislation to make some critique of American slavery. Foote, unlike many Southerners, saw no connection between Hungarian independence and American abolitionism.[32]

Foote's isolation, however, was not immediately apparent amid the enthusiastic citizens who greeted the Kossuth entourage when it ventured into the Deep South. Kossuth's first stop was New Orleans. Inhabited by large French and German immigrant populations, the Crescent City treated the Hungarians warmly. Its citizens approached the manager of the American Theater to rent space for a welcome meeting. The manager agreed, but when he asked that admission proceeds from the meeting be divided between the theater and Kossuth, he was sorely rebuked for his "unpatriotic" attitude. City officials escorted Kossuth both to the battleground of Andrew Jackson's victory over a British force in 1815 and to a slave auction, scenes awkwardly suggesting Southerners' tension at hearing the Hungarian preach self-determination for his own country.[33]

Kossuth took both sights in stride, focusing his appeal as a champion of local government, nothing more. In New Orleans he declared he had nothing to do with either abolitionism or "anti-abolitionism," because as a foreigner he had no right to interfere with "domestic concerns." In Mobile, on the other hand, he claimed to see little difference between his cause and that of the slave states, observing, "Of all the great principles guaranteed by your constitution, there is none they more cherish . . . than the principle that their own affairs are to be managed by themselves, without any interference . . . from another state . . . nor from the central government." Kossuth also warned Southerners that to allow monarchies hostile to democracy to dominate Europe would risk shutting off Old World markets to Southern cotton.[34]

Kossuth did win a few conversions, especially among "Young Americans," who envisioned the American mission as more than merely setting an example. And the idea that monarchical Europe might become off-limits to Southern cotton, though far-fetched, prodded the Kentuckian George Sanders, editor of the *Democratic Review*, to argue for the republicanization of Europe as a means of guaranteeing an Atlantic free-trade zone. His calls for U.S. interventionism held appeal for Southerners, who in the 1850s sought to take over Cuba and other vulnerable areas of Latin America, although many of them aimed to spread the sphere of slavery, not universal liberty.[35]

In assuming that Southern audiences embraced democracy, then, Kossuth probably hurt his argument as much as he bolstered it, as some leading Southerners were hardly eager to promote democracy even at home, let alone abroad. The Tennessee senator James Jones expressed wariness, as noted above, and the citizens of Charleston, South Carolina, which the Hungarian soon visited, revealed that they "understood the liberal forces [working] in the world beyond their peninsula . . . [and] began energetically erecting barricades to the erosion of traditional social values." This sentiment applied across most of the South, which typically responded to Kossuth with polite applause in person and with less generous reactions in published sources. Kossuth complained that he was "being charged from one side with being in the hands of abolitionists, and from the other side with being in the hands of slaveholders," but his nonalignment with antislavery did not persuade Southern opinion makers. The Louisiana House of Representatives resolved that Kossuth's conduct toward Henry Clay in Washington had been "arrogant" and that his doctrine of intervention was "anti-American." The *Vicksburg Whig* perceived him as a closet Free Soiler, as did the *Montgomery Advertiser*. Kossuth had been in Charleston two days before the local paper even announced his visit, and he canceled a planned stopover in Richmond, so negligible was the advance publicity. In Virginia a reflective colonel in the U.S. army, Robert E. Lee, captured the abiding sentiment in the South as Kossuth's retinue returned northward: "I fear I do not admire [Kossuth]. . . . I look solely to the good of my country. I wish him every . . . success in accomplishing . . . independence. But we are not called on to engage in the quixotic scheme of righting European wrongs. Nor would it advance the principle of self-government by destroying the only nation where it exists, or depriving the world of . . . the asylum we now offer to all lovers of liberty." Lee was right when he spoke of America as an asylum, although by the early 1850s it was an exceptional asylum not of liberty, but order, which many Southerners felt Kossuth ultimately jeopardized.[36]

The presidential campaign of 1852 is customarily considered vacuous and forgettable, other than as the swan song of the Whig Party. The 1850

Compromise had in large part undermined the drive for a third party, Democrat and Whig leaders maintaining that it had permanently solved the slavery question. The Free Democratic Party—the renamed Free Soil Party—received only half of its 1848 total vote. But in 1852, perhaps precisely because the candidates did not debate slavery as a moral issue, they did pay attention, as in 1848, to the less volatile issue of U.S. foreign relations.[37]

Louis Kossuth was obviously the most visible element of the European revolutions in the 1852 election. Contradicting his earlier avowal of disinterest in American domestic politics, in the West he urged the formation of a German American voting bloc, "without party respect," for the political candidate who would pledge to support U.S. intervention in Europe. Democrats at first responded favorably to Kossuth's pleas. At a banquet in Washington sponsored by the Democratic Party, Kossuth heard one speaker after another endorse the principle of intervention, either as a reflection of new American power or as a reciprocation of the European intervention through which the colonies had gained their independence.[38]

Two of Kossuth's admirers attending the affair were both front-runners for the Democratic nomination: Lewis Cass and Stephen Douglas. Cass's reputation for equivocation had doomed him in 1848, and unfortunately, in 1852 he did nothing to improve his image. At the banquet he declared that the United States should "insist" that Russia not interfere with Hungary—a weak statement, perceived as worse than either silence or assertiveness. Douglas, on the other hand, affirmed his willingness to consider the use of force to assist Hungarian as well as Irish peoples in achieving self-determination. But ultimately, Douglas's presidential campaign faltered amid publicity he received from George Sanders, who exhorted readers of the *Democratic Review* to embrace Douglas as a Westerner untainted by Old World luxury—unlike Cass, the former minister to France—and therefore an advocate of aggressive policy in Europe. A misreading of Westerners' enthusiasm for Kossuth as national support for intervention, Sanders's zealous portrayal of Douglas helped to do in the Illinois senator, frightening voters as the Democratic national convention approached.[39]

Reflecting the emerging emphasis among all parties on protecting American freedom from foreign risks, the Democratic platform of 1852 resolved "that in view of the condition of popular institutions in the Old World, [we have] a high and sacred duty . . . to uphold the rights of every State . . . and to sustain among us constitutional liberty." Democrats subsequently nominated Franklin Pierce, a former U.S. senator from New Hampshire and a veteran of the Mexican War, whose appeal lay in his independence from Washington; his support for the 1850 Compromise; and his lack of interest in Europe, other than as a venue for achieving reciprocal trade and preserving the western hemisphere for American expansion. The choice of Pierce revealed the decline of Democratic fervor regarding the potential for change in Europe, amounting to a stark repudiation of Kossuth.[40]

Whigs were even less circumspect than Democrats, categorically rejecting the idea of an American liberation of Europe in their plans for the presidency. In 1852 the Whigs did publish a platform pledging the party's sympathy for "struggling freedom everywhere," but, as in 1848, they again invoked the teachings of "the Father of the Country" against "imposing upon other countries our forms of government . . . [except for] teaching by example . . . the blessings of self-government." Whigs nominated the old war hero Winfield Scott, who, like Pierce, was attractive for his lack of opinions about foreign intervention and the sensitive issue of slavery.[41]

At the same time, though, Whigs attempted to exploit the lingering presence of Kossuth. The Hungarian had condemned Roman Catholicism on several occasions, including in a speech to Henry Ward Beecher's three-thousand-seat church in Brooklyn and in a St. Louis lecture that revealed that the Jesuits wished to take over the world. Catholic spokesmen unanimously condemned Kossuth. The *Boston Pilot* demonstrated that the prophetic number "666" could be derived from the letters LUDOVIC K (Louis Kossuth), proving that the Hungarian exile might be the anti-Christ. Orestes Brownson warned that Kossuth represented not liberty, but "red republican[ism]." Other Catholic spokesmen declared the Democratic Party atheist in its embrace of Kossuth. But when some Catholic voters rallied to the Whig flag in response to exposés of Kossuth's anti-Catholicism, nativist Whigs allied with the Democrats in protest.[42]

The Free Democratic Party most hearkened to Kossuth's plea for a national U.S. policy of activism in Europe. In 1852 the Free Democratic Party consisted principally of Massachusetts and Ohio antislavery Whigs, as most of 1848's Barnburner Democrats had by now returned to the main party. The Free Democratic platform condemned the 1850 Compromise, especially the Fugitive Slave Law. Perhaps to attract supporters still eager to intervene in Europe, or in tacit acknowledgment of the idealism of their cause, the Free Democrats resolved that "every nation has a right to alter its government. . . . Especially is it the duty of the American government, the chief republic of the world, to protest against . . . the intervention of kings and emperors against nations seeking to establish for themselves republican or constitutional governments." This was precisely the kind of endorsement that Louis Kossuth had asked for, and it conformed to his pleas, while touring the West, for "German citizens [to] unite with a third independent party" espousing interventionism. But in the national election many German and Irish immigrants remained Democrats, their resentment of Whig nativism still more powerful than their desire to see Europe Americanized by force. The Massachusetts senator Charles Sumner supported the Free Democrats in 1852, but he nonetheless—like Robert E. Lee—voiced the isolationism that connected the main political parties by that time. "Individuals may do as they please," wrote Sumner, "[but] Kossuth errs—all err who ask any intervention by GOVERNMENT. . . . I am [an] enthusiast for Freedom, but that is not practical." In 1852 Americans thus pledged themselves to practical isolationism, which Kossuth's interventionist pleas had uncovered but could not overcome.[43]

Americans' changing sentiments for Kossuth revealed their interest in him as an idealized character, a fallen European revolutionary celebrity. Many attributed to his exploits in Europe qualities that they distilled from the American revolutionary experience, praising his quest for freedom from an empire, his military genius, and his parliamentary skill—qualities that enabled them to link up with what they perceived to be their own heroic past, as distant as the exotic but benighted land of Hungary. Indeed, these two "distant revolutions"—one far in the past, one far away—help explain Americans' peculiar, limited, romantic enthusiasm for revolution at the time. But the more Americans became acquainted with Kossuth and his mission, the more they sensed that his agenda was different from what they had anticipated, driving a wedge between the Hungarian hero and his potential American backers. Kossuth's visit to America exemplified the inherent difficulties attending the peaceful assimilation of the European revolutions into American culture. It also, ironically, provided a further demonstration of how Americans, in light of the failure of the 1848 revolutions, could cling ever more tightly to their notion of a distinctive American revolutionary consciousness and identity.

In his inaugural address in March 1853, Franklin Pierce referred proudly to the differences between the two sides of the Atlantic: "Of the complicated European systems of national polity we have heretofore been independent. From their wars, their tumults, and anxieties we have been, happily, almost entirely exempt." Only in their disinterested sympathies for freedom were Americans remotely connected to the European scene, said Pierce. There were, moreover, no signs that American tranquility would not continue: "The apprehension of dangers from extended territory, multiplied States, accumulated wealth, and augmented population has proved to be unfounded." Unlike in revolutionary Europe, standing armies in America were dangerous and unnecessary. But events that Americans would perceive as European revolutionism descending on a halcyon America would shortly shatter Pierce's tranquilizing assurances.[44]

8. THE ANTISLAVERY MOVEMENT AS A CRISIS
OF AMERICAN EXCEPTIONALISM

Many Americans at the outset of the 1848 revolutions considered the prospect that, at least politically, the United States and Europe were growing closer together. But Americans viewed the revolutions' lack of success as a debacle, and many inferred that the ingredients necessary for revolutionary success resided only on the western side of the Atlantic. Only in the United States were citizens capable of gaining constitutional rights through minimal violence and maintaining the prosperity that accompanied those rights. Thus, in the early 1850s many Americans saw themselves alone, with a fate to be determined by historically unique circumstances and internal events, rather than as contributing or receiving members of a transatlantic world. In conjunction with rising tension over the question of the expansion of slavery, however, this assumption would soon reverse.

The 1848 revolutions had prodded many Americans to affirm the conservative character of their own national beginning. The 1848 revolutions presented complicated conditions of conflict between groups—as in France, where parties struggled over local, not universal issues; or, in Germany and among the Slavic peoples, where they struggled over divided political and ethnic loyalties. The revolutions involved wars over contested sovereignty between Hungary, Austria, and Russia, and between Hungary and Slavic peoples. They included conflicts in which peoples of a supposedly backward religion rose against the authorities of a supposedly backward political regime, as in Italy. Amid such distinctions most Americans embraced a more idealistic narrative of revolution, a popular majority using universal legal precepts and organic attitudes to oust a clearly corrupt foreign tyrant.

One famous history of the American Revolution that appeared shortly after the 1848 revolutions reflected this understanding of revolution. The historian George Bancroft issued his *History of the United States* beginning in 1852, its first volumes focused on the American Revolution, completed during and shortly after his tenure as the U.S. minister to Great Britain. Thus, his account of the American past was written in the context of the turbulent European present. Accordingly, Bancroft's account conveys an unmistakable trace of his musing over contemporary events:

> For Europe, the crisis foreboded the struggles of generations. . . . In the chaos of states, the ancient forms of society, after convulsive agonies, were doomed to be broken in pieces. . . . In America, the influences of time were molded by the creative force of reason, sentiment, and nature. Its political edifice rose in lovely proportions, as if to melodies of the lyre. Peacefully and without crime, humanity was to make for itself a new existence. . . . The American Revolution . . . was most radical in its character, yet achieved with such benign tranquility, that even conservatism hesitated to censure.

Bancroft's description of a chaotic Europe and a serene America seems curious, given his stated purpose of recounting an forceful overthrow of colonial government and the destruction of its defenders. But such was the paradoxical lesson that someone like Bancroft, an apostle of the notion of an organic and harmonious American democracy and a firsthand observer of European upheaval, took from Europe. Conservatism in America had fled underground in the late eighteenth century with the triumph of radical republicanism.[1] During 1848 American conservatism had resurfaced, couched in images of an American revolutionary identity framed by negative perceptions of European turbulence.[2]

At the time that Bancroft's salute to America's organic identity appeared, however, the troublesome topic of slavery was becoming the central focus of debate over America's differences from Europe. Did American slavery make the United States more or less stable than the Old World? Some Northern writers joined Southern apologists in affirming slavery's benevolent social influence. Bancroft, for example, claimed that Europeans had foisted slavery on the New World. He rationalized the institution's perpetuation as a tragedy of racial incompatibility: if slaves had been white, the problem of slavery would have been remedied "by the benevolent spirit of colonial legislation." Nonetheless, black slavery, over time, would perform "the office of advancing and civilizing the Negro." Slavery, in Bancroft's view, was a vestige of Old World corruption. Not only would American democratic institutions gradually eradicate the institution from the New World, but their global spread could also redeem Africa. Likewise, Solon Robinson, the agricultural editor of the *New York Tribune,* after touring the South, wrote about "God's providence, in his wise provisions for . . . the [slaves]. Let [abolitionists] inquire how it happens, that guards of armed soldiery cannot prevent in Europe, violence and bloodshed among their 'white slaves,' while here . . . no force is required to make him quietly and faithfully obey and serve his master." For some Americans slavery represented American political and social stability, in contrast to a Europe beset by corruption and violence.[3]

Not all Americans, however, reflexively held up a triumphant American revolutionary identity against a Europe in chaos, much less justified slavery as an American bulwark. In the early 1850s the most celebrated of these skeptics was the abolitionist Harriet Beecher Stowe, whose *Uncle Tom's Cabin* appeared in book form in March 1852, after being printed earlier as a serial by the *National Era.* In despair over the new Fugitive Slave Law passed as part of the 1850 Compromise, Stowe wrote a series of sketches that eventually grew to the book's forty-five chapters, responding to her sister-in-law's entreaty that Stowe "write something that will make this whole nation feel what a cursed thing slavery is." By year-end the book had sold three hundred thousand copies in America and a million copies in Britain. Circulation in the latter country was so wide that it was reported that even remote villages, ignorant of the February 1848 revolution in France, now contained "scarcely a cottage" where the inhabitants had not wept or laughed at Stowe's characters.[4]

Like other abolitionists at midcentury, Harriet Beecher Stowe referred to revolutionary Europe in her attempt to spur Americans to radical action. In the novel Alfred scoffs at Augustine's suggestion that the "lower class" may get "the upper hand" as "republican humbug," boasting that "they [the slaves] must be kept down, consistently, steadily. . . . We'll take care of that, in this country." Augustine warns him that "Austria and Pius IX" also believed that no popular revolution was possible in Europe, but again Alfred smirks that Augustine is uttering "red republican humbug." Meanwhile, in her "Concluding Remarks," Stowe directly urged her readers to heed foreign events: "Nations are convulsed. A mighty influence is abroad, heaving the world as with an earthquake. Is America safe?" Stowe saw events in America and abroad together beckoning "the day of his appearing" and asked, "Is not this the spirit of HIM whose kingdom is yet to come? . . . A day of grace is yet held out to us . . . [but] every nation that carries in its bosom great and unredressed injustice has in it the elements of this last convulsion." Like other Americans, from Margaret Fuller to Protestant clerics, Stowe saw transatlantic turmoil as a precursor to an apocalyptic fulfillment of history.[5]

Was fear of a slave insurrection, responding to the international upheaval Americans had witnessed over the preceding five years, the source of the book's wild acclaim? Probably not. *Uncle Tom's Cabin* was serially published at the same time that Louis Kossuth was making his way to the United States, and it appeared as a book when he was not quite halfway through his American tour. In June 1852 Kossuth lectured in New York, warning, like Stowe, that no nation could be confident of its future: "As long as the fragile wisdom of political exigencies overrules the doctrines of Christ, there is no freedom on earth firm, and the future of no nation sure." The Hungarian and Uncle Tom both served as popular lightning rods in America.[6]

Yet Kossuth came and went and, upon settling as an exile in London, spent the 1850s brooding over the failure of Americans to share his view that the United States, as a leading republic, should intervene to help Hungary establish its own republic. Meanwhile, *Uncle Tom's Cabin* provoked Abraham Lincoln to remark in 1862 at its role in moving the United States toward Civil War. If Lincoln exaggerated the book's causal influence, he nevertheless attested to its rapidly developing legendary status.[7]

What was the difference between these two transatlantic icons? Integral to the dramatic impact of *Uncle Tom's Cabin* was its portrayal of individuals on American soil embroiled in the slavery debate. Sympathetic readers could grow frustrated with the lethargy of St. Clare, resent the moral piety of Miss Ophelia, and hate the planter Simon Legree. They could imagine the tragedy of ordinary slaves' suffering through Uncle Tom himself. Whereas William Lloyd Garrison had called Kossuth a hypocrite for accepting comparisons to Christ, he remarked, "Like Jesus himself, Tom was willing to be led as a lamb to the slaughter, anxious only for the salvation of his enemies." This captures the difference between the two: Stowe's depiction of a besieged black family appealed to a peculiar

American domesticity in a way Kossuth never could. Still, Stowe, like the Hungarian, portrayed distant scenes of despotism: both Hungarian rebels and African American slaves were unfamiliar to their American audiences (*Uncle Tom's Cabin* was read mainly outside the South). And both placed lurking American trouble over slavery in an international context.[8]

In assessing the impact of *Uncle Tom's Cabin,* Stowe's proslavery critics insisted that foreign elements were manufacturing the furor over the book because they resented American peace and prosperity. Moreover, they argued, Europeans, more than Americans, needed to heed any moral lessons the book might contain. The *United States Democratic Review* declared, "Had [Stowe's] work consisted of pictures of [the] tyranny and degradation . . . of . . . all Europe, it would . . . have passed quietly . . . to oblivion. . . . [Instead, Europeans] use . . . the fictions of a female romancer for materials to aid in undermining our prosperity and destroying our domestic peace." The *New York Herald* warned "the aristocrats of England and Europe" that they should look after their own affairs. While they "fancy they are dealing a blow at our institutions by their patronage of Uncle Tom," they themselves "are the Legrees . . . upon whom retribution must fall." Reaction against *Uncle Tom's Cabin* reiterated many Americans' understanding that violence and despotism in Europe explained both European anarchy and American peacefulness.[9]

Worsening the situation for antislavery readers sympathetic to Stowe's novel, the administration of President Franklin Pierce sought to expand the area open to slavery. Following through on the pledge he had made in his inaugural address, Pierce pursued U.S. expansion across Latin America. While it did not actively support filibustering, his administration hardly enforced U.S. neutrality laws against private citizens' military interference in foreign countries. At least three Southerners, John Quitman of Mississippi, Henry Kinney of Texas, and William Walker of Tennessee, laid schemes to stage revolutions in and occupy Cuba, a Spanish colony with a thriving slave-based economy, and Nicaragua, a British-claimed protectorate that had abolished slavery in 1824. All gained assurances that the government would not obstruct their plans. Kinney briefly occupied Nicaragua in 1855, and Walker, when he gained control of Nicaragua in 1856, received U.S. recognition as the country's head of state. Nicaraguans drove him out within a year, but not before he revoked existing slavery-abolition laws. Meanwhile, in 1854, in Ostend, Belgium, U.S. ministers to Britain,

France, and Spain penned a memorandum to the State Department, which soon became public, recommending the U.S. government offer no more than 120 million dollars to acquire Cuba from Spain. Should Spain not sell, they advised that the United States would be justified in taking the island by force. While Spain resisted American expansion in Cuba, the Pierce administration did succeed in purchasing an additional slice of northern Mexico from a Mexican government intimidated by defeat in the recent war. The objective of this purchase was a southern route for a transcontinental railway that would link Los Angeles with New Orleans.[10]

Ironically, in all of its expansionist schemes, the Pierce administration invoked the liberal and idealistic rhetoric of "Young America," espousing the spread of American democratic institutions under the American flag. Arguments for the spread of American influence abroad had initially inspired Americans' enthusiasm for the 1848 revolutions, and they persisted even into the election season of 1852. As in the presidential election campaign in 1848, Whig and Democratic spokesmen again traded accusations that the other side represented "red republicanism." For example, the *American Whig Review* attempted to discredit Democratic proexpansionists by labeling them "a faction . . . which was in truth Jacobinical; since known as the 'Red (or bloody) Republican.'" But in response the *United States Democratic Review* differentiated American interest in acquiring Cuba from a European "propaganda of liberation": the French republic's abolition of West Indian slavery in 1848, the *Democratic Review* claimed, was "consistent with *their* principle of revolution." Thus, it was simply "frightful . . . Red Republican" doctrine to suggest that Cuban slaves would be liberated as a consequence of Cuban annexation. Such "declaration[s] of universal emancipation" were "not the logic of Washington and his compeers, and such will not be ours." "Young American" sentiment gained support in 1852 because it offered the prospect of foreign adventuring within the western hemisphere, safely distant both from European shores and from alien "Red Republican" ideology and, in its antiabolitionism, consistent with American revolutionary doctrine. The American empire itself could remain little disturbed and violence-free in the process.[11]

The Pierce administration's maneuvering served to emphasize the legitimacy of slavery and seemed to reconfirm traditional American stability. In the wake of the uncertainty of 1850, Pierce acknowledged the year's "perilous crisis" but confirmed that the country was now safe, as long as

Americans of his generation consulted the "comprehensive wisdom [of] . . . the founders of the Republic . . . as time has proved." Horace Greeley, the antislavery editor of the *New York Tribune*, did not share the president's sense of triumph. Still, he wrote: "We have been wickedly beaten by a coalition of the Go-Slowly factions against us. I mean now to lie quiet a while and see how the world goes on." Greeley had earlier evinced the most support of any journalist for transatlantic social change during the years of European revolution, but he plodded back to the traditional Whig Party in 1852. Both America and Europe seemed to be returning to the *status quo ante bellum.*[12]

Yet Harriet Beecher Stowe's question, "Is America safe?" lingered. Again, by the end of the 1848 revolutions, many Americans had been per-suaded that America *was* safe from European-style storms. The American Revolution had established a historical political framework that rendered America unique, preserving its peace, capable of manufacturing resolu-tion of conflict. But by the mid-1850s developments concerning slavery effectively reversed assumptions about the distance of European turmoil from America's political culture. The earlier reception of *Uncle Tom's Cabin* in many ways fostered the intellectual atmosphere for this change, but it took political events, and a particular interpretation of them, to direct the clamor Stowe's work had caused.

Specifically, events in the territory of Kansas, stemming from the ap-plication of the 1854 Kansas-Nebraska Act, took on a transatlantic sig-nificance. While disruption to the American political system caused by antagonism over the Kansas territory has been well-documented, studies have commonly framed the Kansas conflict only as a domestic event, not considering the international context to explain the controversy or its sig-nificance. But images of European violence informed the ways Americans, especially antislavery Northerners, interpreted the Kansas struggle as an apparent American corollary to events in Europe. Because Americans largely had sworn off the violence of European revolutions, and counter-revolutions, as events having nothing to do with the United States, the violence in Kansas had a shocking and disruptive effect on the American political system, to the point that antislavery forces increasingly decided they must act against what seemed European-style violence erupting on the American plains. They must themselves disavow law and order, around which Americans had constructed an ideological shrine useful for distinguishing the United States from Europe, and instead consider and even welcome defiance of the laws in terms of what many began to call "revolution." In effect, the antislavery movement, galvanized by domestic scenes reminiscent of distant violence in Europe, shifted from peripheral nonviolent protest to a widespread movement tolerant of violent subversion of the political and social order.[13]

In 1854 Congress established Kansas as a territory under the doctrine of "popular sovereignty"—the position on slavery that Lewis Cass had enunciated in his presidential campaign of 1848. Popular sovereignty implied that the voters of Kansas alone were responsible for deciding whether to ban or welcome slavery. Coveted by land-hungry settlers and speculators both North and South, and adjacent to the slave state Missouri, the territory became a battleground. While land speculation, promotion of the transcontinental railroad, and spoliation of Indian reservations contributed to loss of life in the territory, the Northern antislavery press attributed the violence to "border ruffians"—armed Missourians who crossed the border to fraudulently swell proslavery votes on election days. President Pierce, continually solicitous of Southern counsel in hopes of maintaining national harmony, sent Kansas a series of territorial governors either sympathetic to proslavery interests or too weak to oppose them. Meanwhile, antislavery forces, called "jayhawkers," were hardly pious. Some were supplied by a Massachusetts venture, the New England Emigrant Aid Company, with hundreds of deadly Sharps breech-loading rifles, as well as cannons and a howitzer. But antislavery settlers frequently boycotted elections they believed were rigged. Consequently, despite a majority antislavery population, by 1856 Kansas had elected a delegate to Washington and a territorial legislature that both endorsed slavery and had ratified a territorial constitution friendly to the institution's expansion. In the process the Free Soil town of Lawrence was destroyed, and several hundred people lost their lives, including five proslavery settlers who were slain, execution-style, by John Brown, an Eastern abolitionist.

David Potter wrote that to gauge the significance of such events, "it is less important to know what happened in Kansas than to know what the American public thought was happening in Kansas." Potter demonstrated how "Bleeding Kansas" served to coalesce Northern opinion around drastic measures to halt the course of events in the territory. For example, headlines in the *New York Tribune* for 28 May 1856 read, "Startling news

from Kansas—The War Actually Begun—Triumph of the Border Ruffians—
Lawrence in Ruins—Several Persons Slaughtered—Freedom Bloodily
Subdued." Such apocalyptic descriptions bore a strong resemblance to evo-
cations of violent developments in Europe, to which Americans were by
now accustomed. And Americans, attuned to that alarming transatlantic
alignment, responded. One *Tribune* reader, for example, actually felt the
newspaper was falling behind the radical vanguard of Northern opinion,
not shaping it. Referring to a *Tribune* editorial arguing "against resistance
to the general government," the reader declared that such a policy would
essentially "yield Kansas to the slave power." "Resort to a revolution" was
only a matter of time: "Some of Greeley's arguments against resistance are
good. Others will disappear as soon as the first blow is struck."[14]

Abolitionists, who had objected to the federal government's tolerance of
slavery for decades, were swift to condemn the Kansas situation. New in
the abolitionist critique at this time, however, was a call for direct action
against a nearby evil, not simply moral suasion. For example, the abolitionist newspaper the *National Anti-Slavery Standard* resolved "that constitutional liberty has ceased to exist . . . that we are living under . . . 'Border-
Ruffianism,' incarnated in the person of Franklin Pierce—no longer the
legitimate President of the United States, but one deserving of . . . removal
for his . . . treason as the . . . tool of the Slave Power; and, therefore, that
we are in the midst of a revolution, to throw off the chains of a slaveholding oligarchy a thousand times more intolerable . . . than any ever imposed
upon our Revolutionary fathers by the mother country." Abolitionists used
Kansas to turn earlier invocations of the American Revolution on their
head. Instead of commemorating the Revolution for the precedent-setting
tranquility allegedly maintained during the movement for independence,
abolitionists embraced its example of radical change. This outlook was not
new by 1856. What was new was the abolitionists' embrace of the revolutionary generation's validation of violence—now against an American
authority whose form of rule had become that of a European tyrant.[15]

The fiery writings of Thomas Wentworth Higginson bear witness to this
abolitionist understanding of the presence of European-like conditions on
American soil. A Unitarian minister and journalist, as well as an abolitionist, Higginson had led an 1854 attack on the Boston Court House in a failed
attempt to free the remitted runaway slave Anthony Burns. Two years later
Higginson traveled to Kansas as a correspondent for the *New York Tribune*.

Contrary to the thrust of earlier American opinion, which scoffed at the possibility of violent European conditions breaking out in the United States, Higginson confirmed precisely these conditions' existence. For Higginson Free Soilers were the "Kossuths of Kansas," because they faced not only their "natural enemy," proslavery Missourians, whom he likened to the troops of Austria, but also "the troops of the United States," which, like the forces of Russia, represented the interests of a distant authoritarian government. Higginson met these "Free State men," who were being "driven out" of Kansas under pressure from Missourians, who "had only to point at a man as identified with any measure of public defense, and he was seized at once." "It was like entering Hungary just after the treachery of Görgey," reported Higginson, his readers already familiar with this black-hearted Hungarian general.[16]

But more than simply comparing Kansas to Hungary, Higginson went further, observing that the differences between American slave and free interests were no less stark than the differences among the various nations of Europe. Traveling on the Missouri River, he shared a meal with some sixty other male passengers, "not half of whom," Higginson remarked, "belong[ed] to the same nation with [him]self." Most of the passengers aboard were from various Southern states. "I find myself more alone than I should be among English, French, or Russians," was this Northerner's telling observation. Back in Boston Higginson would again remark that his Kansas experience had convinced him that "there are no two nations in Europe so absolutely antagonistic as the Free-State and the Slave-State men of this Union"—a sentiment shared by other abolitionists and free-labor workingmen who in 1856 moved into the emergent Republican Party. The recent revolutionary conflicts of Europe had conditioned men like Higginson, though they already opposed slavery, to see the conflict in Kansas as a clash between "two nations."[17] In such a clash antislavery forces became the forces of revolution, attempting, as had many European revolutionaries, to match geographic boundaries with nationalistic identity.[18]

Comments by Americans beyond radical antislavery circles attested to the fact that fear had spread that events in Kansas were aligning with European treachery and therefore marked apocalypse for American political fortunes. A New England minister preached, "Kansas is our Sebastopol. . . . [After] a fanatical war . . . some Napoleon III will take the reins of empire; and so many white men as may be left will make up with the

negro the slave population of America. . . . And when the Union is dissolved, Freedom bids the Western Hemisphere farewell." According to
a popular magazine: "It is obvious . . . that the great conflict is drawing
to a head. . . . The coming presidential election [1856] . . . is marshaling
the two orders of civilization to a final encounter. . . . Kansas[,] . . . the
geographical centre of the western continent, is also the pivot of its most
vital and determinative controversy. . . . What France is to Europe—this
region of Kansas will be to the great valley of the west. It holds the key to
. . . civilization. . . . From its capacious womb shall proceed the busy millions destined to redeem or to disgrace the extensive fields beyond. . . .
The character to be impressed on the early society of Kansas is profoundly
important." Elsewhere, an Episcopal minister in Kansas wrote that the
rituals and antiabolitionist fury of a gang of border ruffians "had but one
parallel—the famed Jacobin Club, in France, with Robespierre at its head."
Whereas Americans had earlier shuddered over events across the Atlantic,
"a most vital and determinative controversy" was now raging within the
present and future keystone of the republic. How could citizens hope to
"redeem . . . the extensive fields beyond" if they allowed allegedly distant
violence to take root at home? Recent scenes from Europe clarified the
threat slavery posed to the current generation of Americans and to anyone
who might seek America or come under its sway in the future.[19]

Meanwhile, a host of important antislavery politicians, representing a
broad Northern constituency, reached similar conclusions. Charles Sumner of Massachusetts rose in the Senate in May 1856 to condemn what
he called the "Crime Against Kansas," describing how proslavery settlers
were committing "the rape of a virgin Territory, compelling it to the hate-
ful embrace of slavery." For him the besmirching of Kansas resembled a
corrupt Roman governor's plundering of Sicily and Apollo's lustful pursuit
of Daphne. Such lurid images from antiquity and mythology dramatized
Sumner's speech.[20]

But Sumner's address also suggested a replication in Kansas of more
recent scenes of European suffering. His reference to Sicily called upon
Americans' awareness of the tortuous underground prisons in which Ferdinand, King of Sicily, had placed republican rebels in the denouement of
1848. The prisons were "hell triumphant," in the words of Frederick Law
Olmstead, places whose inmates "go mad, become idiots, or die," reported
Harper's Magazine. Sumner compared the "self-sacrifice" of the women of

the sacked town of Lawrence to the sacrifices of the "matrons of Rome" and the "wives of Prussia," who had given up jewels and spun soldiers' clothing to help repel Napoleon. In attesting to the unlikelihood of violent European despotism coming to America, Abraham Lincoln in 1837 had scoffed at the prospect of a Napoleon watering his horses on the Ohio. Now, ironically, proslavery hordes seemed like the emperor's legions. Sumner was shocked that such a crime could occur "here in our Republic," because it showed "force—aye, sir, force—has been openly employed in compelling Kansas to this pollution." Sumner's descriptions, especially of female suffering, suggested that the pristine United States was losing its purity to an invader perpetrating sexual violence. Stunningly, Sumner's implied censure of Southern sexual morality provoked South Carolina congressman Preston Brooks to assault him on the Senate floor, administering a beating so severe that Sumner had to leave Congress until 1859. Brooks's attack was evidence to Northern newspapers that "violence has now found its way into the Senate chamber. . . . Violence is the order of the day; the North is to be pushed to the wall by it," and "now the enemy is within our borders."[21]

But this was only the beginning. In the summer of 1856 President Pierce sent an appropriations bill to Congress asking that the U.S. military enter Kansas in order to support the territorial government and ensure the maintenance of law and order. Such an apparently sensible provision created a firestorm among Northern members of Congress, who interpreted it to mean, in the words of New York senator William Seward, that Kansas was not a "civil community, with a republican system of government. In other words, it is [not] . . . a Republic—an American Republic." Recall how Americans abroad had ridiculed the ongoing military presence in revolutionary Europe as an emphatic sign of American difference from the Old World. Seward's statement testified to the prospect of transatlantic violence that now influenced American political culture. Only in this way could Kansas, "the geographical centre of the western continent," on whose "capacious womb" the future depended, not seem an "American Republic."[22]

Other politicians also testified to this view. Proclaiming Kansas's territorial constitution a "code of tyranny and oppression," Indiana congressman Schuyler Colfax illustrated the point by cataloging the draconian actions of Louis Napoleon in France since 1850: "The mockery of the pretended freedom of elections . . . the shackles upon the freedom of speech; all . . . emanate from an autocrat who . . . governs France with a strong arm and an iron rule." Based on the measuring stick of French authoritarianism, reasoned Colfax, "no man can rise from a candid perusal of this [Kansas] code without being convinced that it . . . was dictated and enacted by usurpers and tyrants."[23]

Congressman Timothy Day of Ohio shared Colfax's concern and drew particular attention to the alarming similarity of voting procedures in Kansas and France. Day declared that Kansas's political practices were "the [kind of] 'popular sovereignty' the present usurper of France permitted its people to have after the coup d'etat, by which he won his way to a throne through blood and carnage: if you vote as directed, you can vote—if not, not." Day referred to the 1851 plebiscite organized by Louis Napoleon to legitimize his new regime, in which American observers suspected voter intimidation. Universal male suffrage was sacred in American society, partly explaining the controversy surrounding the women's movement of 1848. Thus, abuses of the institution deeply disturbed Americans, as Day's recall of an infamous French day five years in the past attested. The American fear of European-style political violence made reports out of Kansas take on an inordinately sinister significance.[24]

Most significant, American spokesmen began to question the long-standing assumption that "law and order" should prevail, if such a concept connoted the authoritative violence that Americans had earlier shunned across the Atlantic. It might be better, in other words, if law and order of the kind gripping Kansas were not sanctioned, but replaced by a morally authoritative lawlessness. The use of the U.S. military to enforce order in Kansas seemed particularly foreboding. The commander of the U.S. cavalry sent to the town of Lawrence told its mayor, "Without obeyance to the law there is an end to order." But order gained at the point of the bayonet was precisely what frightened antislavery observers; the situation evoked ghastly European scenes. The *New York Times,* for example, warned against "the seizure of our political rights by a foreign foe," while a Northern magazine characterized U.S. military force in administering Kansas's first election for the territory's legislative constitution as perpetrated by "a foreign army," which "marched into the polling places, as the French army, in 1848, filed through the streets of Rome."[25]

Politicians shared these sentiments. Ohio governor Salmon Chase

THE DAY OF
OUR ENSLAVEMENT!!

To-day, Sept. 15, 1855, is the day on which the ini-

quitous enactment of an illegitimate, illegal and fraudulent Legislature have declared commences the prostration of the Right of Speech and the curtailment of the LIBERTY OF THE PRESS!! To-day commences an Era in Kansas which, unless the sturdy voice of the People, backed, if necessary, by "strong arms and the sure eye," shall teach the tyrants who attempt to enthrall us the lesson which our Fathers taught to kingly tyrants of old, shall prostrate us in the dust, and make us the slaves of an Oligarchy

Worse than the veriest Despotism on Earth!

To-day commences the operation of a law which declares: "Sec. 12. If any free person, by speaking or by writing, assert or maintain that persons have not the right to hold slaves in this Territory, or shall introduce into this Territory, print, publish, write, circulate or cause to be introduced into this Territory, written, printed, published or circulated in this Territory, any book, paper, magazine, pamphlet or circular, containing any denial of the right of persons to hold slaves in this Territory, such person shall be deemed guilty of Felony, and punished by imprisonment at hard labor for a term of not less than two years."

Now we DO ASSERT and we declare, despite all the

bolts and bars of the iniquitous Legislature of Kansas, that

"PERSONS HAVE NOT THE RIGHT TO HOLD SLAVES IN THIS TERRITORY."

And we will emblazon it upon our banner in letters so large and in language so plain that the infatuated invaders who elected the Kansas Legislature, as well as

THAT CORRUPT AND IGNORANT LEGISLATURE

Itself, may understand it — so that, if they cannot read,

they may SPELL IT OUT, and meditate and deliberate upon it; and we hold that the man who fails to utter this self-evident truth, on account of the insolent enactment alluded to, is a poltroon and a slave worse than the black slaves of our persecutors and oppressors.

The Constitution of the United States, the great Magna Charta of American Liberties,

Guarantees to every Citizen the Liberty of Speech and the Freedom of the Press!

And this is the first time in the history of America that a body claiming Legislative powers has dared to attempt to wrest them from the people. And it is not only the right, but the bounden duty of every Freeman to spurn with contempt and trample under foot an enactment which thus basely violates the rights of Freemen. For our part we DO and SHALL CONTINUE to utter this truth so long as we have the power of utterance, and nothing but the brute force of an overbearing tyranny can prevent us.

Will any citizen — any free American — brook the insult of

AN INSOLENT GAG LAW!!

the work of a Legislature elected by bullying ruffians who invaded Kansas with arms, and whose drunken revelry, and insults to our peaceable, unoffending, and comparatively unarmed citizens, were a disgrace to manhood, and a burlesque upon popular Republican Government! If they do, they are slaves already, and with them Freedom is but a mockery.

FIGURE 7. [Lawrence] *Kansas Tribune*, 15 September 1855, reporting developments in Kansas as "worse than the veriest Despotism on Earth!" In the mid-1850s many Americans interpreted territorial violence in the context of European revolution and counter-revolution. (Courtesy of Kansas State Historical Society) denounced the capture of one hundred antislavery partisans by U.S. troops in Kansas as "illegal violence against citizens," who were "prompted by the same motives, which led our fathers in the days of the revolution to organize for the defence of life, home, and property against the tools of tyranny." Likewise, Representative Galusha Grow of Pennsylvania used ugly scenes from Europe to illustrate the magnitude of the abuse of "law and order" in the Kansas territory:

> With the shout of law and order you seize law-abiding citizens, and by mob law exile them from their homes. . . . With the shout of law and order you arrest and put in chains order-loving citizens . . . for peaceably petitioning the Government for a redress of grievances. . . . Law and order is the excuse of despotism, the world over. . . . It was to preserve law and order that . . . the dungeon and the rack silenced the voice of patriotism in Hungary. To preserve law and order, the streets of Naples are crowded with chained gangs . . . guilty of no offence save that they hate oppression and love liberty.

The maintenance of peaceful domestic relations, a system on which American commentators had built an ideology for the purpose of keeping dangerous Europe at a distance, seemed, amid the Kansas conflict, to mean something entirely different: the promiscuity of violence in the name of law and order. Poland, Grow noted ominously, saw "its streets red with the best blood of its citizens," not before but after a Russian general had suppressed a popular uprising and delivered to the czar the notorious report, "Order reigns in Warsaw." Once again, but now on the American plains, "the scaffold sends its victim to a quiet rest, and order reigns over his grave," Grow warned. Now the governor of Kansas intended to "send a like dispatch to his superior, 'Order reigns in Kansas.'"[26]

William Seward, perhaps the most prominent antislavery member of Congress, echoed Grow's warning in the Senate. Under the prevailing conditions Seward found it necessary to remind his listeners that "according to the theory of our Government . . . if the laws [of Kansas] are really the statutes of . . . a republican government truly existing there, then . . . the laws will be acquiesced in . . . and executed with [popular] consent against all offenders." Such conditions had prevailed in the past and indeed, according to Seward, continued to prevail "from the Gulf of St. Lawrence to the Gulf of Mexico." On account of its violence, therefore, Kansas presented an illegitimate aberration, given Americans' assumptions about their domestic stability, which Seward reconfirmed.

Kansas's significance, however, lay not only in its current circumstances but in what it portended for the erstwhile peaceful American republic. As Seward continued, "A proposition to employ the standing army of the United States as a domestic police [should be] universally denounced as a premature revelation of a plot, darkly contrived in the chambers of conspiracy, to subvert the liberties of the people, and to overthrow the Republic itself." Historians have shown how the invocation of "conspiracy" to explain menacing developments dates to the early days of American political culture, so Seward's identification of its existence in Kansas was hardly original.[27] But his interpretation of events was momentous because he reiterated his summons to defiance of "law and order" and emphasized that failure to consider such action would sentence the republic to a fate reminiscent of the doomed revolutionaries of Europe: "I know the value of peace, and order, and tranquility. I know how essential they are to prosperity. . . . But I know also the still greater value of Liberty. When you hear me justify the despotism of the Czar of Russia over the oppressed Poles, or the treachery by which Louis Napoleon rose to a throne on the ruins of the Republic in France, on the ground that he preserves domestic peace among his subjects, then you may expect me to vote supplies of men and money to the President . . . to execute the edicts of the Missouri borderers in the Territory of Kansas." William Seward joined other Northern political leaders in confirming that treatment of the slavery issue in Kansas was unprecedented in American political practice. In particular, violence committed by federal military forces violated the principle of governmental noninterference in territorial affairs, as well as the spirit of popular sovereignty. For Seward and others such deployment bore too striking a resemblance to the draconian steps taken by European rulers in asserting ultraconservative authority.[28]

Most important, Seward's protest of federal enforcement reflected a new Northern mindset that would with time contribute to armed conflict on a massive scale. In the context of the Kansas conflict mimicking the restoration of authoritarian stability in counterrevolutionary Europe, calls for "law and order" actually had become inflammatory among antislavery Northerners by the mid-1850s. They began to call instead for "revolution"

and saw the Republican Party as either the fulfillment of a new revolutionary impulse or as a penultimate step before replacing political efforts to
change the government with violence. Just as a journalist described the
formation of the Republican Party in 1856 as a "revolution," a citizen in
Massachusetts wrote that the Republican presidential candidate that year
needed to "be a man all lovers of freedom can unite on, as that seems to be
the only hope—short of a bloody revolution." Defenders of slavery in the
South and the North quickly began to describe the Republican Party as an
alien "Jacobin" and "Red Republican" force, on the basis of the party's rapid
mobilization against the legitimacy of slavery and the two-party system as
a means to negotiate its solution.[29] These proslavery critics were correct.
Beginning with their reaction to Kansas, the Republicans reenacted the
recent European revolutionary movements, rejecting the traditional belief
that the United States was a place immune to revolutionary violence of
the sort that troubled the Old World, an alleged bequeathal of America's
revolutionary origins. Violence in Kansas thus became an opening episode
of the ultimate U.S. response to the violent midcentury upheavals of Europe: a resort to bullets, not ballots. Only through this reenactment could
Americans join "the world of the nineteenth century," in the words of Carl
Schurz in 1860.[30]

That Schurz, before he became a Republican leader, was a "forty-
eighter," having arrived in America only in 1852, suggests the importance
of German revolutionary refugees to the formation of the Republican
Party and the radicalization of the antislavery movement after 1848. In
1848 Secretary of State James Buchanan had reminded Andrew Donelson,
the U.S. minister to Prussia and to the Frankfurt Assembly, of the "large
portion of our population consist[ing] of Germans and their descendants."
Thus, any helpful action Donelson could take to support republicanism
in the German states would of course play favorably among this growing constituency. In 1848 German Americans normally supported the
Democratic Party, less nativist and less supportive of temperance and
sabbatarianism than the Whigs. But with the Kansas-Nebraska Act, many
of them, especially urban revolutionary refugees, swung to Republican
ranks, coming to view slaveholders in the same light as European aristocrats. In 1852 a German American congress met in Wheeling, Virginia,
led by the self-styled "red republican" Amand Gögg, a recent immigrant,
and Karl Goepp, a former Free Soiler. The congress issued a manifesto

comparing the United States to ancient Rome and declaring the "historical necessity" that America absorb the states of Europe into a global republic dominated by "the universality of the American character." Many German Americans longer resident in the United States, the "Grays," believed that such "Green" radicals were troublemakers and labeled their Wheeling manifesto absurd, making a point of contrasting the forty-eighters with the more practical American revolutionaries of 1776 and 1787. The "Grays" joined nativist politicians such as Henry Winter Davis of Baltimore, who also perceived the divided allegiances of the forty-eighters. In 1855 Davis complained, "Generally foreigners were Free-Soilers or Abolitionists— deeply prejudiced against Southern institutions," and "Foreigners owing allegiance to European Sovereigns now have a final voice in deciding . . . the question of freedom or slavery in its fundamental law." Davis exaggerated the uniformity of antislavery opinion among immigrants, but he correctly understood that the German forty-eighters questioned the relevance of the American revolutionary tradition to emerging circumstances and saw Republican mobilization as a way to bring a radical European influence to combat reactionary aristocracy. Their desire for a vindicated American global role fitted with an emerging Republican ideology.[31]

Indeed, the convergence of fears about the entry onto American soil of European-style coercive government and the ambition that America should gain, or regain, its stature as an exemplar of liberal democracy explains the influence of the 1848 revolutions on the rise of the Republican Party, as well as its energizing tension. As various antislavery Americans had declared in reaction to the 1848 revolutions, the existence of slavery undermined any claim that the United States might positively influence Europe and the world. Notable Republican leaders explained how this awareness had motivated them. William Seward opposed slavery because it represented national retardation, not progress, and gave comfort to European aristocracy in arresting the 1848 revolutions. He envisioned emancipation as a compensating "democratic revolution," positioning America on the crest of "the tide of social progress." Parke Godwin, a former Fourierite socialist, lamented that slavery "enable[d] [European despots] to depict us one and all as slave drivers and oppressors. . . . Behold, they exclaim, the model republic, behold democracy in practice, behold the boasted freedom of America. . . . It is in vain that the leaders of the liberal movement try to explain away this imputed disgrace." Charles Sumner complained, "Slavery degrades our country," preventing its "example" from leading the world to the "universal restoration of power to the governed." Abraham Lincoln emphasized, "I hate [slavery] because it deprives our republican example of its just influence in the world—enables the enemies of free institutions, with plausibility, to taunt us as hypocrites."[32]

As the Free Soilers had, the Republican Party leadership understood and sought to protect America's unique opportunity for economic independence. But to this concern Republicans added another crucial element, which the 1848 revolutions had implanted in Northern opinion: the cause of human rights. Thus, Congressman Joshua Giddings of Ohio called for the 1860 Republican Party platform to endorse the egalitarian sentiments of the Declaration of Independence, not because he felt Republicans should pay homage to the American Revolution, but because omission of this "declaration of human rights" would be "low" and "insidious." Only through the realization that new revolutionary violence would be appropriate in America, no less so than in Europe, could both American exemplarism be preserved and American influence extended. Harriet Beecher Stowe's question, "Is America safe?" really was a question about whether American "exceptionalism" was intact. Acceptance of justifiable and even necessary violence by a broadening Northern antislavery movement in the 1850s revealed that America, in fact, was not. The Civil War, "as the final disturbance of the earthquake that convulsed Europe in 1848," would dramatically confirm this.[33]

Epilogue
From 1848 to 1863

The relationship between the European upheavals of 1848 and the American reaction beginning in 1849, the disruption of the American political system in the 1850s, and the North's prosecution of the Civil War may be recapitulated by a focus on two Northern antislavery men, John Brown and Abraham Lincoln. Brown was considered insane by some contemporaries and earlier historians, although scholars have more recently asserted his unflinching commitment to the antislavery cause and his apparently rational view of what his raid at Harpers Ferry, whether or not it sparked a slave uprising, would do to exacerbate sectional hostility.[1]

While historians have restored Brown's sanity, however, until recently they have overlooked his manifestation of ideas and actions grounded in European politics and warfare. His guerrilla military tactics, as well as his sense of the stakes of America's impending sectional conflict, should be emphasized: they locate Brown as a "cis-Atlantic" revolutionary, observing radical developments in the Atlantic world and applying interpretations of those developments to American conditions.[2] Before he went to Kansas, Brown acquainted himself with guerrilla warfare in European history, reading accounts of Portuguese and Spanish resistance to Napoleon in the Pyrenees Mountains. He traveled to Europe in 1849 on a business trip but took time to study notable battlefields. He gathered around himself associates sharing experience in the 1848 revolutions, including Hugh Forbes, a British soldier who had served under Giuseppe Garibaldi; Charles Leonhardt, a Polish revolutionary; the Bavarian Charles Kaiser and August Bondi of Vienna, two soldiers who had fought with Louis Kossuth; and Richard Hinton, who had fled England to avoid arrest for his Chartist activities. Brown's notorious tactics in Kansas—the size of his guerrilla band, his belief in the capacity of slaves to rise up and organize, once inspired; and his choice of Virginia terrain for his anticipated slave rebellion—all reflect, as historians have noted, his admiration for enslaved Africans who had overthrown their masters and established free communities in Florida, Jamaica, and Haiti. But these aspects of his strategy also parallel the doctrines of the Italian revolutionary Giuseppe Mazzini. Brown, like Mazzini, sought to provoke a revolutionary uprising among peasants against despotic authorities, and Brown surrounded himself with sources and individuals that could teach him about the violent nationalist uprisings in Europe.[3]

In Kansas, moreover, before going east to Virginia, Brown voiced concern that should the new Republican Party somehow gain power, "there will be war," because Southern proslavery interests "will go out" of the Union. Brown believed the slave power would hardly find itself without allies, however, because it would "get the countenance and aid of the European nations, until American republicanism and freedom are overthrown." Earlier in the 1850s Brown had joined most other Americans in rejoicing at the arrival of Kossuth in America. "The last news . . . that all Europe will soon again be in a blaze" excited Brown then because of his "full belief that God is carrying out his eternal purpose in them all." But his later effort to vindicate the antislavery cause through violence and his methods for doing so undoubtedly had some roots in his sense that encroachments of the slave power represented not only the threat but also the arrival of hostile European conditions in America.[4]

Brown's trial and especially his execution at Harper's Ferry provoked a swell of antislavery sympathy in the Northern states and in Europe. Brown became seen as a martyr among antislavery groups on both sides of the Atlantic, a role that Mazzini said a guerrilla revolutionary must be willing to play to encourage nationalist uprising. Virginia state authorities tried and executed Brown for treason, but his fate seemed confirmation of the gathering in America of a malevolent Atlantic host.[5]

For example, in his "Plea for Captain John Brown," Henry David Thoreau observed: "We dream of foreign countries, of other times and races of men, placing them at a distance in history or space; but let some significant event like the present occur in our midst, and we discover, often, this distance and this strangeness between us and our nearest neighbors. They are our Austrias, and Chinas, and South Sea Islands." Thoreau meant to criticize more moderate antislavery supporters' attempt to distance themselves from Brown's fanatical scheme and demise. But his words also suggested the alienation of Americans one from another, the sense that opponents in the mounting slavery crisis were a foreign menace. Likewise, for Thoreau what happened to John Brown punctuated the national government's abandonment of republican principle and complicity with or takeover by European powers intent to destroy liberal democracy. He continued: "'All is quiet at Harper's Ferry,' say the journals. What is the character of that calm which follows when the law and the slaveholder prevail? I regard this event as a touchstone designed to bring out, with glaring distinctness, the character of this government. . . . It is more manifest than ever that tyranny rules. I see this government to be effectually allied with France and Austria in oppressing mankind. . . . This most hypocritical and diabolical government . . . inquires . . . 'What do you assault me for? Cease agitation on this subject, or I will make a slave of you, too, or else hang you.'" Articulating the central question that animated antislavery Northerners, who had decided that America needed to emulate the European revolutionaries of 1848, Thoreau asked, "Are laws to be enforced simply because they were made?"[6]

Abraham Lincoln was one of the antislavery moderates who sought to distance the Republican Party from Brown's dramatic raid. But Lincoln did see the Republican Party itself as part of a transatlantic liberal movement, because its ascension to power and the Southern secession that his election precipitated would create the opportunity to save American republicanism—as he put it in his 1862 message to Congress, the "last best hope of earth." Lincoln's opposition to secession suggests a contradiction of his support in the 1840s for Hungary's right to declare independence from Austria. Then Lincoln argued that all people had the right to overturn the existing government and to establish one more suitable for themselves. Several historians have offered explanations of Lincoln's rationale for suppressing the secession movement even though he declared himself in favor of the fundamental right of all nations to self-determination. James McPherson and Thomas Bender argue that the South in the Civil War was attempting not a revolution, but a counterrevolution; thus, Lincoln was consistent in his opposition to reactionary regimes in both Europe and America. Kenneth Stampp asserts, conversely, that Lincoln was inconsistent in his opposition to Southerners' right of self-determination, that he held two standards of acceptable wars of independence—one foreign, one domestic. What is important to realize about Lincoln's thought and

policies regarding the right of revolution, however, is that his earlier experience of the 1848 revolutions shaped and rationalized his wielding of
political and military authority beginning in 1861. Lincoln committed to
stop the secession movement because he, like other Republican spokesmen, had been both inspired and embarrassed by events in Hungary and
elsewhere in Europe a decade before antislavery forces gained power in
the United States. He thus became committed to consolidating American
power, even at great human sacrifice, so that the country might fulfill its
role as a global model.[7]

Symbolic of Lincoln's twin sympathies to the lessons of the European
revolutions and the legitimacy of coercing the slave states back into the
Union, his explanation of the circumstances he commemorated at Gettysburg in 1863 is worth reconsidering. In his dedication of the battleground, Lincoln explained the ongoing national conflict as a struggle over
the American proposition that "government of the people, by the people,
for the people, shall not perish from the earth." But Lincoln here echoed
the words of Louis Kossuth in an 1852 speech in Ohio.[8] Kossuth himself
probably took the famous expression from Giuseppe Mazzini, who wrote
as early as 1833 that "Young Italy" sought revolution "in the name of the
people, for the people, and by the people." Such imitation reflected Lincoln's admiration for these Europeans' eloquence. It further symbolized
the transatlantic project of democratic reform in the nineteenth century.
But it was also a reminder that this project would be achieved only via
violent national civil wars. The Europeans Kossuth and Mazzini had argued for a right of revolution. As their American counterpart, Lincoln ultimately enforced the same right, for the same purpose. As the careers of
the Hungarian, the Italian, and the American attest, history does not show
popularly accountable governments being achieved or sustained without
significant violence.[9]

The 1848 revolutions allow an international perspective on the American republic in its formative years. In their failed quests for greater liberty,
these revolutions did not follow the American example of a republican
revolution. Instead, in the way that they revealed a deep-seated conservatism in American politics and society and then helped create destabilizing
changes that would lead to the Civil War, they had even more dramatic
consequences for the United States, as did the French Revolution of the
eighteenth century and the Russian Revolution of the twentieth. The 1848

revolutions reveal antebellum Americans' understanding of their relations with the outside world and how these relations affected American society, challenging and redirecting, if not ending, belief and practice in American exceptionalism. Their impact should signal us that while our comparison of foreign revolutions to what we believe about our own revolutionary origins may be unavoidable, judgment of foreign revolutionaries on such a standard is dangerous. The legacy of 1848 is that our cultivation and preservation of democracy, both abroad and at home, depends not only on tolerance for other possible democrats' eccentricities but also on a willingness to act on our own democratic shortcomings.

Chronology of Events, 1848–1854

1848

12 January	Revolt in Palermo
10 February	Constitution in Naples
21 February	Publication of *Communist Manifesto* in London
22–24 February	Revolution in Paris Abdication of Louis Philippe, King of the French Proclamation of the French Second Republic Proclamation of the abolition of colonial slavery Establishment of national labor workshops
28 February	U.S. Minister Richard Rush recognizes French Second Republic
2 March	Universal manhood suffrage proclaimed in France
3 March	Louis Kossuth's revolutionary speech for Hungarian self-government
10 March	U.S. Senate ratifies Treaty of Guadaloupe Hidalgo, ending U.S.–Mexican War
13–15 March	Insurrection in Vienna Prince Klemens von Metternich resigns
14 March	Constitution in Papal States
15–20 March	Violent "March Days" in Berlin Frederick William IV pledges national elections Prussia to be absorbed into a united Germany
18–22 March	Five Days of Milan: insurrection there and in Venice, where republic is proclaimed Kingdom of Piedmont declares war on Austria
26 March	Nicholas I condemns revolutionary events in Europe
10 April	Chartist demonstration in London
12–20 April	Republican uprising in Baden led by Friedrich Hecker

23 April	Popular elections to French national assembly
25 April	Constitution announced for the Austrian empire
29 April	Pope Pius IX proclaims Papal States' neutrality
15 May	Ferdinand suppresses Neapolitan parliament: collapse of revolt in Sicily
17 May	Renewed insurrection in Vienna Hapsburg dynasty flees to Innsbruck
18 May	German national assembly, elected by universal male suffrage, meets in Frankfurt
22 May	Prussian national assembly convenes Democratic Party convention, Baltimore
2–17 June	Slav Congress in Prague Slavic uprising quelled by Austrian force under Prince Alfred Windischgrätz
7 June	Whig Party convention, Philadelphia
23–26 June	"June Days" violence in Paris Suppression of national workshops General Louis Eugène Cavaignac defeats the insurrection and becomes head of government
5 July	Hungarian National Assembly meets in Pest
19 July	Seneca Falls convention on women's rights
29 July	Young Irelander uprising fails in County Tipperary
9 August	U.S. Minister Andrew Jackson Donelson appointed minister to "the Federal Government of Germany" Free Soil Party convention, Buffalo
12 August	Austrian imperial court returns to Vienna
7 September	Emancipation from serfdom in the Hapsburg Empire
17 September	Austrian empire invades Hungary
21 September	Outbreak of second republican uprising in Baden, led by Gustav Struve, who proclaims a "German Republic"
6–31 October	Student and worker insurrection in Vienna Dynasty flees to Olmütz Insurrection quelled by Windischgrätz
7 November	Zachary Taylor elected U.S. president over Lewis Cass and Martin Van Buren
9 November	Austrians execute Robert Blum, of the Frankfurt Assembly, for supporting Viennese revolutionaries

16–25 November	Insurrection in Rome Flight of Pius IX to Gaeta
2 December	Abdication of Emperor Ferdinand of Austria, succeeded by Franz Joseph
5 December	Military occupation of Berlin Prussian national assembly dissolved
10 December	Presidential election in France: victory of Louis Napoleon

1849

21 January	Popular elections in the Papal States for constitutional government
9 February	Establishment of Roman Republic
4–7 March	Constitution dictated in Austria, no special status given to Hungary
22 March	Battle of Novara: Austrian troops defeat forces of Sardinia and Piedmont Charles Albert abdicates throne to Victor Emmanuel II
2–3 April	Frankfurt Assembly produces all-German constitution and invites Frederick William IV to become German emperor; he rejects the offer
14 April	Hungarian Parliament declares independence from Austria Recognition of German constitution by twenty-eight German states
16 April	France sends troops against Roman Republic to restore Pius IX
6–17 June	Under pressure from Prussian military, "Rump" of Frankfurt Assembly meets at Stuttgart, then dissolves
16 June	Russian armies invade Hungary
18 June	President Taylor nominates envoy to Hungarians
1–2 July	Fall of Roman Republic
9–13 August	Final defeat of Hungarian armies Kossuth abdicates to General Arthur Görgey and escapes to Turkey
28 August	Fall of Venetian Republic to Austria

1850

29 January	Henry Clay presents compromise measures to the U.S. Senate over issue of slavery
31 March	Death of John C. Calhoun

3–12 June	First secession convention in Nashville
9 July	President Taylor dies, succeeded by Millard Filmore
19 July	Margaret Fuller, returning from Europe, drowns off New York coast
18 September	Compromise of 1850 passed by U.S. Congress, including the Fugitive Slave Act
11–18 November	Second Nashville convention
Secession impulse defeated

1851

7 April	British Member of Parliament William Gladstone exposes the cruel prison system of the Kingdom of Naples
5 June	*Uncle Tom's Cabin* first appears in serial form in the *National Era*
2 December	Coup d'état of Louis Napoleon and dissolution of the National Assembly
5 December	Kossuth's arrival in the United States

1852

14 July	Kossuth leaves the United States
7 November	Franklin Pierce elected U.S. president over Winfield Scott and John Hale
21–22 November	Plebiscite confirms end of French Second Republic and establishes Second Empire
2 December	Louis Napoleon proclaimed Emperor Napoleon III

1853

31 May	Nicolas dispatches Russian troops to protect Christians in Turkey, precipitating the Crimean War
12–13 October	Last Universal Peace Congress, Edinburgh

1854

20 March	Mass political meeting in Ripon, Wisconsin, advocates establishment of the Republican Party
27–28 March	Britain and France declare war on Russia, widening Crimean War
30 May	Kansas-Nebraska Act passed, opening Western territories to slavery
24 May–2 June	Trial and rendition of Anthony Burns pursuant to Fugitive Slave Law

Notes

Introduction

1. U.S. Congress, House, "Dedication . . . of a Bust of Lajos (Louis) Kossuth." This work will use the spelling of Kossuth's first name (Louis) used by most Americans during the European Revolutions of 1848.

2. Literature on this idea is large, but see Americans' various early assertions of their differences from Europe in Greene, *Intellectual Construction of America*, chapter 6; R. Ellis, *American Political Cultures*, chapter 2; Glickstein, *American Exceptionalism*; Cohen, *Cambridge History of American Foreign Relations*; and B. Perkins, *Creation of a Republican Empire*. For more contemporary applications see Shafer, *Is America Different?*; McEvoy-Levy, *American Exceptionalism and U.S. Foreign Policy*; and "Defining America."

3. U.S. Congress, House, "Dedication . . . of a Bust of Lajos (Louis) Kossuth," 8, 14, 73–75.

4. Pells, *Not Like Us*, xiv.

5. Different viewpoints are Serfaty, *European Unity*; Kagan, *Of Paradise and Power*; and Rifkin, *European Dream*.

6. Armitage and Braddick, *British Atlantic World 1500–1800*, 23 (quotation), 24. Recent surveys of American history from a global perspective are Bender, *Nation among Nations*; Davies, *United States in World History*; Guarneri, *America in the World*; and Tyrrell, *Transnational Nation*.

7. My interpretation is informed by B. Perkins, *Creation of a Republican Empire*; D. B. Davis, *Revolutions*; and Williams, *America Confronts a Revolutionary World*.

8. B. Perkins, *Creation of a Republican Empire*, 13.

9. Sked, "Metternich System"; Sauvigny, *Metternich and His Times*, 157–300; Church, *Europe in 1830*; Broers, *Europe after Napoleon*, 9–18, 106–20; Gildea, *Barricades and Borders*, 20–79.

10. Brands, *What America Owes the World*, vii, 2–9; Pappas, *United States and the Greek War*; Whitaker, *United States and the Independence*.

11. Karl Marx to Friedrich Engels, 7 June 1849, in Marx and Engels, *Collected Works*, 38: 199; Price, *French Second Republic*, 31–94; Agulhon, *Republican Experiment*, 22–48; Fortescue, *Alphonse de Lamartine*, 151–73; Drescher, "British Way, French Way."

12. *London Times*, 21 Mar. 1848. The best surveys of the 1848 revolutions are Sperber, *European Revolutions;* Evans and Pogge von Strandmann, *Revolutions in Europe 1848–1849;* Dowe et al., *Europe in 1848;* and P. Robertson, *Revolutions of 1848.*

13. Valentin, *1848,* 52–59, 176–85, 223–37; Eyck, *Frankfurt Parliament of 1848–1849,* 42–56; Noyes, *Organization and Revolution,* 57–86.

14. R. J. W. Evans, "1848–1849 in the Habsburg Monarchy," 181–88; D. M. Smith, "Revolutions of 1848–1849 in Italy," 62; D. M. Smith, *Mazzini,* 49–60; Ginsborg, *Daniele Manin,* 79–125.

15. Deák, *Lawful Revolution,* 60–138.

16. See A. Hunt, *Haiti's Influence on Antebellum America;* Langley, *Americas in the Age of Revolution,* 102–42.

17. Sperber, *European Revolutions,* 1; Agulhon, *Republican Experiment,* 40–63; Price, *French Second Republic,* 127–92; Tocqueville quoted in G. Ellis, "Revolution of 1848–1849 in France," 41, 42; Bernstein, *New York City Draft Riots,* 5, 60.

18. Valentin, *1848,* 272; Eyck, *Frankfurt Parliament of 1848–1849,* 42–46, 57–95, 288–332; Sperber, *European Revolutions,* 138–40. A copy of the Frankfurt Assembly's constitution appears in Hucko, *Democratic Tradition,* 3–23.

19. Deák, *Lawful Revolution,* 155–210.

20. Trevelyan, *Garibaldi's Defence,* 44–50; Price, "'Holy Struggle against Anarchy,'" 40; Langeweische, "Role of the Military," 702.

21. D. M. Smith, *Mazzini,* 12–39; Soldani, "Approaching Europe"; Palmerston quoted in Griffith, *Mazzini,* 220.

22. Agulhon, *Republican Experiment,* 69–80. For American perceptions of Louis Napoleon, see Casper, *American Attitudes.*

23. D. M. Smith, *Mazzini,* 64–149; McArthur, *Oregon Geographic Names,* 253.

24. Plessis, *Rise and Fall.*

25. Proudhon quoted in G. Ellis, "Revolution of 1848–1849 in France," 45.

26. Valentin, *1848,* 361–75; Eyck, *Frankfurt Parliament of 1848–1849,* 214–46, 332–43; Wittke, *Refugees of Revolution,* 36–57.

27. Deák, *Lawful Revolution,* 210–348.

28. Hohenberg, *Foreign Correspondence,* 13–21; Bjork, "Commercial Roots"; J. H. Wilson, *Life of Charles A. Dana,* 62–96; L. Reynolds, *European Revolutions,* 5.

29. Lévêque, "Revolutionary Crisis of 1848/51"; G. Ellis, "Revolution of 1848–1849 in France," 28; University of Virginia Library, "Historical Census Browser." On the history of American suffrage, see Keyssar, *Right to Vote.*

30. *Luther v. Borden,* 48 U.S. 1 (1849); *Right of the People; U.S. Constitution,* Article IV, section 4; Gettleman, *Dorr Rebellion;* Wiecek, "'Peculiar Conservatism.'"

31. Holt, *Rise and Fall,* 368.

32. McLeod, *Religion and the People,* 1–74; Rémond, *Religion and Society,* 53–66; Hatch, *Democratization of American Christianity;* Gaustad, *Historical Atlas of Religion,* 37–112.

33. Guarneri, *Utopian Alternative.*

34. Kammen, *Season of Youth*, 99; W. F. Craven, *Legend of the Founding Fathers*, 59–64 (quotation on 60); Purcell, *Sealed with Blood*, 1.

35. A. J. P. Taylor, *Revolutions and Revolutionaries*, 3.

36. Studies that assess these American phenomena within an international context are Glickstein, *American Exceptionalism*; D. B. Davis, *Slavery and Human Progress*; Anderson, *Joyous Greetings*; and Messer-Kruse, *Yankee International*.

37. Blumenthal, *Reappraisal of Franco-American Relations*, 4–32; Curti, "Impact of the Revolutions of 1848"; Curti, "Austria and the United States"; Curtis, "American Opinion"; Gazley, *American Opinion of German Unification*; Marraro, *American Opinion*, 312 (quotation); A. J. May, *Contemporary American Opinion*; Whitridge, *Men in Crisis*, 283–326.

38. Gemme, *Italian Risorgimento*; Komlos, *Louis Kossuth in America*; B. Levine, *Spirit of 1848*; Livingston, "Eyes on 'the Whole European World'"; Mize, "Defending Roman Loyalties"; Morrison, "American Reaction to European Revolutions"; L. Reynolds, *European Revolutions*; Rohrs, "American Critics of the French Revolution"; Spencer, *Louis Kossuth and Young America*; Tuchinsky, "Bourgeoisie Will Fall.'"

39. Bender, *Nation among Nations*, 122–24; Potter, "Civil War"; Degler, "One among Many"; McPherson, "Whole Family of Man.'"

40. L. Reynolds, "Righteous Violence."

1. The Ambivalence of Americans Abroad

1. Philip Claiborne Gooch diary, entries for 24 Feb., 2 Mar., 5 Apr., 24 June 1848, Gooch Family Papers; Elizabeth Stiles to Catherine MacKay, 2 July 1848, MacKay and Stiles Family Papers.

2. Sauvigny, "American Travelers in France," 15–18; Mulvey, *Anglo-American Landscapes*, 6–66; Earnest, *Expatriates and Patriots*; Salomone, "Nineteenth Century Discovery of Italy," 1373 (quotation).

3. William Cullen Bryant to Frances Bryant, 13 Aug. 1849, William Cullen Bryant Papers; Mary Emily Donelson Album, entry for 25 Sept. 1848, Andrew Jackson Donelson Papers; Bullard, *Sights and Scenes in Europe*, 87–88; Bryant, *Letters of a Traveller*, 23.

4. Gooch diary, entry for 6 Mar. 1848; *New York Tribune*, 29 Mar. 1848; Duyckinck and Goodrich quoted in L. Reynolds, *European Revolutions*, 10, 6.

5. Richard Rush to James Buchanan, 5 Mar. 1848, and Buchanan to Rush, 31 Mar. 1848, in Buchanan, *Works*, 8: 3–4, 33; Rush, *Occasional Productions*, 368; Peterson, *Recognition of Governments*, 92–93; Goebel, *Recognition Policy*, 171–72; Blumenthal, *Reappraisal of Franco-American Relations*, 12.

6. James Buchanan to Andrew Jackson Donelson, 15 Aug. 1848, in Buchanan, *Works*, 8: 167–69; Wittke, *Refugees of Revolution*, 37; Gazley, *American Opinion of German Unification*, 23.

7. Andrew Jackson Donelson to James Buchanan, 10 Apr., 16, 23, 26 Oct. 1848,

in U.S. Department of State, *Despatches . . . to the German States,* reels 5, 18; Buchanan to Donelson, 18 Dec. 1848, in Buchanan, *Works,* 8: 267; A. J. May, *Contemporary American Opinion,* 48; Adams, *Prussian-American Relations,* 62.

8. C. Brown, *Agents of Manifest Destiny;* R. May, *Manifest Destiny's Underworld.*

9. See Horsman, *Race and Manifest Destiny,* parts 2 and 3.

10. Curti, "George N. Sanders"; Curti, "Young America"; Wittke, *Refugees of Revolution,* 36–38; Nevins, *Ordeal of the Union,* 217; Wilson and Fiske, *Appleton's Cyclopaedia of American Biography,* 5: 215; Wilentz, *Chants Democratic,* 354–87; Szilassy, "America and the Hungarian Revolution," 186.

11. Belchem, "Nationalism, Republicanism and Exile," 114 (quotation); Belchem, "Waterloo of Peace and Order," 245 (quotation); Sloan, *William Smith O'Brien.*

12. James Buchanan to George Bancroft, 23, 28 Oct., 18 Dec. 1848, and Buchanan to William E. Robinson, 15 Nov. 1848, in Buchanan, *Works,* 8: 220, 230–31, 243–44, 266; Bancroft to William H. Prescott, 28 July 1848, William H. Prescott Papers.

13. Steele, *Captain Mayne Reid,* 22–24; Wittke, *Refugees of Revolution,* 38, 101; O'Connor, *Boston Irish,* 68, 74.

14. Thomas Gold Appleton to William Appleton, 10, 16 May 1848, Appleton Family Papers; "Thomas Appleton," in UUA, *Dictionary of Unitarian and Universalist Biography;* L. Hunt, *Politics, Culture, and Class,* 81.

15. L. Reynolds, *European Revolutions,* 47–48 (Dana quotation on 48); Guarneri, *Utopian Alternative,* 336–42 (Dana quotation on 342).

16. Kime, *Donald G. Mitchell,* 10–11; Copeland, *Kendall of the Picayune,* 151–69.

17. *New Orleans Picayune,* 20, 23 July 1848; L. Reynolds, *European Revolutions,* 46–48; Copeland, *Kendall of the Picayune,* 242–47 (quotation on 246).

18. Thomas Gold Appleton to William Appleton, 27 Apr., 27 May 1849, 6 Jan. 1850, Appleton Family Papers.

19. William Stiles to James Buchanan, 16 Mar. 1848, in U.S. Department of State, *Despatches . . . to Austria,* reel T-2; Curti, "Austria and the United States," 150–51.

20. Stiles, *Austria in 1848–49.*

21. Elizabeth Stiles to Catherine MacKay, 2 July 1848, MacKay and Stiles Family Papers; William Stiles to James Buchanan, 18 May 1848, in U.S. Department of State, *Despatches . . . to Austria.*

22. Taking note of the liberal reforms of Pope Pius IX, the Polk administration appointed and the Senate confirmed Jacob Martin as the first American representative ever to the Papal States in April 1848. But Martin died shortly after arriving in Rome, and the post remained vacant until late 1849 (Marraro, *Diplomatic Relations,* 1: 60–61).

23. Marraro, "Unpublished American Documents," 461–62; Marraro, *Diplomatic Relations,* 1: 26; Marraro, *American Opinion,* 70.

24. James Buchanan to John Marston, 31 Oct. 1848, in Buchanan, *Works,* 8: 234; Marraro, *American Opinion,* 71.

25. Margaret Fuller, a columnist for the *New York Tribune* in Rome, wrote an article complaining about the incongruity in U.S. policy regarding France and Italy (*New York Tribune*, 23 June 1849, in Fuller, *These Sad but Glorious Days*, 282–83).

26. Nathaniel Niles to James Buchanan, 24 Dec. 1848, in Marraro, "Unpublished American Documents," 460; John Rowan to Buchanan, 31 May, 3 Mar. 1849, in Marraro, *Diplomatic Relations*, 1: 672–73, 667–71.

27. Clayton quoted in Sioussat, "Selected Letters," 266 n. 38.

28. A. Dudley Mann to John Clayton, 13 June, 27, 9 Sept. 1849, in U.S. Congress, Senate, Senate Documents, 61st Cong., 2nd sess., docs. no. 215, 279 (Washington, D.C., 1979), U.S. serial set no. 5657; Spencer, *Louis Kossuth and Young America*, 24–27; Adams, *Prussian-American Relations*, 60, 58.

29. Barnes, *Life of Thurlow Weed*, 2: 203.

30. Theodore Fay to John Clayton, 24 May 1850, in U.S. Department of State, *Despatches . . . to the German States*, reel 6; William Stiles to James Buchanan, 1 Mar. 1849, in U.S. Department of State, *Despatches . . . to Austria*, reel T-2. Walsh's comment appeared in the *New York Journal of Commerce* (quotation from Casper, *American Attitudes*, 173).

31. "Financial and Commercial Review"; U.S. Congress, House, Select Committee on the Tobacco Trade, *Report [of] the Select Committee;* James Buchanan to Andrew Jackson Donelson, 15 Aug. 1848; [F. Hunt,] "Commercial Chronicle and Review," July 1848; Gildea, *Barricades and Borders*, 12–13; Eckes, *Opening America's Market*, 20–26, 62–67.

32. *New York Commercial Advertiser*, 28 Mar. 1848; [F. Hunt,] "Commercial Chronicle and Review," Apr. 1849; [F. Hunt,] "Commercial Chronicle and Review," Aug. 1849; M'Cay, "Review of the Cotton Trade"; *New York Herald*, 5 Nov. 1849; Gildea, *Barricades and Borders*, 149–50.

33. H. Watson, *Liberty and Power*, 144.

34. Corcoran & Riggs stock and bond records 1843–90, Riggs Family Papers.

35. H. Cohen, *Business and Politics in America*, 53, 59, 261; Thomas F. Ward to W. W. Corcoran, 30 June 1848, Riggs Family Papers.

36. H. Cohen, *Business and Politics in America*, 54, 56.

37. Thomas F. Ward to W. W. Corcoran, 3 Nov. 1848, Riggs Family Papers.

38. Baring Brothers to Corcoran and Riggs, 20 Oct. 1848, and Elisha Riggs Jr. to W. W. Corcoran, 24 Sept. 1849, both Riggs Family Papers.

39. D. Johnson, *Guizot*, 49; Sauvigny, *Metternich and His Times*, 256, 257.

40. L. Reynolds, *European Revolutions*, 35, 36; Packer, "Establishment and the Movement."

2. The Rise and Fall of the 1848 Revolutions in American Public Culture

1. Gooch diary, entries for May 5, July 27, 1849.

2. Brinton, *Anatomy of a Revolution*, 248–49; M. Hunt, *Ideology and U.S. Foreign Policy*, 13; Travers, *Celebrating the Fourth*, 6–7.

3. Ryan, *Civic Wars*, 13. For the formation of American national public identity, see Waldstreicher, *In the Midst of Perpetual Fetes*, esp. 9–13, 135, 293.

4. Kammen, *Machine That Would Go of Itself*, xi–xx, 397–406 (quotation on 399).

5. Quoted in L. Reynolds, *European Revolutions*, 22.

6. "Histoire des Girondins," 53; Fortescue, *Alphonse de Lamartine*, 128–30; *Alphabetical List of Towns and Counties*; Gannett, *American Names*; Southworth, *Colorado Mining Camps*.

7. *New York Tribune*, 31 Mar. 1849, quoted in Fuller, *These Sad but Glorious Days*, 247–48.

8. *Wisconsin Argus* (Madison), 30 May 1848; *New York Tribune*, 1 Apr. 1848; Ginsborg, *Daniele Manin*, 81.

9. Chaffin, *Fatal Glory*, 75, 234; Harris, "Red Cap of Liberty," 283–312.

10. Chaffin, *Fatal Glory*, 109–10.

11. Mary Emily Donelson to Andrew Jackson Donelson Jr., 24 Feb. 1849, Andrew Jackson Donelson Papers.

12. Benjamin Harrison VIII to Ann Harrison, Feb. 1845, Harrison Family Papers; Strong, *Diary*, 1: 318; Saul, *Distant Friends*, 174; Nemes, "Politics of the Dance Floor," 802–23.

13. Durang, *Durang's Terpsichore*, 150, 161 (emphasis original).

14. Silverman, *Cultural History*, 545–67; Grimsted, *Melodrama Unveiled*, 67–68; Kasson, *Rudeness and Civility*, 217–22.

15. *New York Tribune*, 29 Mar. 1848; *Wisconsin Argus*, 19 Apr. 1848; Brandt, *Theatre in Europe*, 331–32.

16. *Charleston Courier*, 3 Apr. 1848; L. Reynolds, *European Revolutions*, 18; Odell, *Annals of the New York Stage*, 5: 321–22, 350, 413–14.

17. *New York Herald*, 20 July 1848, 4 Nov. 1849; Odell, *Annals of the New York Stage*, 5: 412; Crouthamel, *Bennett's New York Herald*, 70–88; Guarneri, *Utopian Alternative*, 335–67; Tuchinsky, "'Bourgeoisie Will Fall,'" 490–91.

18. L. Levine, *Highbrow Lowbrow*, 21–22.

19. Odell, *Annals of the New York Stage*, 5: 412; L. Levine, *Highbrow Lowbrow*, 56–60; Kasson, *Rudeness and Civility*, 217–28; Grimsted, *Melodrama Unveiled*, 51, 55–56, 104; Lott, *Love and Theft*, 85–88.

20. Grimsted, *Melodrama Unveiled*, 144 (emphasis original).

21. Broadside reference 8981.f, Broadside Collection.

22. J. McDermott, *Lost Panoramas of the Mississippi*; McLanathan, *American Tradition in the Arts*, 302–8; Dondore, "Banvard's Panorama."

23. *New York Tribune*, 5 Dec. 1851.

24. Twain, *Tramp Abroad*, 104.

25. Elson, *Guardians of Tradition*, 101–85; Callcott, *History in the United States*, 90–97.

26. *Wisconsin Argus*, 9 May 1848, quoting the *New York Observer*; Callcott, *History in the United States*, 166; Kaestle, *Pillars of the Republic*, 15–20.

27. Randal William McGavock, diary entries, Spring 1848, in McGavock, *Pen and Sword*, 140, 118.

28. [Bowen], "War of the Races in Hungary," 82 (quotation).

29. "Resolutions of Sympathy with the Cause of Hungarian Freedom," [*Springfield Illinois Journal*, 7 Sept. 1849], in Lincoln, *Collected Works*, 2: 62; Spencer, *Louis Kossuth and Young America*, 25–39; A. J. May, *Contemporary American Opinion*, 55–60.

30. Carter, *Hungarian Controversy*; newspaper accounts quoted in Morison, "Francis Bowen," 508–9, and Morison, *Three Centuries of Harvard*, 292.

31. Ryan, *Civic Wars*, 96.

32. *Richmond Enquirer*, 14, 28 Apr. 1848; *New York Tribune*, 27 Mar. 1848 (emphasis original); *New York Herald*, 10 Apr. 1849.

33. *New York Tribune*, 4 Apr. 1848.

34. *New York Tribune*, 4 Apr. 1848; Raeder, *America in the Forties*, 171–72.

35. *New York Tribune*, 4 Apr. 1848. Foresti eventually returned to Europe as the U.S. consul to Genoa, in Sardinia, in 1858 (Marraro, *American Opinion*, 10, 206).

36. Such stories appeared in many newspapers in the spring of 1848, including the *New Orleans Delta*, as reported in the *Richmond Enquirer*, 25 Apr.; *New York Tribune*, 20 Mar., 6 Apr; *Boston Daily Evening Transcript*, 2, 5 Apr.; *Wisconsin Argus*, 2, 9 May; *Nashville Union*, 1 Apr.; *Daily National Intelligencer* (Washington, D.C.), 21 Mar.; *Richmond Enquirer*, 2 May; and *Charleston Courier*, 31 Mar. See also Raeder, *America in the Forties*, 171. Louis Philippe in fact settled in England, dying in Surrey in 1850.

37. *Philadelphia Public Ledger*, 21 Aug. 1849; Raeder, *America in the Forties*, 237.

38. *Philadelphia Public Ledger*, 21 Aug. 1849; A. Johnson, *Dictionary of American Biography*, 3: 526–27.

39. *Philadelphia Public Ledger*, 21 Aug. 1849.

40. Washington and Henry were Virginians, Pinckney and Marion were South Carolinians, Ames was from Massachusetts, Greene came from Rhode Island, and Wayne was a Pennsylvanian (Lossing, *Field-Book of the American Revolution*).

41. Deák, *Lawful Revolution*, 1–9, 91–106.

42. Quoted in Feldberg, *Turbulent Era*, 14.

43. Welter, *Mind of America*, 38–54. On the importance of "rites of commemoration," see Travers, *Celebrating the Fourth*; and Waldstreicher, *In the Midst of Perpetual Fetes*.

3. The Presidential Campaign of 1848

1. See the first three weeks of Apr. 1848 for the *New Orleans Daily Picayune*, *New York Tribune*, *Charleston Courier*, *Daily National Intelligencer*, *Cincinnati Atlas*, and *Weekly Ohio State Journal* (Columbus).

2. *National Intelligencer*, 7 Apr. 1848; *Charleston Courier*, 8 Apr. 1848.

3. Burnham, *Critical Elections*; Gerring, *Party Ideologies in America*.

4. Many works describe America's antebellum political culture, but see Alt-

schuler, *Rude Republic;* H. Watson, *Liberty and Power;* and Pasley, Robertson, and Waldstreicher, *Beyond the Founders.*

5. Rayback, *Free Soil;* Blue, *Free Soilers;* Blue, *No Taint of Compromise.*

6. Meyers, *Jacksonian Persuasion,* vii.

7. J. Baker, "Ceremonies of Politics," 166.

8. Rayback, *Free Soil,* 288; Hamilton, "Election of 1848"; Morrison, *Slavery and the American West,* 66–95; Alexander, "Harbinger of the Collapse."

9. Porter and Johnson, *National Party Platforms,* 13.

10. Charles Francis Adams diary, entry for 16 June 1848, Adams Family Papers; Donald, *Charles Sumner,* 142; Gatell, "'Conscience and Judgment,'"41.

11. Lester, *Life and Public Services,* 166; Gatell, "'Conscience and Judgment,'" 34.

12. Parker, "Free Soil Movement," 192; *National Era* (Washington, D.C.), 20, 6 July 1848.

13. "Address of the Democratic Members of the Legislature," reel 30; L. Hoyt to Samuel Tilden, 25 May 1848, Samuel Tilden Papers (emphasis original); Curtis, "American Opinion," 261.

14. *Free Soil Minstrel,* preface, 119, 158; Howard and Clark, *Clarion of Freedom,* 3–5, 12, 14; Gardiner, *Great Issue,* preface.

15. Porter and Johnson, *National Party Platforms,* 13.

16. Porter and Johnson, *National Party Platforms,* 12.

17. Merk, *Manifest Destiny and Mission,* 54–55; Widmer, *Young America,* 3–11; Curti, "Young America." Cass is quoted in Klunder, *Lewis Cass,* 164–65, 199.

18. Potter, *Impending Crisis,* 18–23, 57–59; Klunder, *Lewis Cass,* 178–80.

19. F. L. Mott, *American Journalism,* 255–57; *Richmond Enquirer,* 21 Sept. 1849.

20. *Richmond Enquirer,* 14 Apr. 1848.

21. *Richmond Enquirer,* 25 July 1848; *Charleston Courier* and *Harrisburg Torch Light,* quoted in the *Daily National Intelligencer,* 24, 28 Mar. 1848. See also citations in Rohrs, "American Critics of the French Revolution," 370–72.

22. Pyles, "American Political Terms," 224; Sperber and Trittschuh, *American Political Terms,* 218–19; Formisano, "Political Character," 695–96; A. Robertson, *Language of Democracy,* 73.

23. *New York Tribune,* 28 Oct. 1848; *Congressional Globe,* 30th Cong., 1st sess., Appendix, 1041–43; *Richmond Enquirer,* 8 Aug. 1848; Hamilton, *Zachary Taylor,* 76–85.

24. Porter and Johnson, *National Party Platforms,* 14–15; NIUL, "Campaign Songbooks"; Gales, *Sketch of the Personal Character;* Morrison, *Slavery and the American West,* 88–90.

25. John Forsyth to Lewis Cass, 21 July 1840, John Y. Mason Papers; Lewis Cass, *France, Its King, Court, and Government,* quoted in Klunder, *Lewis Cass,* 98; *Albany Argus,* 27, 30 May, 1, 6 June 1848.

26. *Richmond Whig and Public Advertiser,* 2 June 1848. See also the *Louisville*

Journal, excerpted in the same issue, and the *Daily National Intelligencer,* 27 Mar. 1848.

27. Ames, *History of the* National Intelligencer, 113, 279–80, 292; F. L. Mott, *American Journalism,* 255–57; Hamilton, *Henry Clay and the Whig Party,* 186–87.

28. *Daily National Intelligencer,* 10 June 1848.

29. *Daily National Intelligencer,* 27 Mar. 1848 (emphasis original).

30. M. Hunt, *Ideology and U.S. Foreign Policy,* 46–124.

31. *New York Sun,* 2 Mar. 1848; *New York Herald,* 14 Nov. 1849.

32. *Daily National Intelligencer,* 27 Mar. 1848; Belohlavek, *George Mifflin Dallas.*

33. *Daily National Intelligencer,* 27 Mar. 1848.

34. R. Ellis, *Union at Risk,* 91–93, 160–65. During Nullification and the Dorr Rebellion, the *Intelligencer* actually called for the use of military troops to suppress acts of insurrection. See *Daily National Intelligencer,* 16, 21 May 1842; Ames, *History of the* National Intelligencer, 206–7.

35. *Daily National Intelligencer,* 27 Mar. 1848; Arendt, *On Revolution,* 148.

36. [Greeley], "Election of 1848," 4.

37. Greeley and Raymond, *Association Discussed,* 4; Guarneri, *Utopian Alternative,* 25–35; Tuchinsky, "'Bourgeoisie Will Fall.'"

38. *New York Commercial Advertiser,* 28 Mar. 1848; Isely, *Horace Greeley and the Republican Party,* 35–36; Burke quoted in Arendt, *On Revolution,* 113.

39. Strong, *Diary,* entry for 21 Oct. 1848, 1: 332.

40. Murdock, *Address on the Free-Soil Question,* 12, 19, 40.

41. [Leisler], *Letters to the People of Pennsylvania,* 2, 14, 20, 21 (emphasis original); entries for Jacob Leisler in Wilson and Fiske, *Appleton's Cyclopaedia of American Biography.*

42. Daniel Webster, "Speech at Marshfield, September 1, 1848," in Webster, *Papers,* 2: 506; James A. Seddon to Robert M. T. Hunter, 16 June 1848, in Ambler, "Correspondence of Robert M. T. Hunter," 2: 91.

43. Burnham, *Presidential Ballots;* Hamilton, "Election of 1848," 2: 878–94; Potter, *Impending Crisis,* 81–82.

44. Salmon Chase to Charles Sumner, 19 Sept. 1849, in Chase, *Papers,* 2: 258.

45. Van Deusen, *Horace Greeley,* 123; Greeley, *Recollections of a Busy Life,* 214–15 (emphasis original); Howe, *Political Culture of the American Whigs,* 18–22, 137.

4. American Reform

1. James Russell Lowell, "Shall We Ever Be Republican?" *National Anti-Slavery Standard* (Boston), 20 Apr. 1848.

2. McInerney, *Fortunate Heirs of Freedom;* Bolt, *Women's Movements,* 79–125; DuBois, *Feminism and Suffrage,* 21–52; Messer-Kruse, *Yankee International,* 12. For discussions of the extent and limits of abolitionists' thinking in transnational terms, see Guarneri, "Abolition and American Reform"; Lynd, *Intellectual Origins,*

130–59; and McDaniel, "'Our Country Is the World.'" My thanks to Dr. McDaniel for citing his work.

3. D. B. Davis, *Slavery and Human Progress*, 168–229; Rice and Crawford, *Liberating Sojourn*; Fladeland, *Men and Brothers*. Garrison quoted in Lynd, *Intellectual Origins*, 137.

4. Sklar, "'Women Who Speak'"; Huxman, "Mary Wollstonecraft"; Anderson, *Joyous Greetings*, 67–98.

5. Wilentz, *Chants Democratic*, 190–220, 243–44; Laurie, *Working People of Philadelphia*, 77, 164–68; Guarneri, *Utopian Alternative*, 292–301; Bronstein, *Land Reform and Working-Class Experience*.

6. Deák, *Lawful Revolution*, 91–106; Stearns, *1848*, 101–2, 150–57; Sewell, *Work and Revolution in France*, 245–72; Guarneri, *Utopian Alternative*, 300. The German states disenfranchised paupers, criminals, and servants, and Hungary required voters to know the Magyar language.

7. Kolchin, *Unfree Labor*, 49; Blackburn, *Overthrow of Colonial Slavery*, 473–515. After 1848 only Russia, Hungary, and Romania clung to serf labor in Europe, while Holland and Spain remained the sole practitioners of slavery in the Caribbean.

8. Parker, "Free Soil Movement," 190–92, 209.

9. Parker, "Abolition of Slavery," 169–70; *Liberator* (Boston), 14 Apr. 1848.

10. Lucretia Mott, "Law of Progress," in L. Mott, *Complete Speeches and Sermons*, 72–75 (emphasis original).

11. "Address of H. W. Johnson," *Rochester North Star*, 21 Aug. 1848; *Syracuse Impartial Citizen*, 11 Apr. 1849; Frederick Douglass, "The 1848 Revolution in France; An Address Delivered in Rochester, New York, on 27 April 1848," in Douglass, *Frederick Douglass Papers*, 2: 116; *Report of the Proceedings of the Colored National Convention, Held at Cleveland, Ohio, on Wednesday, September 6, 1848* (Rochester, 1848), in Ripley, *Black Abolitionist Papers*, 4: 43, 46, 55.

12. Frederick Douglass, "A Day, A Deed, An Event, Glorious in the Annals of Philanthropy: An Address Delivered in Rochester, New York, on 1 August 1848," and "The 1848 Revolution in France," both in Douglass, *Frederick Douglass Papers*, 2: 136, 2: 115–16; McFeely, *Frederick Douglass*, 138–41, 155–57 (Douglass quotation on 141).

13. *Liberator*, 26 May 1848. On white workers' anxiety about "wage slavery," see Roediger, *Wages of Whiteness*, 43–93.

14. Industrial Congress quoted in Wilentz, *Chants Democratic*, 383; Commons, *History of Labour*, 1: 565–68, 616–18; Wittke, *Refugees of Revolution*, 101, 171–74, 276–77; Nadel, "From the Barricades of Paris."

15. D. Reynolds, *George Lippard*, 9–10, 17–21, 51.

16. D. Reynolds, *George Lippard*, 47–48, 62–69 (Lippard quotation on 63); Lippard, *George Lippard*, 130–53.

17. Whitman quotation from Wilentz, *Chants Democratic*, 389; Commons, *History of Labour*, 1: 569–71 (quotation on 571); *Congressional Globe*, 32nd Cong., 1st sess., *Appendix*, 583.

18. New York workers' resolution quoted in Bernstein, *New York City Draft Riots*, 96; Rayback, "American Workingman"; Osofsky, "Abolitionists, Irish Immigrants"; Foner, *Reconstruction*, 479–80; Roediger, *Wages of Whiteness*, 34–35, 43–44, 59–60 (quotation of Irish workers on 136).

19. Douglass, "Editorial from *The North Star*," 84–85.

20. *Report of the Woman's Rights Convention*, 1. For the Seneca Falls Convention, see Wellman, *Road to Seneca Falls*.

21. *Report of the Woman's Rights Convention*, 2; "Declaration of Sentiments and Resolutions."

22. Ginzberg, *Women and the Work of Benevolence*, 112; DuBois, *Feminism and Suffrage*, 40–41.

23. *New Orleans Picayune*, 20, 23 July 1848; *Wisconsin Argus*, 20 June 1848; "Gossip of the Month," *United States Democratic Review* 23 (Aug. 1848), 189; L. Reynolds, *European Revolutions*, 46–48 (quotation from *New York Herald* on 55).

24. Stanton, *Eighty Years and More*; Ginzberg, *Women and the Work of Benevolence*, 90; Marilley, *Woman Suffrage*, 50; Anderson, *Joyous Greetings*, 168.

25. Deák, *Lawful Revolution*, 98; Anderson, *Joyous Greetings*, 14–17, 155–78; Hewitt, "Re-rooting American Women's Activism."

26. Anderson, *Joyous Greetings*, 161–66, 178–82, 190, 205 (Stanton quotation on 172); Jane Elizabeth Jones quoted in "Woman's Rights Convention," *New York Herald*, 12 Sept. 1852; Elizabeth Cady Stanton, "Address by Elizabeth Cady Stanton to the legislature of New York," *Albany Evening Journal*, 15 Feb. 1854, in Stanton and Anthony, *Papers*; "Appeal by Elizabeth Cady Stanton to the Women of the State of New York," *New York Tribune*, 26 Dec. 1854.

27. W. W. Brown, *Narrative of William Wells Brown*; W. W. Brown, *Clotel*; Farrison, *William Wells Brown*; Fuller, *Woman in the Nineteenth Century*; Capper, *Margaret Fuller*.

28. Elihu Burritt to George Thompson, 2 June 1848, Lant Carpenter Papers; Phelps, *Anglo-American Peace Movement*, 43–84; Brock, *Pacifism in the United States*, 641–43; Tyrrell, "Making the Millennium."

29. W. W. Brown, *American Fugitive in Europe*, 39; W. Stowe, *Going Abroad*, 70; Coleman, "William Wells Brown," 53.

30. W. W. Brown, *American Fugitive in Europe*, 71, 72, 141, 57 (emphasis original); Phelps, *Anglo-American Peace Movement*, 55.

31. Margaret Fuller to Caroline Sturgis, 10 July 1845, and Fuller to Samuel G. and Anna B. Ward, 3 Mar. 1846, both in Fuller, *Letters*, 4: 132, 193.

32. *New York Tribune*, 3 Mar., 19, 2 Feb. 1847, 13 Nov. 1846, in Fuller, *These Sad but Glorious Days*, 102–3, 96, 88, 72. For the story of American associationism, see Guarneri, *Utopian Alternative*.

33. Von Mehren, *Minerva and the Muse*, 240; Rossi, *Image of America*, 51; Margaret Fuller to Richard F. Fuller, 27 Sept. 1846, and Fuller to Caroline Sturgis, 16 Nov. 1846, both in Fuller, *Letters*, 4: 228, 240.

34. Von Mehren, *Minerva and the Muse*, 113, 246–47; Fuller, *Letters*, 5: 175–76

n. 2; Margaret Fuller to Elizabeth Hoar, 18 Jan. 1847, in Fuller, *Letters*, 4: 256–57; Fuller to Hoar, 17 Mar. 1847, in Chevigny, *Woman and the Myth*, 362. George Sand was the pseudonym of Aurore Dupin, baronne Dudevant. Sand was an aristocrat and novelist, but she incorporated themes of socialism and women's intellect into her writing.

35. Fuller, *Letters*, 5: 258–59; *New York Tribune*, 3 Mar. 1847, in Fuller, *These Sad but Glorious Days*, 109.

36. *New York Tribune*, 29 May, 27 Nov. 1847, 1 Jan. 1848, 5 June 1849, in Fuller, *These Sad but Glorious Days*, 129–30, 160, 164, 274 (emphasis original); Barolini, "Italian Side of Emily Dickinson"; Salomone, "Nineteenth-Century Discovery of Italy."

37. Margaret Fuller to William Henry Channing, 28 Aug. 1849, in Fuller, *Letters*, 5: 258.

38. Kearns, "Margaret Fuller"; Guarneri, *Utopian Alternative*, 257.

39. *New York Tribune*, 1 Jan. 1848, in Fuller, *These Sad but Glorious Days*, 166.

40. Thomas Hicks, *Eulogy on Thomas Crawford*, quoted in Gale, *Thomas Crawford*, 63; Yellin, "Caps and Chains," 801 (quotation). When Powers presented the statue to officials in Washington, they rejected it because of its elements' likeness to abolitionist iconography, even after Powers changed the name of the statue from *Liberty* to *America* and replaced its controversial liberty cap with a tiara. It is now at the Smithsonian American Art Museum.

41. *New York Tribune*, 27 Nov. 1847, 4 Apr. 1849, in Fuller, *These Sad but Glorious Days*, 159, 257 (emphasis original); Dwight, *Roman Republic of 1849*, 16, 34, 41, 237; Jefferson, *Notes on the State of Virginia*, 180; J. B. Stewart, *Holy Warriors*, 127–49.

42. *New York Tribune*, 13 Mar. 1848, 23 June 1849, in Fuller, *These Sad but Glorious Days*, 205, 278; Fuller, "Narrative of the Life of Frederick Douglass," 136–38 (quotation on 136).

43. *New York Tribune*, 24 July 1849, in Fuller, *These Sad but Glorious Days*, 294. Fuller accused the *Times* of being funded by the Austrian government and noted how foreign journals described red flags mounted on the houses of Rome as evidence of Roman bloodthirstiness. "The fact is," she corrected, "these flags are put up where there is no barricade, as a signal that coachmen and horsemen can pass freely." See *New York Tribune*, 23 June, 24 July 1849.

44. Gitlin, *Sixties*, 81–97, 127–29, 244–56, 285–88; Scott and Smith, "Rhetoric of Confrontation."

45. *New York Tribune*, 26 Jan., 23 June 1849, in Fuller, *These Sad but Glorious Days*, 245, 282. The U.S. minister to Rome, Lewis Cass Jr., declined to present his credentials to the Roman republic, instead awaiting the return of the papal government in late 1849 (Marraro, "Unpublished American Documents," 462–63).

46. *New York Tribune*, 13 Feb. 1850, in Fuller, *These Sad but Glorious Days*, 321.

47. Margaret Fuller to Constanza Arconati Visconti, 22 June 1848, in Fuller,

Letters, 5: 73; *New York Tribune,* 6 Oct. 1849, in Fuller, *These Sad but Glorious Days,* 313.

48. E. B. Browning, *Letters,* 1: 428 (emphasis original); Fuller, *Memoirs;* Lucy Henry to John Bigelow, 4 May 1849, John Bigelow Papers; Chevigny, "Long Arm of Censorship."

49. Pease and Pease, "Confrontation and Abolition"; Di Scala, *Italy,* 90–100.

5. THE CONSERVATIVE CHRISTIAN ALLIANCE

1. Hughes, *Church and the World,* 3–4.

2. Hatch, *Democratization of American Christianity,* 185, 186 (quotations); Noll, *Old Religion in a New World,* 95–112.

3. Carey, *People, Priests, and Prelates,* 140–53, 277 (Hughes quotation on 196); Noll, *America's God.*

4. Noll, *History of Christianity,* 227–29; Carwardine, *Evangelicals and Politics,* 36–40.

5. Hughes, *Church and the World,* 23; Hughes, *Decline of Protestantism,* 17.

6. Quoted in Franchot, *Roads to Rome,* 101; George Martin to brother, 16 Apr. 1848, in Erickson, *Invisible Immigrants,* 288–90. The seminal work on American anti-Catholicism remains Billington, *Protestant Crusade.*

7. Benson, *Concept of Jacksonian Democracy;* Hatch, *Democratization of American Christianity;* Carey, *People, Priests, and Prelates.*

8. "Revolutions of 1848," *Methodist Quarterly Review* 30 (Oct. 1848): 539.

9. Kirk, *Church Essential to the Republic,* 12, 18; Moorhead, "Between Progress and Apocalypse." On antebellum perceptions of the relation between the American Revolution and the Reformation, see Butler, *Awash in a Sea of Faith,* 284–86; Franchot, *Roads to Rome,* 3–5. Among the many books on Edwards, see G. McDermott, *One Holy and Happy Society.*

10. Mathews, *Religion in the Old South,* 175; Daniel 11:21–23, 41; Revelation 7:2.

11. "An American Layman," *The Second Advent, or, Coming of the Messiah in Glory,* cited in Gribbin, "Covenant Transformed," 303–4; "Religion in Europe," *Southern Religious Telegraph* 12 (1833), quoted in Colbenson, "Millennial Thought," 69–70. Millennial associations with Europe in the 1790s are traced in Nash, "American Clergy."

12. McGill commenced with the year 606 A.D., when Pope Boniface III assumed the title of "Universal Bishop," which his predecessor Gregory the Great had disavowed as a "blasphemous antichristian assumption." To 606 McGill added 1,260, the sum of the days in Boniface's three-and-a-half-year reign, allowing 360 days for a "prophetic year." This sum was 1866. He then subtracted 18, which was the (rounded) product of 5, the days' subtraction from each temporal year in the first calculation, and 3.5, the years in Boniface's reign. The result of this tortured analysis was 1848 (McGill, *Popery the Punishment of Unbelief,* 40; Schaff, *History of*

the Christian Church, 4: 230–31; Wilson and Fiske, *Appletons' Cyclopædia of American Biography,* 4: 117).

13. "Remarkable Exposition of Prophecy," *Louisville Baptist Banner,* 3, 31 May 1848; "Revolutions of 1848," 538; Thomas Russell, "Address to the Society of Alumni of Randolph Macon College, Richmond, Va., 1848," quoted in Colbenson, "Millennial Thought," 71–72.

14. Bushnell quoted in Bodo, *Protestant Clergy and Public Issues,* 237; Bushnell, *Barbarism the First Danger;* Conkin, *Uneasy Center,* 234–47.

15. Thornwell, *Life and Letters,* 303; Farmer, *Metaphysical Confederacy,* 156–67; Startup, "'Mere Calculation of Profit and Loss,'" 219.

16. Thornwell quoted in Farmer, *Metaphysical Confederacy,* 172; *Baptist Banner,* 26 Apr. 1848; "Promiscuous Dancing," *Christian Magazine of the South* (Columbia, S.C.), 7 Jan. 1849, 12; Palmer, "Social Dancing."

17. Thornwell quoted in Clarke, *Our Southern Zion,* 194, and in Farmer, *Metaphysical Confederacy,* 189. On perfectionism see Thomas, "Romantic Reform in America"; T. Smith, "Righteousness and Hope"; and Quist, *Restless Visionaries.*

18. Bozeman, "Inductive and Deductive Politics"; Howe, *Unitarian Conscience,* 274–86.

19. Thornwell quoted in Farmer, *Metaphysical Confederacy,* 174, 222, and in Bozeman, "Inductive and Deductive Politics," 710. On Southern clergy see Loveland, *Southern Evangelicals.*

20. Noll and Niemczyk, "Evangelicals and the Self-Consciously Reformed," 204–7; Nevin quoted in Hatch, *Democratization of American Christianity,* 164–65, and in Nichols, *Romanticism in American Theology,* 57.

21. Nevin quoted in Hanley, *Beyond a Christian Commonwealth,* 71, and in Nichols, *Romanticism in American Theology,* 215. See also Conkin, *Uneasy Center,* 173–76; Nichols, *Romanticism in American Theology,* 259–60; Hatch, *Democratization of American Christianity,* 170–83.

22. Thornwell, *Life and Letters,* 310–11 (emphasis original).

23. *Proceedings of a public meeting . . . ;* Marraro, *American Opinion,* 93–94. See also "Present Reforms of Pope Pius IX."

24. Mize, "Defending Roman Loyalties," 480.

25. *Catholic Herald* (Philadelphia), 4 May 1848.

26. *Boston Pilot,* quoted in McGreevy, *Catholicism and American Freedom,* 22.

27. *Catholic Herald,* 20 July, 3 Aug. 1848.

28. Carey, "Introduction"; McGreevy, *Catholicism and American Freedom,* 49; Brownson quoted in Schlesinger, *Pilgrim's Progress,* 90–92, 106.

29. Howe, *Unitarian Conscience,* 10, 135; Carey, "Introduction," 27–30; Orestes Brownson, "Nature and Grace," and "The Mediatorial Life of Jesus," in Brownson, *Selected Writings,* 286, 211.

30. Brownson, "Conservatism and Radicalism," 455, 456, 465; Brownson, "Cooper's *Ways of the Hour,*" 276, 277, 278.

31. Brownson, "Socialism and the Church," 149.

32. Brownson, "Conservatism and Radicalism," 464, 465, 457, 456, 478; Brownson, "Know-Nothings," 481.

33. Hassard, *Life of John Hughes*, 211–16; Meenaugh, "Archbishop John Hughes"; R. L. Moore, "Insiders and Outsiders," 402–3.

34. Hassard, *Life of John Hughes*, 286–88; Hughes, *Church and the World*, 10; Hughes, *Decline of Protestantism*, 22–23; [John Hughes], "'The Present Position of Pius IX,' preached at St. Patrick's Cathedral," *New York Tribune*, 9 Jan. 1849; Schlesinger, *Pilgrim's Progress*, 129; Howe, *Unitarian Conscience*, 174–300; Macauley, *Unitarianism in the Antebellum South*, 144–57; Fox-Genovese and Genovese, *Mind of the Master Class*, 48; Livingston, "Eyes on 'the Whole European World,'" 94 (quotation).

35. Hughes, *Church and the World*, 13; Hughes, *Decline of Protestantism*, 16–17; Howe, *Unitarian Conscience*, 1–23; Foner, *Tom Paine*.

36. *Freeman's Journal and Catholic Register* (New York), quoted in Casper, *American Attitudes*, 123. Hughes owned the *Journal* from 1846 to 1848, directing its editorial positions during that period as well as afterward.

37. Hughes, *Church and the World*, 25, 28–29.

38. Beman, *Characteristics of the Age*; "Wonder of the Nineteenth Century"; Bercovitch, *American Jeremiad*, 93–94.

39. The first English translation of the *Communist Manifesto* appeared in a London Chartist periodical, the *Red Republican*, beginning on 9 Nov. 1850. Excerpts from the *Manifesto* were first printed in the United States in the *New York World*, 21 Sept. 1871. See *Red Republican*, 1: ix–xi.

40. Noll, *History of Christianity*, 348–58.

41. Winders, *Mr. Polk's Army*, 139–57; Carwardine, *Evangelicals and Politics*, 8, 13, 184; Heimert, "*Moby-Dick* and American Political Symbolism," 514.

6. Secession or Revolution?

1. Trescot, *Position and Course of the South*, 6. For discussion of "conservatism" see Huntington, "Conservatism as an Ideology," 454–73.

2. Dormon, *Theater in the Antebellum South*, 131, 153; C. Watson, *Antebellum Charleston Dramatists*, 129 ff.; R. Clark, "German Liberals in New Orleans," 149.

3. *Richmond Enquirer*, 25 Apr. 1848; *New Orleans Daily Picayune*, 12 Apr. 1848; Gazley, *American Opinion of German Unification*, 21;Raeder, *America in the Forties*, 170; R. Clark, "German Liberals in New Orleans," 137–51.

4. Lieber, *Life and Letters*, 213–14; W. Taylor, *Cavalier and Yankee*, 275. On the Young American literary movement, see Widmer, *Young America*.

5. For samples of Northern opinion, see "Fourierism and France, and the *Tribune*," *New York Herald*, 20 July 1848; "French Ideas of Democracy," 315, 316.

6. David Outlaw to Emily Outlaw, 29 Mar. 1848, David Outlaw Papers; Trescot, *Position and Course of the South*, 9, 13. For an assessment of Congress's skepticism

about the Second French Republic, see Rohrs, "American Critics of the French Revolution."

7. [J.], "National Anniversary," 180; Curtis, "American Opinion," 258. For the impact of the Haitian revolution, see Langley, *Americas in the Age of Revolution*, 87–144; A. Hunt, *Haiti's Influence in Antebellum America*.

8. Genovese, *Political Economy of Slavery*, 231–32; Berlin and Gutman, "Natives and Immigrants," 1175–76 (*Richmond Whig* quotation on 1197).

9. David Outlaw to Emily Outlaw, 28 July 1848, David Outlaw Papers; Schecter, "Free and Slave Labor"; B. Levine, *Spirit of 1848*, 91–95; Eaton, *Freedom-of-Thought Struggle*, 340–41; Berlin and Gutman, "Natives and Immigrants," 1198.

10. Thornton, *Politics and Power*, 213.

11. [Tucker], "Present State of Europe," 285–86, 298; Stiles, *Address Delivered before the Georgia Democratic State Convention*; Faust, *Sacred Circle*, 75; Kammen, *Season of Youth*, 51–54, 155–56. Simms's essay appeared in the July 1848 issue of the *Southern Quarterly Review*.

12. Hassard, *Life of John Hughes*, 211–16; Hughes, *Church and the World*, 8, 25, 28–29; Gleeson, *Irish in the South*, 139; McGreevy, *Catholicism and American Freedom*, 37.

13. Sinha, *Counterrevolution of Slavery*, 5–7, 88; Calhoun, *Disquisition*.

14. "Guizot's Democracy in France," 164; William Gilmore Simms to James Henry Hammond, 20 May 1848, in Simms, *Letters*, 2: 411; "Constitution of France," 504.

15. "Foreign Correspondence," 283; "Absolutism versus Republicanism," 598; "Miscellany," 657.

16. *Liberator*, 7 Dec. 1849; *Congressional Globe*, 31st Cong., 1st sess., 293, and *Appendix*, 47.

17. "Glimpses at Europe in 1848," 8; W. M. Evans, "From the Land of Canaan,'" 24–25.

18. "Hungary."

19. [J.], "National Anniversary," 175; John C. Calhoun to Mrs. Thomas G. Clemson, 7 Mar. 1848, and Calhoun to Thomas G. Clemson, 13 Apr. 1848, both in Jameson, "Correspondence of John C. Calhoun," 745–50; Curti, "John C. Calhoun."

20. Eyck, *Frankfurt Parliament of 1848–1849*.

21. Fritz, "Popular Sovereignty," 52; A. Craven, *Growth of Southern Nationalism*, 78.

22. *Richmond Enquirer*, 14 Apr. 1848, 16 Oct., 25 Dec. 1849, 10 Jan. 1850.

23. Cave Johnson to James Buchanan, 20 Jan. 1850, in Sioussat, "Tennessee," 318; Edward Joy Morris to Secretary of State John Clayton, 5 July 1850, in Marraro, *Diplomatic Relations*, 2: 12–16.

24. Potter, *Impending Crisis*, 100–116; Hamilton, *Prologue to Conflict*; Stegmaier, *Texas, New Mexico*.

25. *Congressional Globe*, 31st Cong., 1st sess., *Appendix*, 117.

26. *Congressional Globe,* 31st Cong., 1st sess., 259.

27. *Congressional Globe,* 31st Cong., 1st sess., 267–68.

28. *Congressional Globe,* 31st Cong., 1st sess., 276.

29. Curti, "Austria and the United States," 157, 162–64; Spencer, *Louis Kossuth and Young America,* 30–42; Daniel Webster to Johann Georg Hülsemann, 21 Dec. 1850, in Webster, *Papers,* 2: 60.

30. Webster to Hülsemann, 21 Dec. 1850, 53, 60.

31. Webster to Hülsemann, 21 Dec. 1850, 52–54.

32. Webster confided his motives in a personal letter to George Ticknor, 16 Jan. 1851. See Webster, *Writings and Speeches,* 16: 586; Shewmaker, "Daniel Webster."

33. Johnson to Buchanan, 20 Jan. 1850, 319; Jennings, *Nashville Convention;* Walther, *Fire-Eaters.*

34. "Southern Convention," 227–28.

35. "Southern Convention," 220; Potter, *Impending Crisis,* 462.

36. Trescot, *Position and Course of the South,* 13; Bryan, *Rightful Remedy,* 67; Benton, *Thirty Years' View,* 2: 783.

37. Jennings, *Nashville Convention,* 174–75, 187–88; Freehling, *Road to Disunion,* 511–35; Lévêque, "Revolutionary Crisis of 1848/51," 114–17; Price, "'Holy Struggle against Anarchy,'" 39–47.

38. "Usurpation of Louis Napoleon," 180; Henry Clay Yeatman diary, entry for 22 Dec. 1852, Yeatman-Polk Papers; Freehling, *Road to Disunion,* 515; Sinha, *Counterrevolution of Slavery,* 122–23.

39. Rogin, *Subversive Genealogy,* 102–9.

40. *Richmond Enquirer,* 28 Nov. 1850; Andrew Jackson Donelson to James Buchanan, 5 June 1848, in U.S. Department of State, *Despatches . . . to the German States and Germany,* reel 5; Cole, "South and the Right of Secession," 378, 384; Freehling, *Road to Disunion,* 528.

41. *New Orleans Louisiana Statesman,* quoted in *Richmond Enquirer,* 28 Nov. 1850; Barney, *Secessionist Impulse,* 235.

42. Freehling, *Road to Disunion,* 519.

43. "Manufactures in South Carolina and the South," 130; Genovese, *Political Economy of Slavery,* 180–220.

44. Cole, "South and the Right of Secession," 396, 392.

45. "Separate Secession," 311–12; Freehling, *Road to Disunion,* 530.

46. "Southern Cotton Mills," 682; Casper, *American Attitudes,* 176.

7. Louis Kossuth and the Campaign of 1852

1. For British reactions to the 1848 revolutions, see Belchem, "Waterloo of Peace and Order"; L. Mitchell, "Britain's Reactions to the Revolutions"; and M. Taylor, "1848 Revolutions and the British Empire."

2. *Kossuth in New England,* 70; *New York Tribune,* 5, 6 Dec. 1851; Headley, *Life of Louis Kossuth,* 300–301. For Lafayette's visit see Somkin, *Unquiet Eagle,* 137–68.

3. Ammon, *Genet Mission;* Elkins and McKitrick, *Age of Federalism,* 330–73.

4. Elkins and McKitrick, *Age of Federalism,* 330–73; Genêt quoted in Waldstreicher, *In the Midst of Perpetual Fetes,* 134. The 1793 Proclamation of Neutrality is in Richardson, *Compilation of the Messages and Papers,* 1: 156.

5. Odell, *Annals of the New York Stage,* 5: 442–43, 448, 6: 141–42, 150; *Louisville Journal,* 6 Mar. 1852.

6. Accounts of Kossuth's welcome are taken from Pulszky and Pulszky, *White Red Black,* 1: 51–75; *New York Times,* 6 Dec. 1851; and Spencer, *Louis Kossuth and Young America,* 5–9.

7. Strong, *Diary,* entry for 12 Dec. 1851, 2: 75.

8. "Louis Kossuth," *Burritt's Christian Union* (Worcester, Mass.), excerpted in *Liberator,* 31 Aug. 1849; "Patriotism and Christianity: Kossuth and Jesus," *Liberator,* 31 Aug. 1849.

9. Redpath, *Roving Editor,* 60; "Proceedings of the Convention of the Colored Freemen of Ohio, held in Cincinnati January 14–19, 1852," in Foner and Walker, *Proceedings of the Black State Conventions,* 1: 276; Spencer, *Louis Kossuth and Young America,* 69; Morrison, "American Reaction to European Revolutions," 115.

10. "Proceedings of the Convention of the Colored Freemen," 277; Everett, "Emigres and Militiamen"; Langley, *Americas in the Age of Revolution,* 211–13; Hickey, *War of 1812,* 26–51. A recent treatment of the War of 1812 is Langguth, *Union 1812.*

11. Miller, "American Christians," 11.

12. W. L. Garrison, *Letter to Louis Kossuth; Liberator,* 12 Dec. 1851.

13. Kossuth's first speech in the United States, printed in the *New York Tribune,* 7 Dec. 1851; W. L. Garrison, *Letter to Louis Kossuth,* 17, 19.

14. McInerney, *Fortunate Heirs of Freedom,* emphasizes the relevance of the American Revolution to antebellum abolitionists and their rhetorical use of it, not the ways it failed to serve their purposes.

15. W. L. Garrison, *Letter to Louis Kossuth,* 52.

16. Headley, *Life of Louis Kossuth,* 274.

17. *Welcome of Louis Kossuth,* 30.

18. *Welcome of Louis Kossuth,* ix, xv.

19. *New York Tribune,* 6 Dec. 1851; *Kossuth in New England,* 70.

20. Kossuth, *Selected Speeches,* 200 (emphasis original); Channing quoted in Somkin, *Unquiet Eagle,* 121. Civic ideology during nineteenth-century pedagogy is shown in Kaestle, *Pillars of the Republic,* 75–103, and Elson, *Guardians of Tradition.*

21. Curtiss, *Western Portraiture,* 141; U.S. Congress, *History of Foreign Leaders.*

22. Daniel Webster, "Speech at the Kossuth Banquet," *Boston Daily Advertiser,* 12 Jan. 1852, in Webster, *Writings and Speeches,* 8: 462; Webster, *Works,* 6: 133; Curti, "Austria and the United States," 200–204.

23. Quoted in Spencer, *Louis Kossuth and Young America,* 94.

24. Wittke, *Refugees of Revolution,* 35.

25. *Congressional Globe,* 32nd Cong., 1st sess., 177, 181, 193; *New York Times,* 20 Jan. 1852; *Pittsburgh Gazette,* 29 Dec. 1851, 29 Jan. 1852, quoted in Oliver, "Kossuth's

Appeal to the Middle West," 486, 488; Lincoln quoted in Stampp, "One Alone?" 132; Kossuth, "Kossuth before Ohio Legislature," 116; McGreevy, *Catholicism and American Freedom*, 24.

26. *Kossuth in New England*, 18, 82; *New York Times*, 20 Jan. 1852.

27. *New York Tribune*, 23, 29 Dec. 1851.

28. "Name and Fame," *Liberator*, 31 Aug. 1849; Gale, *Cultural Encyclopedia of the 1850s*, 222; *Alphabetical List of Towns and Counties*; Gannett, *American Names*.

29. Moller, "Accelerated Development Youth," 757–58; *Daily Indiana State Journal*, 12 Mar. 1852, quoted in L. Howard, *Victorian Knight-Errant*, 302–3; J. B. Moore, "Kossuth," 289.

30. *Congressional Globe*, 32nd Cong., 1st sess., 310, and *Appendix*, 247. For tensions regarding America's global obligations at the end of the nineteenth century, see Brands, *What America Owes the World*, 1–21.

31. *Congressional Globe*, 32nd Cong., 1st sess., 310, and *Appendix*, 247, 308, 212–13; *Pittsburgh Post*, 14 Feb. 1852, quoted in Oliver, "Kossuth's Appeal to the Middle West," 491. Jones referred to Seward's "Higher Law" speech of Mar. 1850, placing the morality of antislavery above the Constitution.

32. *Journal of the House of Representatives*, 31st Cong., 2nd sess., 3–7, 362–63, 400–402; *Congressional Globe*, 31st Cong., 1st sess., *Appendix*, 43; Kestenbaum, "Political Graveyard"; Spencer, *Louis Kossuth and Young America*, 73–75. The House voted twice on the resolution, on 27 Feb. 1851 (91 yea, 50 nay) and on 3 Mar. 1851 (126 yea, 42 nay).

33. S. Smith, *Theatrical Management*, 223; Pulszky and Pulszky, *White, Red, Black*, 2: 97–98.

34. Rogers, "'Nation's Guest,'" 361–62.

35. Curti, "Young America," 39; R. May, *Southern Dream*.

36. *Kossuth in New England*, 92; Robert Edward Lee to son, 12 Jan. 1852, Lee Papers; Bellows, *Benevolence among Slaveholders*, 119; Rogers, "'Nation's Guest,'" 359; Spencer, *Louis Kossuth and Young America*, 150; Rogers, "Kossuth's Visit to Alabama," 116. Komlos, Louis *Kossuth in America, 1851–1852*, emphasizes Kossuth's poor judgment of his audiences in the South and elsewhere.

37. Blue, *Free Soilers*, 232–33.

38. *Proceedings to the Banquet.*

39. Spencer, *Louis Kossuth and Young America*, 113–16, 160–61; A. J. May, *Contemporary American Opinion*, 117–18; Curti, "Young America," 42–44.

40. Porter and Johnson, *National Party Platforms*, 18.

41. Porter and Johnson, *National Party Platforms*, 20; Summers, *Plundering Generation*, 187–94.

42. *New York Tribune*, 19, 29 Dec. 1851, 24 Mar. 1852; Miller, "American Christians," 12–13; McGreevy, *Catholicism and American Freedom*, 45; Gienapp, *Origins of the Republican Party*, 23–24.

43. Porter and Johnson, *National Party Platforms*, 19; *New York Tribune*, 26, 28 June 1852; Strong, *Diary*, entry for 27 June 1852, 2: 98; Charles Sumner to John

Bigelow, 13 Dec. 1851, in Bigelow, *Retrospections of an Active Life*, 1: 123; Gienapp, *Origins of the Republican Party*, 28, 31; Lynch, "Antislavery Tendencies of the Democratic Party," 330–31.

44. Franklin Pierce, "Inaugural Address, 4 March, 1853," in Richardson, *Compilation of the Messages and Papers*, 4: 2735.

8. THE ANTISLAVERY MOVEMENT AS A CRISIS OF AMERICAN EXCEPTIONALISM

1. See Wood, *Radicalism of the American Revolution*.

2. Bancroft, *History of the United States*, 4: 3–17, 7: 22–25, quoted in Greene, *Ambiguity of the American Revolution*, 49, 50, 54; Lewis, "Organic Metaphor and Edenic Myth."

3. D. B. Davis, *Problem of Slavery in Western Culture*, 21–24 (Bancroft quotations on 23, 24); Robinson, "Negro Slavery at the South," 214 (quotation).

4. Stowe quoted in McPherson, "Tom on the Cross," in *Drawn with the Sword*, 26–27; Gossett, Uncle Tom's Cabin *and American Culture*, 239–59.

5. H. B. Stowe, *Uncle Tom's Cabin*, 74, 75, 344, 476.

6. Kossuth, *Future of Nations*, 39.

7. Curti, "Young America," 48–53. On the political impact of the book, see Grant, "*Uncle Tom's Cabin* and the Triumph of Republican Rhetoric."

8. *Liberator*, 26 May 1852; Shaw, "Pliable Rhetoric of Domesticity."

9. "Blackwood's Magazine Article," 300; *New York Herald* quoted in Gossett, Uncle Tom's Cabin *and American Culture*, 257.

10. R. May, *Manifest Destiny's Underworld*.

11. "Democratic Nomination," 135 (quotation); "Foreign Policy of the United States," 39 (quotation) (emphasis original). "Manifest destiny" took on a different meaning in the 1890s from its proslavery meaning in the early 1850s. See Merk, *Manifest Destiny and Mission*; Hietala, *Manifest Design*.

12. Franklin Pierce, "Inaugural Address, 4 March, 1853," in Richardson, *Compilation of the Messages and Papers*, 4: 2736; Horace Greeley to Mrs. Bruce Kirby, 6 Dec. 1852, Horace Greeley Papers. See also Higham, *From Boundlessness to Consolidation*.

13. See Rawley, *Race and Politics*; Gienapp, *Origins of the Republican Party*; Stampp, *America in 1857*; Etcheson, *Bleeding Kansas*.

14. Barstow Darrach to S. L. Adair, 27 Nov. 1856, Samuel and Florella Adair Collection; Potter, *Impending Crisis*, 217.

15. *National Anti-Slavery Standard* quoted in Pease and Pease, "Confrontation and Abolition," 937. For the emergence within the antislavery cause of an endorsement of violence, see the essays in McKivigan and Harrold, *Antislavery Violence*.

16. Higginson's articles for the *New York Tribune* are quoted in Meyer, *Magnificent Activist*, 79–80.

17. An alternative explanation of Northern and Southern perceptions of their sectional rival as a foreign enemy—focused on hostility arising because of the sec-

tions' commercial policies competing in an emerging world of national markets—
is Onuf and Onuf, *Markets, Nations, and War,* esp. 176–85.

18. Higginson, *New Revolution,* 110; Fellman, "Theodore Parker and the Abolitionist Role," 667; Foner, *Free Soil,* 40–72; Meyer, *Magnificent Activist,* 95. On
international efforts at this time to match "states" and "nations," see Bender, *Nation
among Nations,* 122–30.

19. *Farmer's Cabinet* (Amherst), 3 July 1856; "Political Aspect," 89; *In Perils By
Mine Own Countrymen,* 41. In its treatment of John Brown's execution of proslavery
settlers, the Eastern antislavery press tended either to not give the story much
attention or to attribute the murders to Native Americans (Potter, *Impending Crisis,* 222).

20. Sumner, *Crime Against Kansas.*

21. Olmstead, *Walks and Talks,* 251; "Monthly Record of Current Events," 855;
Abraham Lincoln, "On the Challenge of Violence to the Perpetuation of Our Political Institutions," in R. Brown, *American Violence,* 8; Gienapp, *Origins of the Republican Party,* 301, 360. Sumner specifically chastised South Carolina senator Andrew
Butler, a relative of Brooks, for keeping a "polluted mistress . . . the harlot, slavery."
This vilification of Brooks's kinsman, and possibly Sumner's ridicule of Butler's
drooling on account of a recent stroke, convinced Brooks of the need to retaliate.

22. Seward, *Army of the United States Not to Be Employed.*

23. Colfax, *"Laws" of Kansas.*

24. Day, *Democratic Party.*

25. "Political Aspect," 90; Mullis, *Peacekeeping on the Plains,* 167; Etcheson,
Bleeding Kansas, 136.

26. Salmon Chase to James Grimes, 8 Nov. 1856, in Chase, *Papers,* 2: 371; Grow,
Admission of Kansas.

27. D. B. Davis, *Fear of Conspiracy;* Wood, "Conspiracy and the Paranoid Style,"
401–6; Hofstadter, *Paranoid Style in American Politics,* 3–40.

28. Seward, *Army of the United States Not to Be Employed;* Seward, *Speeches . . .
on the Army Bill,* 155.

29. Fitzhugh, *Cannibals All!* 8, 192; A. Robertson, *Language of Democracy,* 120–
21; Fermer, *James Gordon Bennett,* 144–48; Faust, *Creation of Confederate Nationalism,* 12–14l; "Reopening of the African Slave Trade," 94.

30. Hiram Hill to Charles Wright, 18 June 1856, Hiram Hill Collection; McPherson, *Battle Cry of Freedom,* 161; Foner, *Free Soil,* 72.

31. Buchanan to Donelson, 15 Aug. 1848; Wittke, *Refugees of Revolution,* 102–8,
161–76, 191–202; Kamphoefner, "Dreissiger and Forty-Eighter"; Gienapp, *Origins
of the Republican Party,* 21–31; B. Levine, *Spirit of 1848,* 151, 217; Towers, *Urban
South,* 101.

32. *Congressional Globe,* 31st Cong., 1st sess., *Appendix,* 268; Godwin, *Political
Essays,* 101–3; Sumner quoted in Bender, *Nation among Nations,* 121; Lincoln, *Selected Speeches and Writings,* 94.

33. Foner, *Free Soil,* 133; L. Reynolds, *European Revolutions,* 53.

EPILOGUE

1. Nevins, *Emergence of Lincoln*, 2: 8–11. Revisions of Nevins's view of Brown as insane include Oates, *Our Fiery Trial*, 22–42; and D. Reynolds, *John Brown*.

2. For this concept see Armitage and Braddick, *British Atlantic World*, 23.

3. Schenone, "John Brown e il pensiero insurrezionale italiano"; Dal Lago, "Radicalism and Nationalism"; von Frank, "John Brown, James Redpath"; D. Reynolds, *John Brown*, 106–10.

4. Brown quoted in Hinton, *John Brown and His Men*, 68; von Frank, "John Brown, James Redpath," 144.

5. D. M. Smith, *Mazzini*, 123; Drescher, "Servile Insurrection."

6. Thoreau, "Plea for Captain John Brown," 404, 410.

7. McPherson, *Battle Cry of Freedom*, 234–75; Bender, *Nation among Nations*, 125; Stampp, "One Alone?" See also McPherson, "'Whole Family of Man.'"

8. Kossuth's words were: "The spirit of our age is Democracy. All for the people and by the people. Nothing about the people without the people. That is Democracy, and that is the ruling tendency of the spirit of our age" (speech to the Ohio legislature, Columbus, 17 Feb. 1852; noted in U.S. Congress, House, "Dedication . . . of a Bust of Lajos [Louis] Kossuth").

9. Rossi, *Image of America*, 135; Pressly, "Bullets and Ballots"; McPherson, *Abraham Lincoln*, 23–42. On the topic of violent nation-building, see Geyer and Bright, "Global Violence and Nationalizing Wars"; and Bender, *Nation among Nations*, 131–32.

Bibliography

Manuscript Collections

Samuel and Florella Adair Collection. Kansas State Historical Society. Topeka.

Adams Family Papers. Massachusetts Historical Society. Boston.

Appleton Family Papers. Massachusetts Historical Society.

Aylett Family Papers. Virginia Historical Society. Richmond.

John Bigelow Papers. New York Public Library.

Broadside Collection. Library Company of Philadelphia.

Bruce Family Papers. Virginia Historical Society.

William Cullen Bryant Papers. New York Public Library.

Lant Carpenter Papers. Manchester College. Oxford, U.K.

George William Curtis Papers. Harvard University. Cambridge, Mass.

Andrew Jackson Donelson Papers. Tennessee State Library and Archives. Nashville.

Gooch Family Papers. Virginia Historical Society.

Horace Greeley Papers. New York Public Library.

Harrison Family Papers. Virginia Historical Society.

Hiram Hill Collection. Kansas State Historical Society.

Amos Adams Lawrence Papers. Massachusetts Historical Society.

Lee Family Papers. Virginia Historical Society.

James Russell Lowell Papers. Harvard University.

Theodore Lyman, Jr. Papers. Massachusetts Historical Society.

MacKay and Stiles Family Papers. University of North Carolina Southern Historical Collection.

Manigault Family Papers. South Carolina Historical Society. Charleston.

John Y. Mason Papers. Virginia Historical Society.

David Outlaw Papers. University of North Carolina Southern Historical Collection. Chapel Hill.

William H. Prescott Papers. Massachusetts Historical Society.

Riggs Family Papers. Library of Congress. Washington, D.C.

Charles Sumner Papers. Harvard University.

Samuel Tilden Papers. New York Public Library.

Cyprian Porter Wilcox Diaries. University of Georgia Hargrett Rare Book and Manuscript Library. Athens.

Yeatman-Polk Papers. Tennessee State Library and Archives.

NEWSPAPERS, 1846–56

Albany Argus, Boston Daily Evening Transcript, [Amherst] *Farmer's Cabinet,* [Boston] *Liberator,* [Boston] *National Anti-Slavery Standard, Boston Pilot, Charleston Courier, Cincinnati Atlas,* [Columbus] *Weekly Ohio State Journal, Congressional Globe, Harrisburg Torch Light, London Times, Louisville Journal,* [Madison] *Wisconsin Argus, Nashville Union, New Orleans Daily Picayune, New York Commercial Advertiser, New York Evening Post, New York Herald, New York Sun, New York Times, New York Tribune,* [Philadelphia] *Catholic Herald, Philadelphia Public Ledger, Pittsburgh Post, Richmond Enquirer,* [Richmond] *Religious Herald, Richmond Whig,* [Washington] *National Era,* [Washington] *Daily National Intelligencer*

BOOKS AND ARTICLES

"Absolutism versus Republicanism: The State of Europe." *United States Democratic Review* 31 (November–December 1852): 592–601.

Adams, Henry. *Prussian-American Relations, 1775–1871.* Cleveland, 1960.

"Address of the Democratic members of the Legislature of the State of New York." *Albany Atlas,* extra issue, April 1848. In *Papers of Martin Van Buren.* Washington, D.C., 1960. Microfilm.

Agulhon, Maurice. *The Republican Experiment, 1848–1852.* Cambridge, U.K., 1983.

Alexander, Thomas. "Harbinger of the Collapse of the Second Two Party System: The Free Soil Party of 1848." In *Crisis of Republicanism: American Politics in the Civil War Era,* edited by Lloyd Ambrosius, 17–54. Lincoln, 1990.

Allen, Margaret. "Political and Social Criticism of Margaret Fuller." *South Atlantic Quarterly* 72 (Autumn 1973): 560–73.

Alphabetical List of Towns and Counties. Alamo, Calif., 1970.

Altschuler, Glenn. *Rude Republic: Americans and Their Politics in the Nineteenth Century.* Princeton, 2000.

Amann, Peter. *Revolution and Mass Democracy: The Paris Club Movement in 1848.* Princeton, 1975.

Ambler, Charles Henry, ed. "Correspondence of Robert M. T. Hunter, 1826–1876." In *Report of the American Historical Association for the Year 1916,* vol. 2. Washington, D.C., 1918.

Ames, William. *History of the National Intelligencer.* Chapel Hill, 1972.

Ammon, Harry. *The Genet Mission.* New York, 1973.

Anderson, Bonnie. *Joyous Greetings: The First International Women's Movement, 1830–1860.* New York, 2000.

[Appel, Theodore]. "Kossuth in America." *Mercersburg Review* 4 (January 1852): 81–89.

Arendt, Hannah. *On Revolution.* New York, 1974.

Armitage, David, and Michael Braddick, eds. *The British Atlantic World 1500–1800.* New York, 2002.

Austin, Erik, and Jerome Clubb. *Political Facts of the United States since 1789.* New York, 1986.

Bailey, Thomas. *A Diplomatic History of the American People.* New York, 1969.

Baird, Robert. *Impressions and Experiences of the West Indies and North America in 1849.* Edinburgh, 1850.

———. *Progress and Prospects of Christianity in the United States of America.* London, 1851.

Baker, Jean. *Affairs of Party: The Political Culture of Northern Democrats in the Mid-Nineteenth Century.* Ithaca, 1983.

———. "Ceremonies of Politics: Nineteenth-Century Rituals of National Affirmation." In *A Master's Due: Essays in Honor of David Herbert Donald,* edited by William Cooper, Michael Holt, and John McCardell, 161–78. Baton Rouge, 1985.

———. "From Belief into Culture: Republicanism in the Antebellum North." *American Quarterly* 37 (Fall 1985): 532–50.

Baker, Paula. "Domestication of Politics: Women and American Political Society, 1780–1920." *American Historical Review* 89 (June 1984): 620–47.

Bancroft, George. *History of the United States.* 10 vols. Boston, 1834–74.

Banner, James, Jr. "France and the Origins of American Political Culture." *Virginia Quarterly Review* 64 (1988): 651–70.

Barnes, T. W. *Life of Thurlow Weed Including His Autobiography and a Memoir.* 2 vols. Boston, 1884.

Barney, William. *Secessionist Impulse: Alabama and Mississippi in 1860.* Princeton, 1974.

Barolini, Helen. "The Italian Side of Emily Dickinson." *Virginia Quarterly Review* 70 (1994): 461–79.

Belchem, John. "Nationalism, Republicanism, and Exile: Irish Emigrants and the Revolutions of 1848." *Past and Present* 146 (February 1995): 103–35.

———. "Republican Spirit and Military Science: The 'Irish Brigade' and Irish-American Nationalism in 1848." *Irish Historical Studies* 29 (May 1994): 44–64.

———. "The Waterloo of Peace and Order: The United Kingdom and the Revolutions of 1848." In Dowe et al., *Europe in 1848,* 242–58.

Bell, Caryn Cossé. *Revolution, Romanticism, and the Afro-Creole Protest Tradition in Louisiana 1718–1868.* Baton Rouge, 1997.

Bellows, Barbara. *Benevolence among Slaveholders: Assisting the Poor in Charleston, 1670–1860.* Baton Rouge, 1993.

Belohlavek, John. *George Mifflin Dallas: Jacksonian Patrician.* University Park, Pa., 1977.

Beman, Nathan Sidney Smith. *Characteristics of the Age: A Discourse Delivered in the First Presbyterian Church, Troy New York, On December 12, 1850.* Troy, 1851.

Bender, Thomas. *A Nation among Nations: America's Place in World History.* New York, 2006.

Benson, Lee. *The Concept of Jacksonian Democracy.* New York, 1961.

Benton, Thomas Hart. *Thirty Years' View; or, A History of the American Government for Thirty Years from 1820–1850.* 2 vols. New York, 1857.

Bercovitch, Sacvan. *American Jeremiad.* Madison, 1978.

Berlin, Ira, and Herbert Gutman. "Natives and Immigrants, Free Men and Slaves: Urban Workingmen in the Antebellum American South." *American Historical Review* 88 (December 1983): 1175–2000.

Bernstein, Iver. *The New York City Draft Riots: Their Significance for American Society and Politics in the Age of the Civil War.* New York, 1990.

Bigelow, John. *Retrospections of an Active Life.* 5 vols. New York, 1909–13.

Billington, Ray Allen. *Protestant Crusade, 1800–1860: A Study of the Origins of American Nativism.* New York, 1938.

Bjork, Ulf Jonas. "Commercial Roots of Foreign Correspondence: The *New York Herald* and Foreign News, 1835–1839." *American Journalism* 11 (Spring 1994): 102–15.

Blackburn, Robin. *Overthrow of Colonial Slavery, 1776–1848.* New York, 1988.

"Blackwood's Magazine Article—'Slavery and the Slave Power in the United States.'" *United States Democratic Review* 32 (April 1853): 289–324.

Blondheim, Menahem. *News over the Wires: The Telegraph and the Flow of Public Information in America, 1844–1897.* Cambridge, Mass., 1994.

Blue, Frederick. *The Free Soilers: Third Party Politics, 1848–1854.* Urbana, 1973.

———. *No Taint of Compromise: Crusaders in Antislavery Politics.* Baton Rouge, 2006.

Blumenthal, Henry. *American and French Culture, 1800–1900.* Baton Rouge, 1975.

———. *A Reappraisal of Franco-American Relations, 1830–1871.* Chapel Hill, 1959.

Bodo, John. *Protestant Clergy and Public Issues, 1812–1848.* Princeton, 1954.

Bolt, Christine. *The Women's Movements in the United States and Britain from the 1790s to the 1920s.* New York, 1993.

Boritt, Gabor, ed. *Lincoln, the War President: The Gettysburg Lectures.* New York, 1994.

[Bowen, Francis]. "War of the Races in Hungary." *North American Review* 70 (January 1850): 78–136.

Bozeman, Theodore Dwight. "Inductive and Deductive Politics: Science and Society in Antebellum Presbyterian Thought." *Journal of American History* 64 (December 1977): 704–22.

Brands, H. W. *What America Owes the World: The Struggle for the Soul of Foreign Policy.* New York, 1998.

Brandt, George. *Theatre in Europe: A Documentary History: German and Dutch Theatre, 1600–1848.* Cambridge, U.K., 1993.

Brinton, Crane. *Anatomy of a Revolution.* New York, 1965.

Brock, Peter. *Pacifism in the United States from the Colonial Era to the First World War.* Princeton, 1968.

Broers, Michael. *Europe after Napoleon: Revolution, Reaction and Romanticism, 1814–1848.* Manchester, U.K., 1996.

Bronstein, Jamie. *Land Reform and Working-Class Experience in Britain and the United States, 1800–1862.* Stanford, 1999.

Brooks, Van Wyck. *Dream of Arcadia: American Writers and Artists in Italy, 1760–1915.* New York, 1958.

Brown, Charles. *Agents of Manifest Destiny: The Lives and Times of the Filibusters.* Chapel Hill, 1980.

Brown, Richard, ed. *American Violence.* Englewood Cliffs, N.J., 1970.

Brown, William Wells. *American Fugitive in Europe.* Boston, 1855.

———. *Clotel; or, the President's Daughter: A Narrative of Slave Life in the United States.* Edited by Robert Levine. [1853]. Rpt., Boston, 2000.

———. *Narrative of William Wells Brown, a Fugitive Slave.* Boston, 1848.

Browning, Elizabeth Barrett. *The Letters of Elizabeth Barrett Browning.* 2 vols. Edited by Frederic G. Kenyon. New York, 1898.

Brownson, Orestes. "Conservatism and Radicalism." *Brownson's Quarterly Review* 10 (October 1848): 453–82.

———. "Cooper's *Ways of the Hour.*" *Brownson's Quarterly Review* 13 (July 1851): 273–97.

———. "Know-Nothings." *Brownson's Quarterly Review* 16 (October 1854): 447–87.

———. *Selected Writings.* Edited by Patrick Carey. New York, 1991.

———. "Socialism and the Church." *Brownson's Quarterly Review* 11 (January 1849): 91–127.

Bryan, Edward. *The Rightful Remedy.* Charleston, S.C., 1850.

Bryant, William Cullen. *Letters of a Traveller; or, Notes of Things Seen in Europe and America.* New York, 1850.

Buchanan, James. *The Works of James Buchanan.* 12 vols. Edited by John Bassett Moore. Philadelphia, 1909–11.

Bullard, Anne Tuttle Jones. *Sights and Scenes in Europe.* St. Louis, 1852.

Burke, Martin. *Conundrum of Class: Public Discourse on the Social Order in America.* Chicago, 1995.

Burnham, Walter Dean. *Critical Elections and the Mainsprings of American Politics.* New York, 1970.

———, ed. *Presidential Ballots, 1836–1892.* Baltimore, 1955.

Bushnell, Horace. *Barbarism the First Danger: A Discourse for Home Missions.* New York, 1847.

Butler, Jon. *Awash in a Sea of Faith: Christianizing the American People.* Cambridge, Mass., 1990.

Calhoun, John C. *Disquisition on Government.* Edited by John Anderson. In *Calhoun: Basic Documents,* 29–97. State College, Pa., 1952.

Callcott, George. *History in the United States, 1800–1860.* Baltimore, 1970.

Capper, Charles. *Margaret Fuller: An American Romantic Life: The Public Years.* New York, 2007.

Capper, Charles, and Cristina Giorcelli, eds. *Margaret Fuller: Transatlantic Crossings in a Revolutionary Age.* Madison, 2007.

Carey, Patrick. "Introduction." In *Orestes A. Brownson: Selected Writings*, edited by Patrick Carey, 7–58. New York, 1991.

———. *People, Priests, and Prelates: Ecclesiastical Democracy and the Tensions of Trusteeism*. Notre Dame, Ind., 1987.

Carter, Robert. *The Hungarian Controversy: An Exposure of the Falsifications and Perversions of the Slanderers of Hungary*. Boston, 1852.

Carwardine, Richard. *Evangelicals and Politics in Antebellum America*. New Haven, 1993.

Casper, Henry. *American Attitudes toward the Rise of Napoleon III*. Washington, D.C., 1947.

Chaffin, Tom. *Fatal Glory: Narciso Lopez and the First Clandestine U.S. War against Cuba*. Charlottesville, 1996.

Chase, Salmon. *Papers*. Edited by John Niven. 5 vols. Kent, Ohio, 1993–98.

Chevigny, Bell Gale. "The Long Arm of Censorship: Myth-Making in Margaret Fuller's Time and Our Own." *Signs* 2 (Winter 1976): 450–60.

———. "To the Edges of Ideology: Margaret Fuller's Centrifugal Revolution." *American Quarterly* 38 (Summer 1986): 173–201.

———. *The Woman and the Myth: Margaret Fuller's Life and Writings*. New York, 1976.

Church, Clive. *Europe in 1830: Revolution and Political Change*. London, 1983.

Clark, Henry Hayden. "The Vogue of Macaulay in America." *Transactions of the Wisconsin Academy of Sciences, Arts and Letters* 34 (1942): 237–92.

Clark, Robert. "German Liberals in New Orleans (1840–1860)." *Louisiana Historical Quarterly* 20 (January–October 1937): 137–51.

Clark, Timothy. *Absolute Bourgeois: Artists and Politics in France, 1848–1851*. Greenwich, Conn., 1973.

Clarke, Erskine. *Our Southern Zion: A History of Calvinism in the South Carolina Low Country, 1690–1990*. Tuscaloosa, 1996.

Coffin, Tristram Potter. *Uncertain Glory: Folklore and the American Revolution*. Detroit, 1971.

Cohen, Henry. *Business and Politics in America from the Age of Jackson to the Civil War: The Career of W. W. Corcoran*. Westport, Conn., 1971.

Cohen, Warren, gen. ed. *Cambridge History of American Foreign Relations*. 4 vols. Vol. 1, *The Creation of a Republican Empire, 1776–1865*, by Bradford Perkins. Cambridge, U.K., 1993.

Colbenson, Pamela Elwyn. "Millennial Thought among Southern Evangelicals, 1830–1865." Ph.D. dissertation, Georgia State University, 1980.

Cole, Arthur. "The South and the Right of Secession in the Early Fifties." *Mississippi Valley Historical Review* 1 (December 1914): 376–99.

Cole, Phyllis. "Stanton, Fuller, and the Grammar of Romanticism." *New England Quarterly* 73 (December 2000): 533–59.

Coleman, Edward. "William Wells Brown as an Historian." *Journal of Negro History* 31 (January 1946): 47–59.

Colfax, Schuyler. *The "Laws" of Kansas: Speech of Schuyler Colfax, of Indiana, in the House of Representatives, June 21, 1856.* Washington, D.C., 1856.

Commons, John. *History of Labour in the United States.* 4 vols. New York, 1921–35.

Conkin, Paul. *Uneasy Center: Reformed Christianity in Antebellum America.* Chapel Hill, 1995.

"Constitutions of France." *Southern Quarterly Review* 16 (January 1850): 502–36.

Copeland, Fayette. *Kendall of the Picayune.* Norman, 1997.

Cott, Nancy. *Bonds of Womanhood: "Woman's Sphere" in New England, 1780–1835.* New Haven, 1977.

Craven, Avery. *Growth of Southern Nationalism 1848–1861.* Baton Rouge, 1953.

Craven, Wesley Frank. *The Legend of the Founding Fathers.* New York, 1956.

Cross, Joseph. *Pizgah-Views of the Promised Inheritance: A Series of Dissertations on the Unaccomplished Prophecies.* New York, 1856.

Crouthamel, James L. *Bennett's* New York Herald *and the Rise of the Popular Press.* Syracuse, 1989.

Cunliffe, Marcus. *Soldiers and Civilians: The Martial Spirit in America, 1775–1865.* Boston, 1968.

Curti, Merle. "Austria and the United States 1848–1852." *Smith College Studies in History* 11 (April 1926): 141–206.

———. "George N. Sanders—American Patriot of the Fifties." *South Atlantic Quarterly* 27 (January 1928): 79–87.

———. "Impact of the Revolutions of 1848 on American Thought." *Proceedings of the American Philosophical Society* 93 (June 1949): 209–15.

———. "John C. Calhoun and the Unification of Germany." *American Historical Review* 40 (1934–35): 476–78.

———. "Young America." *American Historical Review* 32 (October 1926): 34–55.

Curtis, Eugene. "American Opinion of the French Nineteenth-Century Revolutions." *American Historical Review* 29 (January 1924): 249–70.

———. *The French Revolution of 1848 and American Constitutional Doctrine.* New York, 1918.

Curtiss, Daniel. *Western Portraiture, and Emigrant's Guide.* New York, 1852.

Dal Lago, Enrico. "Radicalism and Nationalism: Northern 'Liberators' and Southern Labourers in the USA and Italy, 1830–1860." In *The American South and the Italian Mezzogiorno,* ed. Enrico Dal Lago and Rick Halpern, 197–214. New York, 2002.

Dal Lago, Enrico, and Rick Halpern, eds. *The American South and the Italian Mezzogiorno.* New York, 2002.

Davies, Edward. *The United States in World History.* New York, 2006.

Davis, David Brion, ed. *The Fear of Conspiracy: Images of Un-American Subversion from the Revolution to the Present.* Ithaca, 1971.

———. *The Problem of Slavery in Western Culture.* New York, 1966.

———. *Revolutions: Reflections on American Equality and Foreign Liberations.* Cambridge, Mass., 1990.

———. *Slavery and Human Progress.* New York, 1984.

Davis, Robert Ralph, Jr. "Diplomatic Plumage: American Court Dress in the Early National Period." *American Quarterly* 20 (Summer 1968): 164–79.

Day, Timothy. *The Democratic Party as It Was and as It Is. Speech of Hon. Timothy C. Day of Ohio, In the House of Representatives, April 23, 1856.* Washington, D.C., 1856.

Deák, István. *Lawful Revolution: Louis Kossuth and the Hungarians, 1848–49.* New York, 1979.

"Declaration of Sentiments and Resolutions, Seneca Falls." In Schneir, *Feminism,* 83–85.

"Defining America: Why the U.S. Is Unique." *U.S. News & World Report,* 28 June 2004, 36–72.

Degler, Carl. "One among Many: The United States and National Unification." In Boritt, *Lincoln, the War President,* 89–120.

Deiss, Joseph Jay. *The Roman Years of Margaret Fuller.* New York, 1969.

"The Democratic Nomination." *American Whig Review* 16 (August 1852): 127–37.

Di Scala, Spencer. *Italy: From Revolution to Republic.* Boulder, 1995.

Disturnell, John. *Disturnell's American and European Railway and Steamship Guide.* New York, 1853.

Donald, David. *Charles Sumner and the Coming of the Civil War.* New York, 1960.

Dondore, Dorothy. "Banvard's Panorama and the Flowering of New England." *New England Quarterly* 11 (December 1938): 817–26.

Donelson, Andrew. "Selected Letters, 1846–1856, from the Donelson Papers." Edited by St. George L. Sioussat. *Tennessee Historical Magazine* 3 (1917): 257–91.

Dormon, James, Jr. *Theater in the Antebellum South, 1815–1861.* Chapel Hill, 1967.

Douglas, Ann. *The Feminization of American Culture.* New York, 1977.

Douglass, Frederick. "Editorial from *The North Star.*" In Schneir, *Feminism,* 27–53.

———. *Frederick Douglass Papers Series One: Speeches, Debates, and Interviews.* 5 vols. Edited by John Blassingame. New Haven, 1979–92.

Dowe, Dieter, et al., eds. *Europe in 1848: Revolution and Reform.* Translated by David Higgins. New York, 2001.

Drescher, Seymour. "British Way, French Way: Opinion Building and Revolution in the Second French Slave Emancipation." *American Historical Review* 96 (June 1991): 709–34.

———. *From Slavery to Freedom: Comparative Studies in the Rise and Fall of Atlantic Slavery.* New York, 1999.

———. "Servile Insurrection and John Brown's Body in Europe." In *His Soul Goes Marching On: Responses to the John Brown Raid,* edited by Paul Finkelman, 253–95. Charlottesville, 1995.

DuBois, Ellen Carol. *Feminism and Suffrage: The Emergence of an Independent Women's Movement in America 1848–1869.* Ithaca, 1978.

Dupeux, George. *French Society, 1789–1970.* Translated by Peter Wait. London, 1977.

Durang, Charles. *Durang's Terpsichore; or, Ball Room Guide.* Philadelphia, 1848.

Dwight, Theodore. *The Roman Republic of 1849: with Accounts of the Inquisition, and the Siege of Rome, and Biographical Sketches.* New York, 1851.

Earnest, Ernest. *Expatriates and Patriots: American Artists, Scholars, and Writers in Europe.* Durham, 1968.

Eaton, Clement. *The Freedom-of-Thought Struggle in the Old South.* New York, 1964.

Eckes, Alfred. *Opening America's Market: U.S. Foreign Trade Policy since 1776.* Chapel Hill, 1995.

Ekirch, Arthur. *The Idea of Progress in America, 1815–1860.* New York, 1944.

Elkins, Stanley, and Eric McKitrick. *The Age of Federalism.* New York, 1993.

Ellis, Geoffrey. *The Napoleonic Empire.* Atlantic Highlands, N.J., 1991.

———. "The Revolution of 1848–1849 in France." In Evans and Pogge von Strandmann, *Revolutions in Europe,* 27–53.

Ellis, Richard. *American Political Cultures.* New York, 1993.

———. *Union at Risk: Jacksonian Democracy, States' Rights and the Nullification Crisis.* New York, 1987.

Elson, Ruth. *Guardians of Tradition: American Schoolbooks of the Nineteenth Century.* Lincoln, 1964.

Erickson, Charlotte, ed. *Invisible Immigrants: The Adaptation of English and Scottish Immigrants in 19th-Century America.* Ithaca, 1990.

Etcheson, Nicole. *Bleeding Kansas: Contested Liberty in the Civil War Era.* Lawrence, 2004.

Evans, R. J. W. "1848–1849 in the Habsburg Monarchy." In Evans and Pogge von Strandmann, *Revolutions in Europe,* 181–206.

Evans, R. J. W., and Hartmut Pogge von Strandmann, eds. *The Revolutions in Europe, 1848–1849: From Reform to Reaction.* Oxford, U.K., 2000.

Evans, William McKee. "From the Land of Canaan to the Land of Guinea: The Strange Odyssey of the 'Sons of Ham.'" *American Historical Review* 85 (February 1980): 15–43.

Everett, Donald. "Emigres and Militiamen: Free Persons of Color in New Orleans, 1803–1815." *Journal of Negro History* 38 (October 1953): 377–402.

Eyck, Frank. *Frankfort Parliament, 1848–1849.* New York, 1968.

Farmer, James Oscar. *Metaphysical Confederacy: James Henley Thornwell and the Synthesis of Southern Values.* Macon, Ga., 1986.

Farrison, William. *William Wells Brown: Author and Reformer.* Chicago, 1969.

Faust, Drew. *The Creation of Confederate Nationalism: Ideology and Identity in the Civil War South.* Baton Rouge, 1988.

———. *A Sacred Circle: The Dilemma of the Intellectual in the Old South, 1840–1860.* Baltimore, 1977.

Feldberg, Michael. *The Turbulent Era: Riot and Disorder in Jacksonian America.* New York, 1980.

Fellman, Michael. "Theodore Parker and the Abolitionist Role in the 1850s." *Journal of American History* 61 (December 1974): 666–84.

Fermer, Douglas. *James Gordon Bennett and the* New York Herald: *A Study of Editorial Opinion in the Civil War Era, 1854–1867.* New York, 1986.

Field, James. *From Gibraltar to the Middle East: America and the Mediterranean World, 1776–1882.* Chicago, 1991.

"Financial and Commercial Review." *United States Magazine and Democratic Review* 22 (May 1848): 464–67.

Fitzhugh, George. *Cannibals All! or, Slaves without Masters.* Edited by C. Van Woodward. Cambridge, Mass., 1988.

Fladeland, Betty. *Men and Brothers: Anglo-American Antislavery Cooperation.* Urbana, 1972.

Foner, Eric. *Free Soil, Free Labor, Free Men: The Ideology of the Republican Party before the Civil War.* New York, 1995.

———. *Reconstruction: America's Unfinished Revolution.* New York, 1988.

———. *Tom Paine and Revolutionary America.* New York, 1976.

Foner, Philip, and George Walker, eds. *Proceedings of the Black State Conventions, 1840–1865.* 2 vols. Philadelphia, 1979.

"Foreign Correspondence." *Living Age,* 6 May 1848, 281–87.

"Foreign Policy of the United States in 1825–6. Cuba." *United States Democratic Review* 32 (January 1853): 36–48.

Formisano, Ronald. "Political Character, Antipartyism and the Second Party System." *American Quarterly* 21 (Winter 1969): 683–709.

Forney, John. *Address on Religious Intolerance and Political Proscription.* Washington, D.C., 1855.

Fortescue, William. *Alphonse de Lamartine: A Political Biography.* London, 1983.

Fox-Genovese, Elizabeth, and Eugene Genovese. *The Mind of the Master Class: History and Faith in the Southern Slaveholders' Worldview.* New York, 2005.

Franchot, Jenny. *Roads to Rome: The Antebellum Protestant Encounter with Catholicism.* Berkeley, 1994.

Freehling, William. *Road to Disunion: Secessionists at Bay, 1776–1854.* New York, 1990.

Free Soil Minstrel. New York, 1848.

"French Ideas of Democracy and a Community of Goods." *North American Review* 69 (October 1849): 77–325.

Fritz, Christian. "Popular Sovereignty, Vigilantism, and the Constitutional Right of Revolution." *Pacific Historical Review* 63 (February 1994): 39–66.

Fuller, Margaret. *Letters.* 6 vols. Edited by Robert Hudspeth. Ithaca, 1983–94.

———. *Memoirs of Margaret Fuller Ossoli.* 2 vols. Edited by Ralph Waldo Emerson, William Henry Channing, and James Freeman Clarke. Boston, 1859.

———. "Narrative of the Life of Frederick Douglass, an American Slave." In *Margaret Fuller's New York Journalism,* edited by Catherine Mitchell, 136–38. Knoxville, 1995.

———. *These Sad but Glorious Days: Dispatches from Europe, 1846–1850.* Edited by Larry Reynolds and Susan Belasco Smith. New Haven, Conn., 1991.

————. *Woman in the Nineteenth Century.* Edited by Larry Reynolds. New York, 1997.

Gale, Robert. *Cultural Encyclopedia of the 1850s in America.* Westport, Conn., 1993.

————. *Thomas Crawford: American Sculptor.* Pittsburgh, 1964.

Gales, Joseph. *Sketch of the Personal Character and Qualities of General Zachary Taylor.* Washington, D.C., 1848.

"Gallery of Industry and Enterprise: Daniel Pratt of Prattville, Alabama." *Debow's Review* 10 (February 1851): 225–28.

Gannett, Henry. *American Names.* Washington, D.C., 1947.

Gardiner, Oliver Cromwell. *The Great Issue; or, The Three Presidential Candidates; Being a Brief Historical Sketch of the Free Soil Question in the United States.* New York, 1848.

Garrison, Wendell Phillips, and Francis Jackson Garrison. *William Lloyd Garrison 1805–1879: The Story of His Life. Told by His Children.* 4 vols. New York, 1969.

Garrison, William Lloyd. *A Letter to Louis Kossuth.* New York, 1969.

Gatell, Frank Otto. "'Conscience and Judgment': The Bolt of the Massachusetts Conscience Whigs." *Historian* 21 (November 1958): 18–45.

Gaustad, Edwin Scott. *Historical Atlas of Religion in America.* New York, 1976.

Gazley, John. *American Opinion of German Unification, 1848–1871.* New York, 1926.

Gemme, Paola. *The Italian Risorgimento and Antebellum American Identity.* Athens, Ga., 2005.

Genovese, Eugene. *The Political Economy of Slavery.* New York, 1965.

Gerring, John. *Party Ideologies in America, 1828–1996.* New York, 1998.

Gettleman, Marvin. *The Dorr Rebellion: A Study in American Radicalism 1833–1849.* New York, 1980.

Geyer, Michael, and Charles Bright. "Global Violence and Nationalizing Wars in Eurasia and America: The Geopolitics of War in the Mid-Nineteenth Century." *Comparative Studies in Society and History* 38 (October 1996): 619–57.

Gienapp, William. *Origins of the Republican Party 1852–1856.* New York, 1987.

Gildea, Robert. *Barricades and Borders: Europe, 1800–1914.* New York, 1987.

Ginzberg, Lori. *Women and the Work of Benevolence: Morality, Politics, and Class in the 19th-Century United States.* New Haven, 1990.

Ginsborg, Paul. *Daniele Manin and the Venetian Revolution of 1848–49.* Cambridge, U.K., 1979.

Gitlin, Todd. *The Sixties: Years of Hope, Days of Rage.* New York, 1993.

Gleeson, David. *Irish in the South, 1815–1877.* Chapel Hill, 2001.

Glickstein, Jonathan. *American Exceptionalism, American Anxiety: Wages, Competition, and Degraded Labor in the Antebellum United States.* Charlottesville, 2002.

"Glimpses at Europe in 1848, Part I: Magyar and Croat." *Southern Literary Messenger* 15 (January 1849): 1–10.

Godwin, Parke. *Political Essays.* New York, 1856.

Goebel, Julius, Jr. *The Recognition Policy of the United States.* New York, 1915.

Gossett, Thomas. *Uncle Tom's Cabin and American Culture.* Dallas, 1985.

"Gossip of the Month." *United States Democratic Review* 23 (August 1848): 185–92.

Graburn, Nelson H. H. "Tourism: The Sacred Journey." In *Hosts and Guests: The Anthropology of Tourism,* edited by Valene Smith, 17–31. Philadelphia, 1977.

Grant, David. "*Uncle Tom's Cabin* and the Triumph of Republican Rhetoric." *New England Quarterly* 71 (September 1998): 429–48.

[Greeley, Horace]. "Election of 1848." In *Tribune Almanac for the Years 1838 to 1868.* New York, 1868.

———. *Glances at Europe . . . During the Summer of 1851.* New York, 1851.

———. *Recollections of a Busy Life.* Port Washington, Me., 1971.

Greeley, Horace, and Henry Raymond. *Association Discussed; or, the Socialism of the Tribune Examined being a Controversy between the New-York Tribune and the Courier and Enquirer.* New York, 1847.

Greene, Jack, ed. *The Ambiguity of the American Revolution.* New York, 1968.

———. *The Intellectual Construction of America: Exceptionalism and Identity from 1492 to 1800.* Chapel Hill, 1993.

Greenough, Horatio. "Etchings with a Chisel." *United States Magazine and Democratic Review* 18 (February 1846): 118–26.

Gribbin, William. "The Covenant Transformed: The Jeremiad Tradition and the War of 1812." *Church History* 40 (September 1971): 297–305.

Griffith, Gwilyn. *Mazzini: Prophet of Modern Europe.* New York, 1970.

Grimsted, David. *Melodrama Unveiled: American Theater and Culture, 1800–1850.* Chicago, 1968.

Grow, G. A. *Admission of Kansas. Speech of Hon. G. A. Grow, of Pennsylvania, in the House of Representatives, June 30, 1856.* Washington, D.C., 1856.

Guarneri, Carl. "Abolition and American Reform in Transatlantic Perspective." *Mid-America* 82 (Winter–Summer 2000): 21–49.

———. *Utopian Alternative: Fourierism in Nineteenth-Century America.* Ithaca, 1991.

"Guizot's Democracy in France." *Southern Quarterly Review* 15 (January–April 1849): 114–65.

Gustafson, Sandra. "Choosing a Medium: Margaret Fuller and the Forms of Sentiment." *American Quarterly* 47 (March 1995): 34–65.

Hales, E. E. Y. *Pio Nono: A Study in European Politics and Religion in the Nineteenth Century.* New York, 1954.

Hamilton, Holman. "Election of 1848." In *History of American Presidential Elections, 1789–1968,* 4 vols., edited by Arthur Schlesinger Jr., 2: 865–918. New York, 1971.

———. *Henry Clay and the Whig Party.* Chapel Hill, 1936.

———. *Prologue to Conflict: The Crisis and Compromise of 1850.* Lexington, Ky., 1964.

———. *Zachary Taylor: Soldier in the White House.* Hamden, Conn., 1966.

Hanley, Mark. *Beyond a Christian Commonwealth: The Protestant Quarrel with the American Republic, 1830–1860.* Chapel Hill, 1994.

Harris, Jennifer. "The Red Cap of Liberty: A Study of Dress Worn by French Revolutionary Partisans, 1789–94." *Eighteenth-Century Studies* 14 (Spring 1981): 283–312.

Harrold, Stanley. *Gamaliel Bailey and Antislavery Union.* Kent, Ohio, 1986.

Harvard University. *Annual Catalogue of the Officers and Students of the University at Cambridge, 1847–1852.* Cambridge, Mass., 1847–52.

Hassard, John R. G. *Life of John Hughes First Archbishop of New York.* New York, 1969.

Hatch, Nathan. *Democratization of American Christianity.* New Haven, 1989.

Hawthorne, Nathaniel. *The Portable Hawthorne.* Edited by Malcolm Cowley. New York, 1948.

Headley, Phineas Camp. *Life of Louis Kossuth.* Auburn, N.Y., 1852.

Heimert, Alan. "*Moby-Dick* and American Political Symbolism." *American Quarterly* 15 (Winter 1963): 498–534.

Hewitt, Nancy. "Re-rooting American Women's Activism: Global Perspectives on 1848." In *Woman's Rights and Human Rights,* edited by Patricia Grimshaw, Katie Holmes, and Marilyn Lake, 123–37. New York, 2001.

Hickey, Donald. *The War of 1812: A Forgotten Conflict.* Urbana, 1995.

Hietala, Thomas. *Manifest Design: American Exceptionalism and Empire.* Ithaca, 2002.

Higginson, Thomas. *The New Revolution: What Commitment Requires.* Boston, 1857.

Higham, John. *From Boundlessness to Consolidation: The Transformation of American Culture, 1848–1860.* Ann Arbor, 1969.

Hinton, Richard. *John Brown and His Men.* New York, 1968.

"*Histoire des Girondins:* par A. DeLamartine." *Southern Quarterly Review* 16 (October 1849): 53–76.

"History of the Siege of Boston, and of the Battles of Lexington, Concord, and Bunker Hill." *North American Review* 70 (April 1850): 405–24.

Hobsbawm, Eric. *Age of Revolution, 1789–1848.* New York, 1962.

Hofstadter, Richard. *The Paranoid Style in American Politics and Other Essays.* Chicago, 1979.

Hohenberg, John. *Foreign Correspondence: The Great Reporters and Their Times.* Syracuse, 1995.

Holbrook, Francis, and John Nikol. "Reporting the Sicilian Revolution of 1848–1849." *American Neptune* 43 (July 1983): 165–76.

Holdredge, Helen. *Woman in Black: The Life of Lola Montez.* New York, 1955.

Holt, Michael. *Political Parties and American Political Development: From the Age of Jackson to the Age of Lincoln.* Baton Rouge, 1992.

———. *The Rise and Fall of the American Whig Party.* New York, 2003.

Horgan, John. "The South and the European Revolutions of 1848." In *Consortium on Revolutionary Europe, 1750–1850, Proceedings, 1993,* edited by Gordon Bond and John Rooney Jr., 604–25. Tallahassee, 1993.

Horsman, Reginald. *Race and Manifest Destiny: The Origins of American Racial Anglo-Saxonism.* Cambridge, Mass., 1981.

Howard, E. D., and J. H. Clark. *Clarion of Freedom: A Collection of Free Soil Songs.* Cleveland, 1848.

Howard, Leon. *Victorian Knight-Errant: A Study of the Early Literary Career of James Russell Lowell.* Berkeley, 1952.

Howe, Daniel Walker. *Political Culture of the American Whigs.* Chicago, 1979.

———. *The Unitarian Conscience, 1805–1861.* Middletown, Conn., 1988.

Hucko, Elmar, ed. *The Democratic Tradition: Four German Constitutions.* New York, 1987.

Hughes, John. *The Church and the World: A Lecture.* New York, 1850.

———. *The Decline of Protestantism, and Its Cause: A Lecture.* New York, 1850.

"Hungary." *Southern Literary Messenger* 17 (August 1851): 505–16.

Hunt, Alfred. *Haiti's Influence on Antebellum America: Slumbering Volcano in the Caribbean.* Baton Rouge, 1988.

[Hunt, Freeman]. "Commercial Chronicle and Review." *Merchants' Magazine and Commercial Review* 19 (July 1848): 81–87.

———. "Commercial Chronicle and Review." *Merchants' Magazine and Commercial Review* 20 (April 1849): 419–24.

———. "Commercial Chronicle and Review." *Merchants' Magazine and Commercial Review* 21 (August 1849): 209–14.

Hunt, Lynn. *Politics, Culture, and Class in the French Revolution.* Berkeley, 1984.

Hunt, Michael. *Ideology and U.S. Foreign Policy.* New Haven, 1987.

Huntington, Samuel. "Conservatism as an Ideology." *American Political Science Review* 51 (June 1957): 454–73.

Husch, Gail E. *Something Coming: Apocalyptic Expectation and Mid-Nineteenth Century American Painting.* Lebanon, N.H., 2000.

Huxman, Susan Schultz. "Mary Wollstonecraft, Margaret Fuller, Angelina Grimké: Symbolic Convergence and a Nascent Rhetorical Vision." *Communication Quarterly* 44 (Winter 1996): 16–28.

Hyndman, H. M. *Commercial Crises of the Nineteenth Century.* New York, 1967.

In Perils By Mine Own Countrymen. Three Years On the Kansas Border. By a Clergyman of the Episcopal Church. New York, 1856.

Isely, Jeter Allen. *Horace Greeley and the Republican Party, 1853–1861: A Study of the New York Tribune.* New York, 1965.

[J.]. "The National Anniversary." *Southern Quarterly Review* 2 (September 1850): 170–91.

Jameson, J. Franklin, ed. "Correspondence of John C. Calhoun." In *Annual Report of the American Historical Association for the Year 1899,* 2. Washington, D.C., 1900.

Jefferson, Thomas. *Notes on the State of Virginia.* Edited by David Waldstreicher. New York, 2002.

Jennings, Thelma. *The Nashville Convention: Southern Movement for Unity, 1848–1861.* Memphis, 1980.

Johannsen, Robert. *To the Halls of the Montezumas: The Mexican War in the American Imagination.* New York, 1985.

Johnson, Allen, ed. *Dictionary of American Biography.* 10 vols. New York, 1964.

Johnson, Douglas. *Guizot: Aspects of French History, 1787–1874.* London, 1963.

Jonas, Manfred. *The United States and Germany: A Diplomatic History.* Ithaca, 1984.

Kaestle, Carl. *Pillars of the Republic: Common Schools and American Society, 1780–1860.* New York, 1983.

Kagan, Robert. *Of Paradise and Power: America and Europe in the New World Order.* New York, 2003.

Kammen, Michael. *A Machine That Would Go of Itself: The Constitution in American Culture.* New York, 1986.

———. *Mystic Chords of Memory: The Transformation of Tradition in American Culture.* New York, 1991.

———. *A Season of Youth: The American Revolution and the Historical Imagination.* Ithaca, 1988.

Kamphoefner, Walter. "Dreissiger and Forty-Eighter: The Political Influence of Two Generations of German Political Exiles." In *Germany and America: Essays on Problems of International Relations and Immigration,* edited by Hans Trefousse, 89–102. New York, 1980.

Kaplan, Lawrence. "The Monroe Doctrine and the Truman Doctrine: The Case of Greece." *Journal of the Early Republic* 13 (Spring 1993): 1–21.

Kasson, John. *Rudeness and Civility: Manners in Nineteenth-Century Urban America.* New York, 1990.

Katz, Philip Mark. *From Appomattox to Montmartre: Americans and the Paris Commune.* Cambridge, Mass., 1998.

Kearns, Francis. "Margaret Fuller and the Abolition Movement." *Journal of the History of Ideas* 25 (January–March 1964): 120–27.

Kerber, Linda. *Women of the Republic: Intellect and Ideology in Revolutionary America.* Chapel Hill, 1980.

Kerber, Linda, Alice Kessler-Harris, and Kathryn Kish Sklar, eds. *U.S. History to Women's History: New Feminist Essays.* Chapel Hill, 1995.

Kestenbaum, Lawrence. *The Political Graveyard: A Database of Historic Cemeteries.* 9 August 2008. http://politicalgraveyard.com.

Keyssar, Alexander. *The Right to Vote: The Contested History of Democracy in the United States.* New York, 2001.

Kime, Wayne. *Donald G. Mitchell.* Boston, 1985.

Kirk, Edward Norris. *The Church Essential to the Republic. A Sermon on Behalf of the American Home Missionary Society.* New York, 1848.

Klunder, Willard Carl. *Lewis Cass and the Politics of Moderation.* Kent, Ohio, 1996.

Kolchin, Peter. *Unfree Labor: American Slavery and Russian Serfdom.* Cambridge, Mass., 1987.

Komlos, John. *Louis Kossuth in America, 1851–1852.* Buffalo, 1973.

Kossuth, Louis. *The Future of Nations: In What Consists Its Security, Delivered in New York June 21, 1852.* New York, 1854.

———. "Kossuth before Ohio Legislature." *Ohio Archaeological and Historical Publications* 12 (1903): 114–19.

———. *Select Speeches of Kossuth.* Edited by Francis Newman. London, 1853.

Kossuth in New England: A Full Account of the Hungarian Governor's Visit to Massachusetts; with His Speeches, and the Addresses That Were Made to Him, carefully revised and corrected. Boston, 1852.

Kuklick, Bruce. *Churchmen and Philosophers: From Jonathan Edwards to John Dewey.* New Haven, 1985.

LaFeber, Walter. "Liberty and Power: U.S. Diplomatic History, 1750–1945." In *The New American History,* edited by Eric Foner, 277–301. Philadelphia, 1990.

Langewiesche, Deiter. "The Role of the Military in the European Revolutions of 1848." In Dowe et al., *Europe in 1848,* 694–707.

Langguth, A. J. *Union 1812: The Americans Who Fought the Second War of Independence.* New York, 2006.

Langley, Lester. *The Americas in the Age of Revolution, 1750–1850.* New Haven, 1996.

Laurie, Bruce. *Working People of Philadelphia, 1800–1850.* Philadelphia, 1980.

Leaman, John. *Discourse Delivered on Thanksgiving Day in the Church of Cedar Grove, 12 December 1850.* Lancaster, Pa., 1850.

[Leisler, Jacob]. *Letters to the People of Pennsylvania on the Political Principles of the Free Soil Party.* Philadelphia, 1850.

Lerner, Ralph. *Revolutions Revisited: Two Faces of the Politics of Enlightenment.* Chapel Hill, 1994.

Lester, Charles Edward. *Life and Public Services of Charles Sumner.* New York, 1874.

Lévêque, Pierre. "The Revolutionary Crisis of 1848/51 in France." In Dowe et al., *Europe in 1848,* 91–119.

Levine, Bruce. *Spirit of 1848: German Immigrants, Labor Conflict, and the Coming of the Civil War.* Urbana, 1992.

Levine, Lawrence. *Highbrow Lowbrow: The Emergence of Cultural Hierarchy in America.* Cambridge, Mass., 1988.

Lewis, Merrill. "Organic Metaphor and Edenic Myth in George Bancroft's History of the United States." *Journal of the History of Ideas* 26 (October–December 1965): 587–92.

Lieber, Francis. *Life and Letters of Francis Lieber.* Edited by Thomas Sergeant Perry. Boston, 1882.

Lincoln, Abraham. *Collected Works.* 9 vols. Edited by Roy Basler. New Brunswick, N.J., 1953–55.

———. *Selected Speeches and Writings.* New York, 1992.

Lippard, George. *George Lippard, Prophet of Protest: Writings of an American Radical, 1822–1854.* Edited by David Reynolds. New York, 1986.

Livingston, Craig. "Eyes on 'the Whole European World': Mormon Observers of the 1848 Revolutions." *Journal of Mormon History* 32 (Fall 2005): 78–112.

Lossing, Benson. *Field-Book of the American Revolution.* New Orleans, 1972.

Lott, Eric. *Love and Theft: Blackface Minstrelsy and the American Working Class.* New York, 1993.

Loveland, Anne. *Southern Evangelicals and the Social Order, 1800–1860.* Baton Rouge, 1980.

Luther v. Borden. 48 U.S. 1 (1849).

Lynch, William. "Antislavery Tendencies of the Democratic Party in the Northwest, 1848–1850." *Mississippi Valley Historical Review* 11 (December 1929): 319–31.

Lynd, Staughton. *Intellectual Origins of American Radicalism.* New York, 1968.

Macauley, John. *Unitarianism in the Antebellum South: The Other Invisible Institution.* Tuscaloosa, 2001.

"Manufactures in South Carolina and the South." *Debow's Review* 11 (August 1851): 123–40.

Marilley, Suzanne. *Woman Suffrage and the Origins of Liberal Feminism in the United States, 1820–1920.* Cambridge, Mass., 1996.

Marraro, Howard. *American Opinion on the Unification of Italy, 1846–1861.* New York, 1932.

———, ed. *Diplomatic Relations between the United States and the Kingdom of the Two Sicilies: Instructions and Despatches, 1816–1861.* 2 vols. New York, 1951.

———. "Unpublished American Documents on the Roman Republic of 1849." *Catholic Historical Review* 28 (January 1943): 459–90.

Mathews, Donald. *Religion in the Old South.* Chicago, 1977.

Marx, Karl. *Class Struggles in France, 1848–1850.* New York, 1964.

Marx, Karl, and Friedrich Engels. *Collected Works.* Translated by Richard Dixon et al. 49 vols. New York, 1975.

May, Arthur James. *Contemporary American Opinion on the Mid-Century Revolutions in Central Europe.* Philadelphia, 1927.

May, Robert. *Manifest Destiny's Underworld: Filibustering in Antebellum America.* Chapel Hill, 2002.

———. *The Southern Dream of a Caribbean Empire.* Gainesville, 2002.

Mayfield, John. *Rehearsal for Republicanism: Free Soil and the Politics of Antislavery.* Port Washington, Me., 1980.

McArthur, Lewis. *Oregon Geographic Names.* Portland, Ore., 2003.

M'Cay, C. F. "Review of the Cotton Trade." *Merchants' Magazine and Commercial Review* 21 (December 1849): 595–601.

McCloy, Shelby. *The Negro in the French West Indies.* Lexington, Ky., 1966.

McCoy, Drew. *Last of the Fathers: James Madison and the Republican Legacy.* New York, 1989.

McDaniel, W. Caleb. "'Our Country Is the World': American Abolitionists, Louis Kossuth, and Philanthropic Revolution." Paper presented at the 2004 conference of the Organization of American Historians, Boston.

McDermott, Gerald. *One Holy and Happy Society: The Public Theology of Jonathan Edwards.* University Park, Pa., 1992.

McDermott, John. *Lost Panoramas of the Mississippi.* Chicago, 1958.

McEvoy-Levy, Siobhan. *American Exceptionalism and U.S. Foreign Policy: Public Diplomacy at the End of the Cold War.* New York, 2001.

McFeely, William. *Frederick Douglass*. New York, 1991.

McGavock, Randal William. *Pen and Sword: The Life and Journals of Randal W. Mc-Gavock*. Edited by Herschel Gower and Jack Allen. Nashville, 1960.

McGill, Alexander Taggart. *Popery the Punishment of Unbelief. A Sermon Before the General Assembly of the Presbyterian Church*. Philadelphia, 1848.

McGreevy, John. *Catholicism and American Freedom*. New York, 2003.

McInerney, Daniel. *Fortunate Heirs of Freedom: Abolition and Republican Thought*. Lincoln, 1994.

McKivigan, John, and Stanley Harrold, eds. *Antislavery Violence: Sectional, Racial, and Cultural Conflict in Antebellum America*. Knoxville, 1999.

McLanathan, Richard. *American Tradition in the Arts*. New York, 1968.

McLeod, Hugh. *Religion and the People of Western Europe, 1789–1970*. New York, 1990.

McPherson, James. *Abraham Lincoln and the Second American Revolution*. New York, 1990.

———. *Battle Cry of Freedom: The Civil War Era*. New York, 1988.

———. *Drawn with the Sword: Reflections on the American Civil War*. New York, 1996.

———. "'The Whole Family of Man': Lincoln and the Last Best Hope Abroad." In McPherson, *Drawn with the Sword*, 208–27.

Mead, David. "Brownson and Kossuth in Cincinnati." *Historical and Philosophical Society of Ohio Bulletin*, April 1949, 90–93.

Meenaugh, Martin. "Archbishop John Hughes and the New York Schools Controversy." *American Nineteenth Century History* 5 (Spring 2004): 34–65.

Merk, Frederick. "Dissent in the Mexican War." In *Dissent in Three American Wars*, edited by Samuel Eliot Morison, Frederick Merk, and Frank Freidel, 35–63. Cambridge, Mass., 1970.

———. *Manifest Destiny and Mission in American History: A Reinterpretation*. New York, 1966.

Merriman, John. *The Agony of the Republic: The Repression of the Left in Revolutionary France 1848–1851*. New Haven, 1978.

Messer-Kruse, Timothy. *Yankee International: Marxism and the American Reform Tradition 1848–1876*. Chapel Hill, 1998.

Meyer, Howard, ed. *The Magnificent Activist: The Writings of Thomas Wentworth Higginson*. New York, 2000.

Meyers, Marvin. *The Jacksonian Persuasion: Politics and Belief*. Stanford, 1960.

Miller, Daniel. "American Christians and the Visit of Louis Kossuth." *Fides et Historia* 20 (June 1988): 5–17.

Minutes of the Alabama Conference of the Methodist Episcopal Church, South, held in Tuscaloosa, Alabama, December 7–16, 1853. Mobile, 1854.

"Miscellany." *American Whig Review* 11 (June 1850): 656–61.

Mitchell, Catherine, ed. *Margaret Fuller's New York Journalism*. Knoxville, 1995.

Mitchell, Donald [Ik Marvel]. *The Battle Summer*. New York, 1850.

Mitchell, Leslie. "Britain's Reactions to the Revolutions." In Evans and Pogge von Strandman, *Revolutions in Europe*, 83–98.

Mize, Sandra Yocum. "Defending Roman Loyalties and Republican Values: The 1848 Italian Revolution in American Catholic Apologetics." *Church History* 60 (December 1991): 480–92.

Moller, Herbert. "The Accelerated Development of Youth: Beard Growth as a Biological Marker." *Comparative Studies in Society and History* 29 (October 1987): 748–62.

"Monthly Record of Current Events." *Harper's New Monthly Magazine* 1 (November 1850): 849–57.

Moody, Richard. *The Astor Place Riot*. Bloomington, Ind., 1958.

Moore, Barrington, Jr. "Revolution in America?" *New York Review of Books*, 30 January 1969, 6–10.

Moore, John Bassett. "Kossuth: A Sketch of a Revolutionist. II." *Political Science Quarterly* 10 (June 1895): 257–91.

Moore, R. Laurence. "Insiders and Outsiders in American Historical Narrative and American History." *American Historical Review* 87 (April 1982): 390–412.

Moorhead, James. "Between Progress and Apocalypse: A Reassessment of Millennialism in American Religious Thought, 1800–1860." *Journal of American History* 71 (December 1984): 524–42.

Morison, Samuel. "Francis Bowen, an Early Test of Academic Freedom in Massachusetts." *Massachusetts Historical Society Proceedings* 65 (February 1936): 597–611.

———. *Three Centuries at Harvard, 1636–1936*. Cambridge, Mass., 1936.

Morrison, Michael. "American Reaction to European Revolutions, 1848–1852: Sectionalism, Memory, and the Revolutionary Heritage." *Civil War History* 49 (June 2003): 111–32.

———. *Slavery and the American West: The Eclipse of Manifest Destiny and the Coming of the Civil War*. Chapel Hill, 1997.

Mott, Frank Luther. *American Journalism: A History of Newspapers in the United States through 250 Years, 1690 to 1940*. New York, 1947.

Mott, Lucretia. *Complete Speeches and Sermons*. Edited by Dana Greene. New York, 1980.

Mullis, Tony. *Peacekeeping on the Plains: Army Operations in Bleeding Kansas*. Columbia, Mo., 2004.

Mulvey, Christopher. *Anglo-American Landscapes: A Study of Nineteenth-Century Anglo-American Travel Literature*. New York, 1983.

Murdock, William D. G. *Address on the Free-Soil Question*. Washington, D.C., 1848.

Nadel, Stanley. "From the Barricades of Paris to the Sidewalks of New York: German Artisans and the European Roots of American Labor Radicalism." *American Labor History* 30 (Winter 1989): 47–75.

Nash, Gary. "American Clergy and the French Revolution." *William and Mary Quarterly* 22 (July 1965): 392–412.

Neider, Charles, ed. *The Travels of Mark Twain*. New York, 2000.

Nemes, Robert. "Politics of the Dance Floor: Culture and Civil Society in Nineteenth-Century Hungary." *Slavic Review* 60 (Winter 2001): 802–23.

Nevin, John. *Antichrist; or, The Spirit of Sect and Schism.* New York, 1848.

Nevins, Allan. *The Emergence of Lincoln.* 2 vols. New York, 1950.

———. *The Evening Post: A Century of Journalism.* New York, 1922.

———. *Ordeal of the Union: Fruits of Manifest Destiny.* New York, 1947.

Newman, Francis, ed. *Select Speeches of Kossuth.* London, 1853.

News from the Land of Freedom: German Immigrants Write Home. Edited by Walter Kamphoefner, Wolfgang Helbich, and Ulrike Sommer. Translated by Susan Carter Vogel. Ithaca, 1991.

Nichols, James Hastings. *Romanticism in American Theology: Nevin and Schaff at Mercersburg.* Chicago, 1961.

Noll, Mark. *America's God: From Jonathan Edwards to Abraham Lincoln.* New York, 2002.

———. *History of Christianity in the United States and Canada.* Grand Rapids, 1992.

———. *The Old Religion in a New World: The History of North American Christianity.* Grand Rapids, 2002.

Noll, Mark, and Cassandra Niemczyk. "Evangelicals and the Self-Consciously Reformed." In *The Variety of American Evangelicalism,* edited by Donald Dayton and Robert Johnston, 204–21. Knoxville, 1991.

Northern Illinois University Library (NIUL). "Campaign Songbooks". *Getting the Message Out! National Political Campaign Materials, 1840–1860.* 9 August 2008. http://dig.lib.niu.edu/message/about.html.

Norton, Wesley. *Religious Newspapers in the Old Northwest to 1861: A History, Bibliography, and Record of Opinion.* Athens, Ohio, 1977.

Noyes, P. H. *Organization and Revolution: Working-Class Associations in the German Revolutions of 1848–1849.* Princeton, 1966.

Oates, Stephen. *Our Fiery Trial: Abraham Lincoln, John Brown, and the Civil War Era.* Amherst, 1979.

O'Connor, Thomas. *The Boston Irish: A Political History.* Boston, 1995.

Odell, George C. D. *Annals of the New York Stage.* 15 vols. New York, 1927–41.

Oliver, John. "Kossuth's Appeal to the Middle West—1852." *Mississippi Valley Historical Review* 14 (March 1928): 481–95.

Olmstead, Frederick. *Walks and Talks of an American Farmer in England.* Columbus, Ohio, 1859.

Onuf, Nicholas, and Peter Onuf. *Markets, Nations, and War: Modern History and the American Civil War.* Charlottesville, 2006.

Osofsky, Gilbert. "Abolitionists, Irish Immigrants, and the Dilemmas of Romantic Nationalism." *American Historical Review* 80 (October 1975): 889–912.

Packer, Barbara. "The Establishment and the Movement." In *The Cambridge History of American Literature,* edited by Sacvan Bercovitch, 8 vols., 2: 392–423. New York, 2005.

Palmer, Benjamin Morgan. "Social Dancing Inconsistent With a Christian Profession and Baptismal Vows: A Sermon." *Richmond Watchman and Observer*, 1 November 1849.

Palmer, R. R. *The Age of Democratic Revolutions: A Political History of Europe and America, 1760–1800.* 2 vols. Princeton, 1959–64.

Pappas, Paul Constantine. *The United States and the Greek War for Independence, 1821–1828.* New York, 1985.

Parker, Theodore. "The Abolition of Slavery in the French Republic." In Parker, *Slave Power,* 167–75.

———. "The Free Soil Movement." In Parker, *Slave Power,* 189–217.

———. *The Slave Power.* Edited by James Hosmer. New York, 1969.

Pasley, Jeffrey, Andrew Robertson, and David Waldstreicher, eds. *Beyond the Founders: New Approaches to the Political History of the Early American Republic.* Chapel Hill, 2004.

Pease, Jane, and William Pease. "Confrontation and Abolition in the 1850s." *Journal of American History* 58 (March 1972): 923–37.

Pech, Stanley. *The Czech Revolution of 1848.* Chapel Hill, 1969.

Pells, Richard. *Not Like Us: How Europeans Have Loved, Hated and Transformed American Culture since World War II.* New York, 1997.

Perkins, Bradford. *The Creation of a Republican Empire, 1776–1865.* 4 vols. Vol. 1, *Cambridge History of American Foreign Relations,* edited by Warren Cohen. Cambridge, U.K., 1993.

Perkins, Dexter. *A History of the Monroe Doctrine.* Boston, 1963.

Perry, Lewis. *Boats against the Current: American Culture between Revolution and Modernity, 1820–1860.* New York, 1993.

———. *Childhood, Marriage, Reform: Henry Clarke Wright, 1797–1870.* Chicago, 1980.

Perry, Lewis, and Michael Fellman, eds. *Antislavery Reconsidered: New Perspectives on the Abolitionists.* Baton Rouge, 1979.

Peterson, M. J. *Recognition of Governments.* New York, 1997.

Phelps, Christina. *The Anglo-American Peace Movement in the Mid-Nineteenth Century.* Freeport, N.Y., 1972.

Playfair, Robert. *Recollections of a Visit to the United States.* Edinburgh, 1856.

Plessis, Alain. *The Rise and Fall of the Second Empire, 1852–1871.* Translated by Jonathan Mandelbaum. Cambridge, U.K., 1979.

"The Political Aspect." *Putnam's Monthly Magazine of American Literature, Science and Art* 8 (July 1856): 85–95.

Porter, Kirk, and Donald Bruce Johnson, eds. *National Party Platforms, 1840–1960.* Urbana, 1961.

Postgate, R. W., ed. *Revolutions from 1789 to 1906: Documents.* New York, 1962.

Potter, David. "Civil War." In *The Comparative Approach to American History,* edited by C. Van Woodward, 135–45. New York, 1968.

———. *Impending Crisis, 1848–1861.* Edited by Don Fehrenbacher. New York, 1976.

Powell, J. H. *Richard Rush: Republican Diplomat, 1780–1859.* Philadelphia, 1942.

"Present Reforms of Pope Pius IX." *United States Democratic Review* 22 (April 1848): 301–8.

Pressly, Thomas. "Bullets and Ballots: Lincoln and the 'Right of Revolution.'" *American Historical Review* 67 (April 1962): 647–62.

Price, Roger. *The French Second Republic: A Social History.* Ithaca, 1972.

———. "'The Holy Struggle against Anarchy': The Development of Counterrevolution in 1848." In Dowe et al., *Europe in 1848*, 25–54.

———. *The Revolutions of 1848.* London, 1988.

Proceedings of a public meeting of the citizens of the city and county of Philadelphia, held 6 January 1848, to express their cordial approval of the liberal policy of Pope Pius IX, in his administration of the temporal government of Italy. Philadelphia, 1848.

Proceedings to the Banquet of the Jackson Democratic Association, Washington, Eighth of January, 1852. Washington, D.C., 1852.

"Promiscuous Dancing." *Christian Magazine of the South* 7 (January 1849): 1–17.

Pulszky, Francis, and Theresa Pulszky. *White Red Black: Sketches of Society in the United States during the Visit of Their Guest.* 2 vols. New York, 1968.

Purcell, Sarah. *Sealed with Blood: War, Sacrifice, and Memory in Revolutionary America.* Philadelphia, 2002.

Putnam, George Palmer. *The Tourist in Europe.* New York, 1838.

Pyles, Thomas. "American Political Terms." *American Speech* 38 (October 1963): 223–26.

Quarles, Benjamin. *The Black Abolitionists.* New York, 1991.

Quist, John. *Restless Visionaries: The Social Roots of Antebellum Reform in Alabama and Michigan.* Baton Rouge, 1998.

Raeder, Ole Munch. *America in the Forties: The Letters of Ole Munch Raeder.* Translated and edited by Gunnar Malmin. Minneapolis, 1929.

Rath, R. John. *The Viennese Revolution of 1848.* New York, 1957.

Rawley, James. *Race and Politics: "Bleeding Kansas" and the Coming of the Civil War.* Philadelphia, 1969.

Rayback, Joseph. "The American Workingman and the Antislavery Crusade." *Journal of Economic History* 3 (November 1943): 152–63.

———. *Free Soil: The Election of 1848.* Lexington, Ky., 1970.

Redpath, James. *The Roving Editor: Talks with Slaves in the Southern United States.* Edited by John McKivigan. [1859.] Rpt., University Park, Pa., 1996.

The Red Republican: The Friend of the People. 2 vols. New York, 1966.

"Remarkable Exposition of Prophecy." *Baptist Banner,* 31 May 1848.

Rémond, René. *Religion and Society in Modern Europe.* Translated by Antonia Nevill. Oxford, 1999.

"Reopening of the African Slave Trade." *New Englander* 18 (February 1860): 90–125.

Report of the Woman's Rights Convention, Held at Seneca Falls, New York, July 19 and 20, 1848. Rochester, 1848.

Resolutions of the German Democratic Republican Association of New York City. New York, 1844.

"Revolutions of 1848." *Methodist Quarterly Review* 30 (October 1848): 535–52.

Reynolds, David. *George Lippard.* Boston, 1982.

———. *John Brown, Abolitionist: The Man Who Killed Slavery, Sparked the Civil War, and Seeded Civil Rights.* New York, 2005.

———. *Walt Whitman's America: A Cultural Biography.* New York, 1995.

Reynolds, Larry. *European Revolutions and the American Literary Renaissance.* New Haven, 1988.

———. "Righteous Violence: Margaret Fuller's Revolutionary Example." In Capper and Giorcelli, *Margaret Fuller,* 172–92.

Rice, Alan, and Martin Crawford, eds. *Liberating Sojourn: Frederick Douglass and Transatlantic Reform.* Athens, Ga., 1999.

Richardson, James Daniel, ed. *Compilation of the Messages and Papers of the Presidents.* 20 vols. New York, 1927.

Rifkin, Jeremy. *European Dream: How Europe's Vision of the Future Is Quietly Eclipsing the American Dream.* New York, 2004.

Right of the People to Establish Forms of Government. Mr. Hallett's Argument in the Rhode Island Causes, before the Supreme Court of the United States, January 1848. Boston, 1848.

Ripley, C. Peter, ed. *The Black Abolitionist Papers.* 5 vols. Chapel Hill, 1985–92.

Robertson, Andrew. *The Language of Democracy: Political Rhetoric in the United States and Britain, 1790–1900.* Ithaca, 1995.

Robertson, Priscilla. *Revolutions of 1848: A Social History.* Princeton, 1952.

Robinson, Solon. "Negro Slavery at the South." *Debow's Review* 7 (September 1849): 206–25.

Roediger, David. *Wages of Whiteness: Race and the Making of the American Working Class.* New York, 1991.

Rogers, William Warren. "Kossuth's Visit to Alabama." *Alabama Review* 17 (April 1964): 113–22.

———. "'The Nation's Guest' in Louisiana: Kossuth Visits New Orleans." *Louisiana History* 9 (Fall 1968): 355–64.

Rogin, Michael. *Subversive Genealogy: Politics and Art of Herman Melville.* New York, 1983.

Rohrs, Richard. "American Critics of the French Revolution of 1848." *Journal of the Early Republic* 14 (Fall 1994): 359–77.

Rossbach, Jeffrey. *Ambivalent Conspirators: John Brown, the Secret Six, and a Theory of Slave Violence.* Philadelphia, 1983.

Rossi, Joseph. *The Image of America in Mazzini's Writings.* Madison, 1954.

Rudé, George. *The Crowd in History: A Study of Popular Disturbances in France and England, 1730–1848.* London, 1981.

Rush, Richard. *Occasional Productions, Political, Diplomatic, and Miscellaneous, including, among others, a glance at the Court and Government of Louis Philippe and the French Revolution of 1848.* Philadelphia, 1860.

Ryan, Mary. *Civic Wars: Democracy and Public Life in the American City during the Nineteenth Century.* Berkeley, 1997.

Salomone, William. "The Nineteenth-Century Discovery of Italy: An Essay in American Cultural History." *American Historical Review* 73 (June 1968): 1359–91.

Saul, Norman. *Distant Friends: The United States and Russia, 1763–1867.* Lawrence, 1990.

Saum, Lewis. *The Popular Mood of Pre–Civil War America.* Westport, Conn., 1980.

Sauvigny, Guillaume Bertier de. "American Travelers in France, 1814–1848." In *Diplomacy in an Age of Nationalism: Essays in Honour of Lynn Marshall Case,* edited by Nancy Barker and Marvin Brown, 11–24. The Hague, Netherlands, 1971.

———. *Metternich and His Times.* Translated by Peter Ryde. London, 1962.

———, ed. *La Révolution Parisienne de 1848 vue par les Américains.* Paris, 1984.

Saville, John. *1848: The British State and the Chartist Movement.* Cambridge, U.K., 1987.

Schaff, Philip. *History of the Christian Church.* 8 vols. New York, 1926.

Schecter, Patricia. "Free and Slave Labor in the Old South: The Tredegar Ironworkers' Strike of 1847." *Labor History* 35 (Spring 1994): 165–86.

Schenone, Giulio. "John Brown e il pensiero insurrezionale italiano." In *Atti del I Congresso Internazionale di Storia Americana: Italia E Stati Uniti Dall'Indipendenza Americana Ad Oggi (1776/1976),* 356–66. Genoa, 1978.

Schlesinger, Arthur, Jr. *A Pilgrim's Progress: Orestes A. Brownson.* Boston, 1966.

Schneir, Miriam, ed. *Feminism: The Essential Historical Writings.* New York, 1972.

Schudson, Michael. *Discovering the News: A Social History of American Newspapers.* New York, 1978.

Scott, Robert, and Donald Smith. "Rhetoric of Confrontation." *Journal of Speech* 55 (February 1969): 1–8.

Sears, John. *Sacred Places: American Tourist Attractions in the Nineteenth Century.* New York, 1989.

Sennett, Richard. *The Fall of Public Man.* New York, 1977.

"Separate Secession. Proceedings of Meetings of Delegates from the Southern Right Associations of South Carolina. Held at Charleston. May 1851." *Southern Quarterly Review* 4 (October 1851): 298–317.

Serfaty, Simon. *European Unity and Atlantic Solidarity.* Westport, Conn., 1997.

Seward, William. *The Army of the United States Not to Be Employed As a Police to Enforce the Laws of the Conquerors of Kansas. Speech of William H. Seward in the Senate of the United States, August 7, 1856.* Washington, D.C., 1856.

———.*Speeches of William H. Seward on the Army Bill, at the Extraordinary Session of the Senate Speech August 27, 1856.* Washington, D.C., 1856.

Sewell, William. *Work and Revolution in France: The Language of Labor from the Old Regime to 1848.* Cambridge, U.K., 1980.

Shafer, Byron, ed. *Is America Different? A New Look at American Exceptionalism.* Oxford, U.K., 1991.

Shaw, S. Bradley. "The Pliable Rhetoric of Domesticity." In *The Stowe Debate: Rhetorical Strategies in Uncle Tom's Cabin,* edited by Mason Lowance Jr., Ellen Westbrook, and R. C. De Prospo, 73–98. Amherst, 1994.

Shewmaker, Kenneth. "Daniel Webster and the Politics of Foreign Policy, 1850–1852." *Journal of American History* 63 (September 1976): 303–15.

"Signs of the Times." *Christian Magazine of the South* 7 (September 1849): 260–92.

Silverman, Kenneth. *Cultural History of the American Revolution.* New York, 1976.

Simms, William Gilmore. *Letters of William Gilmore Simms.* Edited by Mary Simms Oliphant, Alfred Taylor Odell, and T. C. Duncan Eaves. 6 vols. Columbia, S.C., 1952–82.

Sinha, Manisha. *The Counterrevolution of Slavery: Politics and Ideology in Antebellum South Carolina.* Chapel Hill, 2000.

Sioussat, St. George, ed. "Selected Letters, 1846–1856, from the Donelson Papers." *Tennessee Historical Magazine* 3 (1917): 257–91.

———. "Tennessee, the Compromise of 1850, and the Nashville Convention." *Mississippi Valley Historical Review* 2 (December 1915): 313–47.

Sked, Alan, ed. *Europe's Balance of Power, 1815–1848.* London, 1979.

———. "The Metternich System, 1815–1848." In *Europe's Balance of Power, 1815–1848,* edited by Alan Sked, 98–112. London, 1979.

Sklar, Kathryn Kish. "'Women Who Speak for an Entire Nation': American and British Women at the World Anti-Slavery Convention, London, 1840." In *Abolitionist Sisterhood: Women's Political Culture in Antebellum America,* edited by Jean Fagan Yellin and John Van Horne, 301–33. Ithaca, 1994.

Sloan, Robert. *William Smith O'Brien and the Young Ireland Rebellion of 1848.* Dublin, 2000.

Smith, Denis Mack. *Mazzini.* New Haven, 1994.

———. "The Revolutions of 1848–1849 in Italy." In Evans and Pogge von Strandmann, *Revolutions in Europe,* 55–81.

Smith, Sol. *Theatrical Management in the West and South, with Anecdotal Sketches.* New York, 1868.

Smith, Timothy. "Righteousness and Hope: Christian Holiness and the Millennial Vision in America, 1800–1900." *American Quarterly* 31 (Spring 1979): 21–45.

Soldani, Simonetta. "Approaching Europe in the Name of the Nation: The Italian Revolution, 1846–1849." In Dowe et al., *Europe in 1848,* 59–88.

Somkin, Fred. *Unquiet Eagle: Memory and Desire in the Idea of American Freedom, 1815–1860.* Ithaca, 1967.

"The Southern Convention." *Southern Quarterly Review* 2 (September 1850): 191–232.

"Southern Cotton Mills." *De Bow's Review* 10 (June 1851): 680–82.

Southworth, Dave. *Colorado Mining Camps.* Round Rock, Tex., 1997.

Spencer, Donald. *Louis Kossuth and Young America: A Study of Sectionalism and Foreign Policy, 1848–1852*. Columbia, Mo., 1977.

Sperber, Hans, and Travis Trittschuh. *American Political Terms*. Detroit, 1962.

Sperber, Jonathan. *The European Revolutions, 1848–1851*. Cambridge, U.K., 1994.

———. *Rhineland Radicals: The Democratic Movement and the Revolution of 1848–1849*. Princeton, 1991.

Stampp, Kenneth. *America in 1857: A Nation on the Brink*. New York, 1990.

———. "One Alone? The United States and National Self-Determination." In *Lincoln, the War President*, edited by Gabor Boritt, 121–44. New York, 1992.

Stanton, Elizabeth Cady. *Eighty Years and More: Reminiscences, 1815–1897*. New York, 1971.

Stanton, Elizabeth Cady, and Susan B. Anthony. *Papers*. Edited by Patricia Holland and Ann Gordon. Wilmington, Del., 1991. Microfilm.

Stanton, Elizabeth Cady, Susan B. Anthony, and Matilda Joslyn Gage, eds. *History of Woman Suffrage*. 6 vols. New York, 1969.

Startup, Kenneth. "'A Mere Calculation of Profit and Loss': Southern Clergy and the Economic Culture of the Antebellum North." In *God and Mammon: Protestants, Money, and the Market, 1790–1860*, edited by Mark Noll, 217–35. New York, 2001.

Stearns, Peter. *1848: The Revolutionary Tide in Europe*. New York, 1974.

———. *The Revolutions of 1848*. London, 1974.

Steele, Joan. *Captain Mayne Reid*. Boston, 1978.

Stegmaier, Mark. *Texas, New Mexico, and the Compromise of 1850: Boundary Dispute and Sectional Crisis*. Kent, Ohio, 1996.

Stewart, George. *Names on the Land: A Historical Account of Placenaming in the United States*. San Francisco, 1982.

Stewart, James Brewer. *Holy Warriors: The Abolitionists and American Slavery*. New York, 1996.

Stiles, William. *Address delivered before the Georgia Democratic State Convention held at Milledgeville 4 July 1856*. Atlanta, 1856.

———. *Austria in 1848–49, Being a History of the late Political Movements in Vienna, Milan, Venice and Prague*. [1852.] Rpt., New York, 1971.

Stowe, Harriet Beecher. *Uncle Tom's Cabin; or, Life among the Lowly*. [1852.] Rpt., New York, 1981.

Stowe, William. *Going Abroad: European Travel in Nineteenth-Century American Culture*. Princeton, 1994.

Strong, George Templeton. *Diary*. 2 vols. Edited by Allan Nevins and Milton Halsey Thomas. New York, 1952.

Summers, Mark. *The Plundering Generation*. New York, 1987.

Sumner, Charles. *The Crime Against Kansas . . . 19th and 20th May, 1856*. Boston, 1856.

Szilassy, Sándor. "America and the Hungarian Revolution of 1848–1849." *Slavonic and East European Review* 44 (January 1966): 180–96.

Taylor, A. J. P. *Revolutions and Revolutionaries.* London, 1978.

Taylor, Bayard. *At Home and Abroad: A Sketch-Book of Life, Scenery and Men.* New York, 1889.

Taylor, Miles. "The 1848 Revolutions and the British Empire." *Past and Present* 166 (February 2000): 146–80.

Taylor, William. *Cavalier and Yankee.* New York, 1961.

Temperley, Harold, and Lillian Penson, eds. *Foundations of British Foreign Policy from Pitt (1792) to Salisbury (1902).* New York, 1966.

Thomas, John. "Romantic Reform in America, 1815–1865." *American Quarterly* 17 (Winter 1965): 656–81.

Thompson, Dorothy. *The Chartists.* London, 1984.

Thoreau, Henry David. "A Plea for Captain John Brown." In *Henry David Thoreau: Collected Essays and Poems,* 396–417. New York, 2001.

Thornton, J. Mills, III. *Politics and Power in a Slave Society: Alabama, 1800–1860.* Baton Rouge, 1978.

Thornwell, James Henry. *Life and Letters of James Henley Thornwell.* Edited by Benjamin Morgan Palmer. Richmond, 1875.

Tocqueville, Alexis de. *Democracy in America.* 2 vols. [1835.] Rpt., New York, 1980.

———. *Recollections: The French Revolution of 1848.* Translated by George Lawrence. Edited by J. P. Mayer and A. P. Kerr. New York, 1970.

Towers, Frank. *The Urban South and the Coming of the Civil War.* Charlottesville, 2004.

Traugott, Mark. "The Crowd in the French Revolution of February, 1848." *American Historical Review* 93 (June 1988): 638–52.

Travers, Len. *Celebrating the Fourth: Independence Day and the Rites of Nationalism in the Early Republic.* Amherst, 1997.

Trescot, William Henry. *The Position and Course of the South.* Charleston, 1850.

Trevelyan, George Macaulay. *Garibaldi's Defence of the Roman Republic.* London, 1907.

Trimble, William. "Diverging Tendencies in New York Democracy in the Period of the Locofocos." *American Historical Review* 24 (April 1919): 396–421.

Tuchinsky, Adam. "'The Bourgeoisie Will Fall and Fall Forever': The *New-York Tribune,* the 1848 French Revolution, and American Social Democratic Discourse." *Journal of American History* 92 (September 2005): 470–97.

[Tucker, Beverly]. "The Present State of Europe." *Southern Quarterly Review* 16 (January 1850): 281–307.

Tuckerman, Henry. *Book of the Artists: American Artist Life.* New York, 1966.

Tuveson, Ernest. *Redeemer Nation: The Idea of America's Millennial Role.* Chicago, 1968.

Twain, Mark. *A Tramp Abroad.* New York. 1996.

Tyrrell, Alexander. "Making the Millennium: The Mid-Nineteenth Century Peace Movement." *Historical Journal* 20 (1978): 75–95.

Tyrrell, Ian. *Transnational Nation: United States History in Global Perspective since 1789*. New York, 2007.

Unitarian Universalist Association (UUA). *Dictionary of Unitarian and Universalist Biography*. Boston. 10 August 2008. http://www.uua.org/uuhs/duub/.

University of Virginia Library. *Historical Census Browser*. 9 August 2008. http://fisher.lib.virginia.edu/collections/stats/histcensus/.

U.S. Bureau of the Census. *Historical Statistics of the United States, Colonial Times to 1970*. Washington, D.C., 1975.

U.S. Congress. House. *House Documents*. 101st Congress, 2nd session, 1990, doc. no. 168. "Dedication by the Congress of a Bust of Lajos (Louis) Kossuth." Washington, D.C., 1990. U.S. serial set no. 13993.

———. *Journal*. 31st Congress, 2nd session, 1851.

———. *Select Committee on the Tobacco Trade. Report [of] the Select Committee, to whom the subject of our tobacco trade with Europe was referred*. H. Rept. 810. 30th Congress, 1st session, 1848.

U.S. Congress. House. Office of the Clerk. *A History of Foreign Leaders and Dignitaries Who Have Addressed the U.S. Congress*. 9 August 2008. http://clerk.house.gov/art_history/house_history/foreignleaders.html.

U.S. Congress. Senate. *Senate Documents*. 31st Congress, 1st session, 1850, docs. no. 40–48. Washington, D.C., 1979. U.S. serial set no. 558.

———. *Senate Documents*. 61st Congress, 2nd session, 1909, docs. no. 215, 279. Washington, D.C., 1979. U.S. serial set no. 5657.

U.S. Department of State. *Despatches from United States Ministers to Austria, 1838–1906*. Washington, D.C., 1958. Microfilm.

———. *Despatches from United States Ministers to France, 1789–1906*. Washington, D.C., 1943. Microfilm.

———. *Despatches from United States Ministers to the German States and Germany 1799–1801, 1835–1906*. Washington, D.C., 1960. Microfilm.

"Usurpation of Louis Napoleon." *Living Age*, 24 January 1852, 171–83.

Valentin, Veit. *1848: Chapters of German History*. Translated by Ethel Talbot Scheffauer. Hamden, Conn., 1965.

Vance, William. *America's Rome*. 2 vols. New Haven, 1989.

Van Deusen, Glyndon. *Horace Greeley: Nineteenth-Century Crusader*. Philadelphia, 1953.

Varg, Paul. *U.S. Foreign Relations, 1820–1860*. East Lansing, 1979.

Von Frank, Albert. "John Brown, James Redpath, and the Idea of Revolution." *Civil War History* 52 (June 2006): 142–60.

Von Mehren, Joan. *Minerva and the Muse: A Life of Margaret Fuller*. Amherst, Mass., 1994.

Waldstreicher, David. *In the Midst of Perpetual Fetes: The Making of American Nationalism, 1776–1820*. Chapel Hill, 1997.

Wallach, Glen. *Obedient Sons: The Discourse of Youth and Generations in American Culture, 1630–1860*. Amherst, 1997.

Walther, Eric. *The Fire-Eaters*. Baton Rouge, 1992.

Warner, Michael. *Letters of the Republic: Publication and the Public Sphere in Eighteenth-Century America*. Cambridge, Mass., 1990.

Watson, Charles. *Antebellum Charleston Dramatists*. Tuscaloosa, 1976.

Watson, Harry. *Liberty and Power: The Politics of Jacksonian America*. New York, 1990.

Webster, Daniel. *Papers of Daniel Webster*. Edited by Charles Wiltse. 15 vols. Hanover, N.H., 1974–89.

———. *Works*. 6 vols. Edited by Edward Everett. Boston, 1851.

———. *Writings and Speeches*. 18 vols. Edited by James McIntyre. Boston, 1903.

Welcome of Louis Kossuth, Governor of Hungary, to Philadelphia, by the Youth. December 26, 1851. Philadelphia, 1852.

Wellman, Judith. *The Road to Seneca Falls: Elizabeth Cady Stanton and the First Woman's Rights Convention*. Urbana, 2004.

Welter, Rush. *The Mind of America, 1820–1860*. New York, 1975.

Wheaton, Henry. *Elements of International Law*. Philadelphia, 1846.

Whitaker, Arthur. *The United States and the Independence of Latin America, 1800–1830*. Baltimore, 1941.

White, Elizabeth Brett. *American Opinion of France: From Lafayette to Poincaré*. New York, 1927.

Whitridge, Arnold. *Men in Crisis: The Revolutions of 1848*. New York, 1947.

Widmer, Edward. *Young America: The Flowering of Democracy in New York City*. New York, 1998.

Wiecek, William. "'A Peculiar Conservatism' and the Dorr Rebellion: Constitutional Clash in Jacksonian America." *American Journal of Legal History* 22 (July 1978): 237–53.

Wilentz, Sean. *Chants Democratic: New York City and the Rise of the American Working Class, 1788–1850*. New York, 1984.

Wilkins, Joe Bassette, Jr. "Window on Freedom: The South's Response to the Emancipation of the Slaves in the British West Indies, 1833–1861." Ph.D. dissertation, University of South Carolina, 1977.

Williams, William Appleman. *America Confronts a Revolutionary World, 1776–1976*. New York, 1976.

Wilson, James Grant, and John Fiske, eds. *Appleton's Cyclopaedia of American Biography*. 7 vols. New York, 1900.

Wilson, James Harrison. *Life of Charles A. Dana*. New York, 1907.

Wilson, Prince. "Anglo-French Diplomatic Relations, 1848–1851." Ph.D. dissertation, University of Chicago, 1954.

Winders, Richard Bruce. *Mr. Polk's Army: The American Military Experience in the Mexican War*. College Station, Tex., 1997.

Wittke, Carl. *Refugees of Revolution: The German Forty-Eighters in America*. Philadelphia, 1952.

"Wonder of the Nineteenth Century." *Baptist Banner*, 12 April 1848.

Wood, Gordon. "Conspiracy and the Paranoid Style: Causality and Deceit in the Eighteenth Century." *William and Mary Quarterly* 39 (July 1982): 401–41.

———. *The Radicalism of the American Revolution.* New York, 1992.

Wright, Nathalia. *Horatio Greenough: The First American Sculptor.* Philadelphia, 1963.

Wunder, Richard. *Hiram Powers: Vermont Sculptor, 1805–1873.* 2 vols. Newark, 1991.

Yellin, Jean Fagan. "Caps and Chains: Hiram Powers' Statue of 'Liberty.'" *American Quarterly* 38 (Winter 1986): 798–826.

Zahler, Helene. *Eastern Workingmen and National Land Policy, 1829–1862.* New York, 1941.

Zucker, Adolph. *The Forty-Eighters: Political Refugees of the German Revolution of 1848.* New York, 1950.

Index